To: Brother [illegible] you

May [illegible]
My Brother-
Peace!/

[illegible signature]
2/23/2019

Controlling the Thought Life

Renewed Minds Change Lives

Barrington C. Hibbert

WESTBOW
PRESS®
A DIVISION OF THOMAS NELSON
& ZONDERVAN

WestBow Press books may be ordered through booksellers or by contacting:

WestBow Press
A Division of Thomas Nelson & Zondervan
1663 Liberty Drive
Bloomington, IN 47403
www.westbowpress.com
1 (866) 928-1240

ISBN: 978-1-9736-5019-5 (sc)
ISBN: 978-1-9736-5018-8 (hc)
ISBN: 978-1-9736-5020-1 (e)

Library of Congress Control Number: 2019900007

Print information available on the last page.

WestBow Press rev. date: 1/31/2019

Contents

Preface

The working of the mind and how it affects our emotions and actions has been for a long time of the deepest fascination for me. As a young Christian, I was often troubled as I observed how some born-again, Spirit-filled Christians acted in ways that did not seem to comport with my understanding of what a Christian should be. I was oriented to believing that Christians should always be happy, kind, gentle, and loving to everyone. In my religious community, a Christian was regarded as lacking faith, or as being fearful, or as not spending enough time in prayer and reading God's Word if he or she confessed to feelings of anxiety, depression, or any other mental health issues. Yet to my observation, many of the Christians who suffered from what seemed to me to be some form of mental health issue were good Christians. They loved the Lord and were confident in their salvation.

This incongruity led me to embark on academic studies in the field of psychology, which eventually resulted in my earning a master of science degree in mental health counseling. This has led me to a conviction that those were good and faithful Christians. Some were dealing with the many stressors of life, and did not have the necessary coping tools to live successful emotional lives. While many of the sufferers could have benefited from the services of a well-trained mental health therapist, I am ever more convinced that in many of those cases, the first line of defense should have been God's Word coupled with fervent prayers. This conviction prompted me to preach a series of sermons on the thought life, the transcript of which forms the basis for this book.

This book fulfills a lifelong dream of mine to put my thoughts in writing for a wider audience than my local church, for which I author the Sunday school lessons. While my academic writings received very positive feedback from various professors and others, I never though them worthy of publication. With the exception of one chapter in an academic text titled *Stress in the Year 2010 and Beyond*, edited by Professor Michael F. Shaughnessy, I have not attempted before now to publish anything else.

I am grateful to those who have encouraged me over the years to publish. They certainly showed more faith in my ability than I had. First, I wish to thank my church family for being my fan club. Their affirmation and praise of me have often lifted my mortified spirit when I was so down that I thought I could not carry on another day. Their response to the ministry God has entrusted me with makes the hard work well worth it.

My great thanks go out to my first reader, Sister Tamika Wisdom, whose insightful comments helped me to clarify the rough draft of the manuscript. I am grateful also to my second reader, the consummate professional, who wishes to remain anonymous. She approached the manuscript as though I were her student. Her many helpful suggestions, while humbling at times, were never condescending, and certainly helped to make the final version a better product than it would be otherwise. Special thanks go out to the good people at WestBow Press for all their help in making this project a reality.

To my lovely wife, Michelle P. Hibbert, who took on the laborious task of transcribing the CDs, my heartfelt thanks. She is a woman of God who loves me, prays for me, and puts up with me as I spend countless hours in my study, writing and editing this book and my sermons. Without her love and support, not just on this project but overall, none of this would be possible.

Finally, if you are reading this book, thank you for spending your money and taking a chance on an unconfirmed author. I pray that your heart will be blessed.

Introduction

Human beings were made in the image of God. As such, we reflect, to some degree, the character of God. One construct of the image of God in humanity regards that image as some unique characteristics or qualities within the human person. That is, humanity is structurally, by these qualities, God's image-bearer. These God-given qualities are psychological or spiritual and are resident in human nature.

Premier among these qualities is reason. Millard Erickson observes, "Although conferred by God, the image resides in humans whether or not they recognize God's existence and his work."[1] Louis Berkhof holds that the image of God includes certain attributes that are uniquely human, such as intellectual power, natural affections, and moral freedom.[2]

Among the many aspects of God's image-bearing status that we could contemplate, this present work is most concerned with the intellectual power of humans—that is, humanity's ability to think and to control what they allow to take residence in their minds. A human being may not be as successful in controlling his or her thought life as could otherwise be achieved through the empowerment of the Holy Spirit. Because our thinking is so critical to our functioning, both on the natural and on the spiritual levels, we must order our thought lives in a manner that will maximize our success. Max Anders observes, "Right thinking is the first step toward righteous living. What is right thinking? It is thinking devoted to life's higher goods and virtues."[3]

This book is a product of the sermon series I preached at our church, titled *Controlling the Thought Life.* The intention was to admonish the church to bring certain dysfunctional thoughts to Christ in order to arrive at cognitive restructuring, resulting in living that is more successful. I meant this to be a two-part series, but it ended up as a fifteen-week endeavor. As I finished one sermon in the series, the Holy Spirit directed my attention to another area of our lives that needed addressing. The Holy Spirit greatly blessed our hearts. After I preached this series, several people asked me to do it again, and to put it in book form. I was at first reluctant to do so. However, as I began reviewing the sermons that my wife so patiently transcribed from the CDs, as well as my notes, it became clear to me that perhaps it would be a worthwhile project to revise the work and offer it as a book. My hope is that it may be a blessing to someone who is favorably disposed to read it.

When I became convinced that I should write this book, my first question concerned the type of book I should write. As a mental health therapist with a master of science degree in mental health counseling, master of divinity in pastoral counseling, and PhD in theology, I thought I would write on the working of the mind from an academic perspective. I quickly abandoned that idea. I contemplated whom I hoped to reach with this book. I quickly concluded that I wanted to speak, not to scholars, but to everyday Christians who may not have had the opportunity to attend a college or university. The end product, I hope, is a book for everyone.

The methodology of this book is simple. Its thesis is that the mind is the place where most of the battles in our lives are won or lost. If the thought life is brought to the obedience of Christ, we can live more spiritually fulfilled and successful lives. That is, if we examine our negative thoughts in light of God's Word, we will experience better outcomes in various areas of our lives.

Much has been written about the mind. It has been observed, "The mind also clusters things and people—for example, men or women, white or black-and automatically categorizes the world around it."[4] The mind can also categorize experiences as threatening or nonthreatening, pleasurable or painful, welcome or unwelcome as they affect the person subjected to such experiences. The mind can develop patterns of responses that may be functional or dysfunctional, liberating or crippling.

The correct ordering of the mind is of vital importance to how we function. It is no wonder that our Lord Jesus Christ and the New

Testament writers spent so much time dealing with the mind. Jesus tells us to love the Lord our God with all our mind (Matt. 22:37; Mark 12:30; Luke 10:27). Paul indicates that those who did not retain God in their knowledge were given over to a reprobate mind (Rom. 1:28). He further states that with the mind, we serve God's law (Rom. 7:27); and that the carnal mind is at war with God (Rom. 8:7). Transformation comes by renewing of the mind (Rom. 12:2). Our minds can be blinded so that we cannot perceive the spiritual things of God (2 Cor. 3:14). Through unbelief, the mind can be blinded by the god of this world, who is Satan (2 Cor. 4:4). It is possible that the mind can be corrupted (2 Cor. 11:3). Paul posits that the mind desires things (Eph. 2:2) and the mind possesses an attitude or a spirit (Eph. 4:23). These are only a few of the New Testament references to the functioning of the mind.

While it is important to attend to the physical and emotional components of our being, it is critical also that we spend the appropriate time and effort in developing a sound mind, because without a well-ordered mind, our spirituality severely suffers. This is the reason that the apostle Paul, after admonishing the Romans to present their bodies as a living sacrifice to God, instructs, "And be not conformed to this world: but be ye transformed by the renewing of your mind, that ye may prove what is that good, and acceptable, and perfect, will of God" (Rom. 12:2).[1] Paul was teaching that spiritual transformation comes by a renewed mind.

One may ask, "How is the mind renewed?" The answer to this question is both simple and complicated. It is simple because to have a sound mind, Christians should think like Christ. In other words, Christians should possess the attitude or the mind-set of Christ (Phil. 2:5). That is more easily said than done however.

The complication comes because, as humans, we are still living in the flesh. As such, there is a war going on in our minds. Paul observes, "But I see another law in my members, warring against the *law of my mind* (emphasis added), and bringing me into captivity to the law of sin which is in my members" (Rom. 7:23). A law is a rule or principle by

---

[1] Unless otherwise noted, all biblical passages referenced are from the Authorized King James Version (Grand Rapids, MI: Thomas Nelson Bibles, 2001).

which a person or object is governed. For example, the law of gravity dictates that if I pick up my Bible and drop it, it will fall to the floor, no matter how much I wish or pray that it will not fall. The law of gravity governs the object's descent. Similarly, there is a law in our minds that dictates how we respond to things around us. The difference between these two laws is that whereas the law of gravity is fixed, the law of the mind is variable and can be influenced to change its responses. How we train our minds, therefore, will determine our functioning.

If we allow certain thought patterns to pervade our being, our minds will naturally respond according to those patterns. If the mind is oriented toward an optimistic perspective, our conclusions and responses to sensory information will be informed by that optimistic orientation. The reverse is also true. The cumulative effect of negative thinking issues forth as cynicism. Pessimistic people look for the negatives in every situation. They somehow find a way to snatch defeat out of the mouth of victory.

I once knew a woman who was a professing Christian. But when it came to her husband, she was the most negative and cynical person. On one occasion, he was trying to agree with her about a position she had taken. She completely misread his motives and began to assail him for not understanding her. With great pains, he tried to explain to her that he was supporting her. It is hard to judge why she took such offense to what was meant to be a supportive statement, but from the outside looking in, it struck me as coming from a very negative place. It may have been that she was so used to hearing him tearing her down that she naturally anticipated criticism from him. It did not really matter what he said on this occasion, because she was programmed to respond to him in a negative way.

Having to live life in such a manner leaves people worn out, tired, and weakened. As such, we do not live optimally satisfying lives. Always living on the edge leads to emotional, mental, and spiritual breakdowns. Knowing that these negative conditions are a result of our thought lives, it is most important that we take steps to develop enriched, Christ-centered thought lives.

While a book of this sort will necessarily draw from many Scripture passages, the focus text that will guide our discussion is 2 Corinthians

10:3–5: "For though we walk in the flesh, we do not war after the flesh: for the weapons of our warfare are not carnal, but mighty through God to the pulling down of strong holds; Casting down imaginations, and every high thing that exalteth itself against the knowledge of God, and bringing into captivity every thought to the obedience of Christ."

Observe the last part of verse 5: "bringing into captivity every thought to the obedience of Christ." We will therefore examine several dysfunctional thoughts, see the possible ways they negatively affect us, and then, using God's Word, take such thoughts to make them obedient to Christ—that is, to make those thoughts conform to the standards of God's Word.

It bears repeating that this book is not intended to be a scholarly work. Neither is it an authoritative treatise on the inner workings of the mind. Rather, it comes from the heart of a pastor and a mental health therapist, who has observed too many born-again believers becoming victims of their thought lives. I wish to offer them some insights as to how they may begin to improve their psychological and emotional functioning. I endeavor to resist the temptation to offer mental health counseling in this book. Instead, I bring God's Word to bear on our daily living, with a view toward fostering a healthy thought life. To the extent that this book accomplishes that purpose in any degree, all praise go to Christ.

A Prayer

Lord, please bless the readers, that today they may experience the power of Your presence. In Jesus's name. Amen!

CHAPTER 1

Understanding the Sphere in which the Battle Is Fought

For though we walk in the flesh, we do not war after the flesh: for the weapons of our warfare are not carnal, but mighty through God to the pulling down of strong holds; Casting down imaginations, and every high thing that exalteth itself against the knowledge of God, and bringing into captivity every thought to the obedience of Christ.
—2 Corinthians 10:3–5

It is safe to assume that many people reading this book have not experienced the challenges of being a soldier on the battlefield. When soldiers go overseas and fight, we hail them as heroes because they have sacrificed so much on behalf of those who cannot or choose not to join the armed services.

Being a soldier is serious business, and it requires many sacrifices. Soldiering demands that a person dispenses with a civilian mind-set and think like a military person. Candidates for the military must not only be physically fit for service, but they must also be emotionally and psychologically conditioned to face combat situations if they are to be successful. While most of us may never know what it is to be a soldier in the secular armed services, as believers, we are soldiers of sorts, the difference being that our soldiering is done in the spiritual realm.

As spiritual soldiers, we will face numerous battles throughout the course of our lives. These battles are won or lost in our minds, as opposed to on foreign shores. If, in our minds, we approach a battle thinking that we are going to lose, we probably will lose. However, if we approach it thinking we are going to win, our chances of winning are much better. When we have a positive, optimistic mind-set, we think positive thoughts. The challenges that others see as the basis for defeat, we see as opportunities for growth and victory.

One who thinks positively has the uncanny ability to pluck victory out of the mouth of defeat. Granted that this assertion is true, we need to control our thought lives, because if we do not control our thought lives and focus on positive things, then we are at the mercies of negative thinking that is self-defeating. When negativity dominates our thought lives, it is difficult to see any positive outcomes. We become the products of our thought lives.

One of the most important challenges that we face is to understand the sphere in which we are doing battle. We must determine whether we are fighting a spiritual or carnal battle. Only when that determination is made can we choose the right weapons to employ. I will have more to say about the weapons in our arsenal in a later chapter, but suffice it here to understand that going to battle with the wrong weapon is a prescription for disaster. To fight a spiritual battle using carnal weapons is worse than sending men on horseback to fight a mechanized infantry unit. It is like sending men into modern military conflict armed with machetes to confront tanks with large sophisticated guns. Clearly, that would not be an intelligent decision.

In the warfare in which we are engaged, we need to figure out how we are going to change our thinking. I believe that at birth, our minds are like blank slates upon which life's experiences will write their own inscriptions. How we are conditioned and what we let into our minds will become part of our personalities, influencing the way we approach problem-solving.

Our socialization influences our worldview. If one is socialized to believe that the world is a bad and hostile place and that no one can be trusted, there is a strong probability that one will grow up embracing that worldview.

We can and do program our minds daily, based on what we allow into our thinking. I have often argued that we become a product of the things to which we listen and upon which we ruminate. For example, if you listen to calypso music long enough, you will begin to hum that type of music almost unconsciously. This is by no means a negative commentary on calypso. Each musical genre has its place. I only observe that what we put into our minds, negative or positive, becomes a part of who we are.

Those who work in the advertising business know this concept well, and have geared television and online commercials to capture our imaginations. They get to us by the ingenious ways they invade our subconscious minds.

In the 1980s, or perhaps the 1990s, there was a cute fast-food commercial with the tag line, "Where's the beef?" That slogan caught on quickly and became a cultural phenomenon. Preachers and politicians alike were asking, "Where's the beef?" They meant, "Where is the substance or veracity?"

Or how could we forget the Folgers coffee commercial? Even if you are not a coffee drinker, when you hear the jingle, "The best part of waking up ..." those of us of a certain age can finish it: "... is Folgers in your cup." We all seem to know that song.

You know what? None of us set out to study that song or to sing it. We can sing it because the advertising industry has programmed our minds. As I have asserted, one does not even have to be a coffee drinker to know that song. One knows it because our minds were programmed through an unconscious or subconscious process.

I have never been a beer drinker. In my entire life, I have drunk perhaps ten beers. My constitution generally cannot tolerate alcohol. But I still remember the Miller Beer commercial from the 1970s. The words and music ring in my head every time I see a sign for Miller Beer. The chorus of their jingle was, "If you've got the time, we've got the beer." How did the Miller Brewing Company get me to learn that song? It programmed me by showing people in that commercial who seemed successful and well-dressed, and were simply having a good time. Then the company exposed me to that image via their television commercials, repeatedly. At the time, I was not aware of what the Miller Brewing Company was doing, but they were very successful at getting my attention.

Some advertisers use subliminal messages to get us to buy their products. Subliminal programming uses a technique of flashing messages before your eyes at a high speed. It is believed that your eyes do not visually process these messages, but your subconscious mind instantly understands and accepts them. The success of these advertising efforts is due in no small measure to the fact that the mind of the receiver is programmed. This programming is planned, systematic, and purposeful. In a similar way, if we are going to control our thought lives in a positive way, it will take planned, systematic, and purposeful actions.

In this series of messages, now transcribed into book form, I want your hearts and minds to be flooded with God's Word so that your thoughts will be changed to be like Christ's. In the mental health counseling profession, practitioners use a behavioral therapeutic method called *flooding*. If a person has a fear of something—say, riding in an elevator—the person is *exposed to* the elevator—that is, made to enter and ride the elevator to neutralize the fear. Through confrontation with the fear, it is hoped that the person will overcome it.

Some Christians, unfortunately, are afraid of the Bible because they do not understand it. They consider it a book of mysteries. It is not so much that they fear it will hurt them; rather, they fear the Bible because they do not understand it. This is particularly true when a new Christian attempts to read the King James Version of the Holy Scripture. However, by continued exposure to Scripture, one will find that the mystery is removed. It is not that difficult a book to understand.

To continue the analogy, as the person with the phobia repeatedly gets into the elevator, and the door closes, and they arrive at their destination, eventually their fear diminishes. In other words, with repeated exposure to the thing feared, the person is no longer fearful. Similarly, one of the objectives of this series is to remove the fear of the Word by repeated exposure, and instead to inculcate in each reader a love for the Word. It is only by getting into the Word that our thought lives will be positively affected.

This foundational chapter aims to define the sphere in which the battle for our souls is being waged. It also aims to show how conditioning for this warfare starts with God's Word. Consistent exposure to the Word keeps us from sin (Ps. 119:9), gives light and understanding to the simple (Ps. 119:130), brings rejoicing to the heart (Ps. 19:8), cleanses us (John 15:3), and helps us to get what we ask from God (John 15:7). The Word is Spirit and life (John 6:63). These are just a few benefits of being exposed to the Word.

I have observed that constant exposure to a thing feared eventually diminishes that fear. When I was a child, I was afraid of firecrackers. My cousins wanted me to be able to safely light one and dispose of it before it could explode in my hand and hurt me. I was deathly afraid and would not touch one.

I had a cousin who had not passed the fourth grade in school, yet evidently knew something about overcoming fear. I am sure he knew nothing about the formal behavioral flooding technique, or anything about academic psychology for that matter. Nevertheless, he figured if he made me hold a firecracker and light it, and then safely threw it away from me before it exploded, that I would overcome my unreasonable fear.

Therefore, he chased me down one Christmas day, until I was out of breath and could run no more. He caught me, opened my hand, put the firecracker in it, and said, "I'm going to beat you if you don't do this."

I believed that he would beat me. He had done so on many previous occasions for simple things, and his beatings were vicious. I had to decide if I was going to take another beating from him—this time on Christmas Day, when all my friends were watching—or try to endure the lighting of this firecracker while I was holding it. I decided that I would take my chances with the firecracker.

I was terrified, and trembled as he lit the firecracker. Once it was lit, he directed me to throw it away. Without an acceptable alternative, I did as he directed me to do. The firecracker exploded harmlessly.

He made me repeat this several times. Each time, my fear became less and less. After a while, I was not only holding the firecracker, I was also holding the match to light it. From that day until it became illegal to set off firecrackers at home, I was able to handle them without being afraid of them.

As I was also deathly afraid of caterpillars, and generally anything that crawled, they tried exposing me to those things too. That did not work quite as well—actually not at all, since I am still afraid of creepy-crawly insects. But in many cases, the principle of flooding does work.

Dear reader, I wish to expose you to God's Word in order that you may have a change in your thinking. I want us to begin to process God's Word so that we can begin to think the way Jesus thought when He lived among us in the flesh. When we begin to think like Jesus, we will have a lot fewer intra- and interpersonal problems. When we begin to think with renewed minds, with transformed thought lives, we will begin to approach life's challenges from a Godlike perspective. I pray that everyone reading this will, by God's grace, bring every dysfunctional thought captive to the obedience of Christ (2 Cor. 10:5).

It merits repeating that there is a battle going on in us, and it starts in our minds. This battle is for our souls and for the quality of the lives we live here and now. It is fought and either won or lost in the sphere of our cognition.

Some folks live very paranoid lives, and drawing conclusions that are far removed from the true nature of the phenomena they observe. Their minds create their own reality. There are pessimists around us who can look at the most joyful situation and make a bad thing out of it. In his play *Julius Caesar*, William Shakespeare, through the character of Cicero, observed, "But men may construe things after their fashion, clean from the purpose of the things themselves."[5]

Stated differently, this means that human beings may choose to interpret observed events in any manner, which may or may not have anything to do with the original meaning of the thing itself.

An example of this battle that rages within us is seen in Romans, where the apostle Paul writes, "I find then a law, that, when I would do good, evil is present with me. For I delight in the law of God after the inward man: But I see another law in my members, warring against the law of my mind, and bringing me into captivity to the law of sin which is in my members" (Rom. 7:21–23). Paul here speaks of two laws, or two principles of living. The one tends to good, but then there is the opposing law that tends to evil.

The evil law that wages war against the good law seems to have the upper hand. This is because, so long as we continue living in the flesh, the flesh wants to do the things that come more naturally to it. If, for example, someone slaps my face, the law of the flesh dictates that I slap that person back, perhaps even harder. The law of the Spirit, by contrast, suggests that I turn the other cheek. Clearly, retaliating comes more naturally than turning the other cheek. It is not difficult to see how this could result in a very hard struggle in the mind. We can only hope to win by understanding that sphere of warfare, and then applying the Word of God.

If the book of Romans ended at the last verse of chapter seven, or if the data of chapter eight were missing, then we would be consigned to a duality that simply amounted to defeat. "I thank God through Jesus Christ our Lord. So then, with the mind I myself serve the law of God; but with the flesh the law of sin" (Rom 7:25). Do you see the duality? Paul seems to be suggesting that we must admit that we serve God's law with our minds, and with the body, we serve the law of sin. If that were the end of the story, we would have a Dr. Jekyll and Mr. Hyde syndrome. Within each person lurk impulses for good and evil that could never be resolved. This would leave us in a permanent state of condemnation.

Happily, Paul did not stop there. Instead of accepting the state of affairs as defined in Romans 7:25, God's Word shows that in Christ Jesus there is a simple, straightforward way of living wholesome lives. The resolution of this dilemma is to recognize that in Christ there is no condemnation if we walk in the Spirit (see Rom. 8:1–4).

When the righteousness of the law is fulfilled in us as we walk in the Spirit, the law of sin and death loses its grip on us. That transformation can only take place when, first, we understand that we are at war, and second, we use God's Word to facilitate that transformation by improving our thought lives.

I will be reiterating several times in this book that my goal is to help the reader change his or her negative thinking where necessary, and to improve the thought lives of those who may have the right idea but are struggling. We need nothing short of what is called in psychology *cognitive restructuring*. This will come about only to the extent that we allow the Lord, by His written Word and the divine intervention of the Holy Spirit, to work on us. Moreover, as I stated earlier, one of the first things we must do in changing our thinking is to understand the sphere of our battle.

Before a country goes to war, that country's military leaders must assess whom they are fighting and what kind of military, political, and economic resources are available to that country. In other words, they must, at the very least, attempt to assess what they are up against. Without a realistic assessment, the invading country cannot adequately plan for this war and is liable to lose.

The twentieth century was called the American Century due to the economic, political, diplomatic, and military prowess of the United States. With few exceptions, its military was unmatched. The United States was instrumental in successfully prosecuting World Wars I and II, both of which ended upon terms favorable to the allied forces of the West. The United States was the first to use atomic weapons, which brought Japan to its knees and finally ended one of history's bloodiest wars. Following that World War, America's reputation and prestige grew exponentially.

One would have expected that a country of this size and power would have no problem overthrowing the Castro regime in Cuba. However, history proved that the United States' intervention resulted in a humiliating defeat at the Bay of Pigs. Why was this the case?

The short answer is that the Americans did not properly assess the capabilities or readiness of the Cubans, in either military or political terms. At the same time, the Americans overestimated the strength of 1,500 Cuban exiles they had trained for the expedition. In addition to that, the Americans had no skin in the game, so to speak. They were not prepared to commit combat troops or heavy weaponry to the fight.

Michael Voss, in a BBC article, reported:

> The American plan was to sneak ashore virtually unopposed, secure the area, take the airfield and fly in a government-in-exile who would then call for direct US support. At the same time, they were relying on a mass uprising in Cuba against the revolutionaries. It could not have gone more wrong: when an advance frogman lit a beacon to show the exiles where to land, it also alerted the Cuban militia to their presence..... The exiles had some air support, but US President John F. Kennedy

> was determined to keep the US involvement a secret and as the initiative turned against the invading force, he backed away from providing further critically needed air cover.[6]

Clearly, while the Unites States wanted the Cuban exiles to succeed, the Americans had not taken enough time to assess the situation on the ground or to plan for contingencies.

Going into battle without knowing the conditions that you will face is a prescription for sure disaster and must be avoided. Our Lord Jesus Christ posed this most salient question: "What king, going to make war against another king, sitteth not down first, and consulteth whether he be able with ten thousand to meet him that cometh against him with twenty thousand? Or else, while the other is yet a great way off, he sendeth an ambassage, and desireth conditions of peace" (Luke 14:31–32). In the battle for our thought lives, we must know the enemy and his capabilities if we are to have a chance of winning. If we are not properly prepared, we may have our own Bay of Pigs experience.

Not only are we at times unaware of our enemy's capabilities, I also think that often we are fighting the wrong enemy and with the wrong weapons. Sometimes, when faced with difficult people in our lives, we believe that they are our problem, when in fact that is an attack of the Devil. At other times when we face difficult situations, we blame the Devil, not realizing that God ordained those difficult situations to make us better Christians.

God uses afflictions as a corrective to lives that do not conform to His designs. Here is how the psalmist assessed the matter:

> Before I was afflicted I went astray:
> but now have I kept thy word....
> It is good for me that I have been afflicted;
> that I might learn thy statutes (Ps. 119:67, 71).

Many times, instead of fighting a battle with prayers, we are fighting a battle with words—our words. Instead of engaging the Enemy of our souls with spiritual weapons—that is, praying and reading the

Word—we fight by quarrelling one with the other. All the while, the Devil is getting the advantage in this warfare. So let us understand the sphere of our battles and bring the appropriate weapons to the fight to assure our victory.

Where did the battle in which we are engaged start? The battle started in the garden of Eden, and it is between God and Satan. In pronouncing the curse upon the serpent for deceiving Eve, God declared, "And I will put enmity between thee and the woman, and between thy seed and her seed; it shall bruise thy head, and thou shalt bruise his heel" (Gen. 3:15).

What does this mean in practical terms for us today? It simply means that due to humanity's disobedience in choosing to listen to the Devil rather than God, there exists a state of hostility between the Devil and God. Since the Devil knows that he cannot defeat God (he tried that in heaven, and it did not work out too well for him), he turns his fury upon the seed of the woman. The ultimate Seed of the woman is Christ, but the hostility is not only between Satan and Jesus. All who are descendants of Adam and Eve, both Jews and Gentiles, are caught in this warfare. This is particularly true of those who belong to Christ.

Paul helps us to identify the seed of the woman in his commentary on Abraham: "Now to Abraham and his seed were the promises made. He saith not, And to seeds, as of many; but as of one, And to thy seed, which is Christ" (Gal. 3:15). God promised Abraham to bless his seed and to make them many. Abraham's children produced many seeds, who are blessed because of Abraham's faithfulness. Yet, in exegeting this text, Paul identified Christ as the Seed. As Adam was the representative head of the human race, Jesus Christ as the new Adam is the representative head of the community of faith found in every corner of the globe.

If the Devil could destroy the work of Christ and thwart God's plan for our redemption, everything would be lost. The sacrificial, substitutionary atonement would have been for naught. Therefore, the Devil is fighting really hard, and we are in the middle.

This means that as we see this war play out in time, we must understand that the battle is not between us as brethren. Rather, the real battle is a spiritual one. It involves the Seed of the woman, Jesus

Christ, and the seed of the serpent, Satan himself. Since we, like Jesus, are God's seed, we are caught up in this spiritual warfare.

Because God is a good parent who protects His children from dangers, God protects us from the attacks of the Devil. We really do not need to fight in this battle, for the battle belongs to God. To the extent that we are engaged in this battle, we must fight it God's way. When we understand the nature of the warfare, it is best we let Christ fight His own battles. To the extent that Christ has recruited us to be involved, we would do well to fight using His methods and His weapons.

The Enemy of our souls is serious, and the warfare is at times fierce and vicious. In this warfare, the Devil has no shortage of means, and he knows no scruples. This means that Satan does not fight fair. He will throw everything in his arsenal at God's people, and he has no remorse. Be prepared, for he is willing to employ anything and everything he has at his disposal. He will use your children, your spouse, your job, your church members, and even your own mind.

Take courage in your battles, for the outcome is assured if you fight the right fight, using spiritual weapons. We must understand that those who stand in violent opposition to us are not the children of God. They are the children of the Devil.

If I must fight a war with the seed of the serpent, and if the sphere of this warfare is really between Jesus and the Devil, why don't I turn over the fight to Jesus? He is ultimately better able and prepared to fight this war than I could ever be. Don't you think it makes sense to let Him take the lead in this fight? We must simply do what He asks us to do. He is the general. He plans the strategies. He sets the objectives. He tells us when to fight and how to fight. If we follow His lead, we will always win.

The apostle Paul wrote, "Now thanks be unto God, which always causeth us to triumph in Christ, and maketh manifest the savour of his knowledge by us in every place" (2 Cor. 2:14). When we follow God's lead, we always triumph!

Please take note that in this warfare, we are indeed captives. But we are not Satan's captives, and we are not led in a shameful procession, to be gloated over by the Enemy. Rather, we are led as captives in Christ's victory procession, and given the job of spreading the sweet aroma of

His knowledge. He has won the victory, and we get to spread the good news!

The sooner we recognize that the fight is Christ's fight after all, and begin to fight the right kind of fight, we are well on our way to total victory. Unfortunately, since we live in the flesh, it is our tendency to fight using fleshly weapons. Although we still walk in the flesh, the Word tells us that we do not war after the flesh. Why is that? Because as God's children, we are more than mere flesh and blood. We are spiritual beings. We are more than a composite of flesh, bones, and sinews. There is something in our being that answers to a higher authority.

As born-again believers, we are "partakers of the divine nature" (2 Pet. 1:4). We are spiritual because in us is the breath of life, breathed in us by God (Gen. 2:7). We have life from God in us because that which "became a living soul," that is, the clay, was animated by the breath that God breathed into it.

The reason God sent His Son, Jesus Christ, to redeem us—that is, to buy us back to Himself—is because we have in us God's breath. The essential nature of redemption is that Christ died to reclaim that which was lost due to sin. The life that He gave to us, lost by Adam's disobedience and subsequent fall, is now purchased by Christ's blood, that He can present us back to God "not having spot, or wrinkle" (Eph. 5:27).

It is important to point out here that Christ died to save our souls and not our physical bodies. That is why our souls can never die: because God is in us. If the intent of Christ's death was to save our bodies from physical sickness and death, then no one for whom Christ died could ever die physically. However, Christians do get sick and physically die. Death simply transforms us from this present mortality to immortality. The Bible says, "This mortal must put on immortality, and this corruptible must put on incorruption" (1 Cor. 15:53). When Christ came, He came that His children may put off the corruptible and put on the incorruptible. Even physical death does not mean our defeat.

I cannot emphasize enough the importance of understanding the nature of this warfare. A good strategic fighter would never fight an opponent using a technique in which that opponent is much better than himself. For example, if you are a boxer and your opponent is a heavy puncher, expert in slugging it out with his opponents, you would be foolish to engage in a slugfest with him. To be successful, you would need to learn how to use the jab, how to stick and move, and how to use the ring to your advantage.

The Devil is the designer, manufacturer, and trainer in the use of carnal weapons. It stands to reason that if we engage in warfare using the Devil's weapons, he will beat us every time, because that is his game.

In fact, there are some fights we should never engage in at all. Why, for example, would I presume to take on the heavyweight boxing champion when he is in prime fighting form, even if I am in the best physical state of my life? I have only fought in the schoolyard and at home a couple of times. I had to do all I could to win those skirmishes. I never had any boxing skills to speak of. I never went to a boxing camp and never learned how to do an upper cut, left hook, or right cross. I have never learned to bob and weave nor to use the boxing ring to my advantage. So I would be rather foolish to challenge a real boxer.

As a child, when I did fight, I threw a few punches and was perhaps a bit more successful throwing stones at my opponents. That certainly did not qualify me as a worthy opponent for the great Muhammad Ali. Why then would I seek out Muhammad Ali when he was in his prime and say, "I'll take you on?" Why would I go into a gym, climb into a professional boxing ring, ill equipped as I am, a non-boxer, and challenge a proven professional fighter? That would be asking to be knocked out, or worse.

If I were so foolish as to do such a thing, and if I were lucky enough to get out alive, I would be completely, and perhaps permanently altered. I would be demolished because I had fought with a person who was expert in his craft. I would simply be outmatched and could not possibly expect to win. We face this outcome when we challenge the Devil on his turf and use his weapons.

We cannot and should not engage the Devil on his turf. We know that the Devil is an expert liar. If, out of convenience or malice, we decide to lie about someone, we would do well to watch ourselves, because the Devil has a bigger lie to tell about us. We must be very careful not to plan an evil device against another person. As big and wicked a device we could think up, the Devil has something bigger in store for us. We just should not fight on the Devil's turf.

Some years ago, a brother was relating a story about a fellow who, having recently arrived in the United States, was desperately looking for a place to live. He could not afford to pay market rent and was willing to settle for an attic or basement until he gained his financial footing. He had learned about a church brother who had a finished attic that, while not legal to rent, was suitable for the purpose. The homeowner, at his own risk, allowed this fellow to live in the attic for a minimal monthly rent.

The newcomer found the apartment comfortable enough, so he lived there for a few years. It seemed like a perfect arrangement because it was convenient and affordable. He had a nice place to live, and the property owner, who was struggling to pay the mortgage, insurance, and taxes, got some much-needed extra cash to fulfill those obligations.

Things were going swimmingly until a coworker told the newcomer that, since the attic apartment was illegal, he could sue the property owner and recover all the money he had paid in rent. Furthermore, he was told that if the property owner lost the case, he would have to pay the fellow's moving expenses. Upon learning of these financial benefits, he promptly sued the property owner and won.

This proved to be a tremendous financial and emotional burden upon the property owner and his wife. Their response was to cry to the Lord for help.

The acquisition of quick money by a less than honorable act encouraged the fellow to pursue other, more devious, and sometimes illegal strategies for getting quick money. To make a long story short, he eventually wove a web of deception, got in a world of trouble with the law, and was deported back to his home country without any chance of returning to the United States legally.

You see, we reap what we sow. When we fight using the Devil's means, the Devil has something else in store for us. The Word of the Lord tells us, "For they have sown the wind, and they shall reap the whirlwind" (Hos. 8:7). God is teaching us that when we employ the Devil's methods, not only will we reap what we sow, but to a greater degree and increased intensity.

It never pays to render evil to anyone. The Golden Rule is still the right way to go: "Therefore all things whatsoever ye would that men should do to you, do ye even so to them" (Matt. 7:12).

In the Old Testament book of Esther, we read about God's people Israel being in captivity under the Persian Empire. Through divine intervention, Esther, a Jew, became queen in Persia. It's a fascinating story that is well worth reading. After Esther became queen, a Persian named Haman became very jealous of the Jews in general, and particularly envious of a Jew named Mordecai. Haman's maneuvering to be promoted by the king backfired, and instead Mordecai was promoted over him. So sure was Haman that Mordecai would fall out of favor with the king that he built a gallows on his property to hang Mordecai.

When Haman's conniving ways were revealed to the king, the king was pretty upset with him. Before the king could even decide what to do with Haman, someone mentioned that Haman had built a gallows in his own yard for Mordecai. How convenient! The king instructed his people to hang Haman on it. The gallows Haman had built for his enemy served as the means of his own execution.

That is what happens when we fight our battles using the Devil's means. We are building our own gallows, so to speak, when we speak against others. We cannot hope to use the weapon of slander and escape slander ourselves. When we indulge in speaking evil, we are setting up ourselves to be spoken against in the same way or worse. We cannot sling mud and not expect to get dirty.

Our text reminds us that although we necessarily live in the world, we do not wage war using the world's methods. Rather we are told, "The weapons of our warfare are not carnal, but mighty through God to the pulling down of strong holds" (2 Cor.10:4). The battle continues to be fought in spiritual realm. It is not a carnal thing. Even when your brother comes to you and says something against you falsely, do not think it is a natural thing. It is rather from the spiritual realm. The Devil is at work trying to bring you down.

I learned this a few years ago. I was used to getting upset when people talked about me. I just wanted to get back at them. I could not wait for the opportunity pay them back in kind. One day God said to me in my spirit, "This is not really about them or you." It was not about them because they really did love God. However, the Devil deceived them and caused them to use their tongues in ways they could not help.

That is the reason we hope to change our thinking and thus our behavior. We want to feed our thought process with positive information so that our behavior will reflect our transformed minds. I am convinced that if good stuff is forced into our thinking, then what comes out will be good. If we put garbage in our thought lives, then garbage will come out.

Years ago, back in the days before we had personal computers, I took a course in computer programming at William Paterson University. We learned very early that the results we got depended upon what we put into the computer. The professor used the now-common saying, "Garbage in, garbage out." We could not reasonably expect to put garbage in the punch cards and expect to get a nice spreadsheet as output.

In the old days in church, our parents in the Lord would say, "What you put in is what you get out." So if we put malice, strife, evil speaking, and envy into our thought process, guess what comes out? That which we put in. When a person speaks negatively about a brother or a sister, the listener is left to wonder what such a person has digested. Upon what meat have we fed, spiritually speaking, for us to have grown so cynical and negative?

I hope to make the case, even at the risk of repeating myself, that the battle is still raging on a spiritual level, even after all these years and so far removed from the garden of Eden. Adamic disobedience in the garden of Eden was, first and foremost, a spiritual infraction. At the highest theological level, Adam's disobedience had very little to do with eating or not eating some fruit. Adam had enough to eat and to spare. He was not deprived of anything that would make him comfortable and happy. Adam's disobedience had everything to do with a hunger for something that he did not have and that was off-limits to him.

Adam's sin was an encroachment on divine prerogatives. That is the seat of envy: the desire to have what does not belong to us. Adam attempted to arrogate to himself divine privilege, for which the human race was thrown into chaos. In his pride, Adam was discontented with what God had allotted to him. Adam sought to encroach upon that which properly belonged to God.

John Calvin summarizes well the nature of Adam's transgression:

> The prohibition to touch the tree of the knowledge of good and evil was a trial of obedience, that Adam, by

> observing it, might prove his willing submission to the command of God. For the very term shows the end of the precept to have been to keep him contented with his lot, and not allow him arrogantly to aspire beyond it. The promise, which gave him hope of eternal life as long as he should eat of the tree of life, and, on the other hand, the fearful denunciation of death the moment he should taste of the tree of the knowledge of good and evil, were meant to prove and exercise his faith. Hence, it is not difficult to infer in what way Adam provoked the wrath of God. Augustine, indeed, is not far from the mark, when he says (in Psa. 19), that pride was the beginning of all evil, because, had not man's ambition carried him higher than he was permitted, he might have continued in his first estate.[7]

That was the battle that Adam and Eve had to fight. They lost. Again, the battle my friends, was spiritual. The battle had less to do with eating or not eating a fruit, and more to do with obedience and humility. It was about who would get the glory, and that was a spiritual matter.

Christians are engaged in a battle against "principalities, against powers, against the rulers of the darkness of this world, against spiritual wickedness in high places" (Eph. 6:12). We must be prepared for this fight, and we do well in our preparation to understand the wiles of the Devil.

What does that mean? It means that we must be perceptive of his trickeries, devices, strategies, and schemes. The Devil does not come at us haphazardly. He comes with a plan of action that appeals to our personalities, proclivities, and predispositions.

The Devil does not come to me for example, with cursing, because he knows I do not curse. He does not come to me with drinking, because I do not drink. Nor does the Devil come to me with drugs. I do not know what crack cocaine looks like close up. I've never seen it, and I never want to see it. I know the smell of marijuana, but I never touched the stuff, and I have no desire to touch it.

However, I know the Devil understands what may get my attention.

A beautiful woman is altogether another matter. The effort to remain sanctified, being saddled with my Hibbertine male nature, has been a monumental struggle for me for most of my adult life. Though now, because of age and maturity, I am much better able to control my impulses, I still feel I must be particularly vigilant to avoid falling into this temptation.

The Devil has his strategic plans for your life. He has figured out how he will get you, and he is planning even now to lay a trap for you. Be aware. After all, "we are not ignorant of his devices" (2 Cor. 2:11).

As we engage in this battle, the Word instructs us to be strong in the Lord and in the power of His might. We are told to put on the whole armor of God, that we may be able to stand against the strategies of the Devil. What is the whole armor of God? Ephesians tells us that the armor consists of loins girt about with truth, the breastplate of righteousness, feet shod with the preparation of the gospel of peace, the shield of faith, the helmet of salvation, and the sword of the Spirit, which is the Word of God. All this is undergirded with prayer. Verse 18 states, "Praying always with all prayer and supplication in the Spirit, and watching thereunto with all perseverance and supplication for all saints."

Let us be prepared for battle. We would not go into battle in Siberia in the dead of winter, dressed in summer clothing and sneakers with no socks. As Hitler's armies discovered in World War II, that is a prescription for disaster. Similarly, unpreparedness for spiritual battle is a recipe for failure.

We need to know the nature of the battle in which we are engaged. We need to know where we stand. We need to know how best to prepare for warfare. And lest you think this is not a war, think again. The Bible tells us to be prepared "because your adversary the devil, as a roaring lion, walketh about, seeking whom he may devour" (1 Pet. 5:8). He does not only want to touch you a little. He wants to devour you. If he had his way (and may that never be), when he is done with you and me, he wants us to be good for nothing. He wants us dead and in hell with him for all eternity. Even then, I do not think he will be satisfied.

Permit me to issue a word of warning here. Let us not deceive ourselves that we can play with the Devil and get away with it. We cannot play with him. I have observed over the years that many Christians seem to take the Devil lightly. At times, we are very spiritual and on our way to glory. At other times, we seem so enamored by the glitter of sin that the things of God are light-years away from us.

There is something radically wrong with that way of living. We cannot have one foot in the church and one foot out. The Enemy of our souls is not going to be satisfied until he destroys us. If the Devil gets you into gambling, he will not be through with you until you lose your home and all that you have. If he gets you into alcohol, he will not release you until you have cirrhosis of the liver. If he gets you into illicit sexual habits, he will not be satisfied until you contract HIV and die from AIDS. If the Devil gets you, you eventually die in your sin.

The final objective of the Enemy is not simply to embarrass us in the here and now. His ultimate objective is to kill our souls in hell. He wants us to be eternally separated from God. He does not want us to lose our homes here on earth, yet nevertheless go to heaven in the end. Rather, he wants us to lose our homes, our spouses, and our children, and then go to hell. He wants our God to say to us in the end, "I tell you, I know you not whence ye are; depart from me, all *ye* workers of iniquity" (Luke 13:27).

In the book of Genesis, we learn of the war between the seed of the woman and the seed of the serpent (3:15). That conflict did not stop and will not stop until Jesus comes to finally bind that old serpent and cast him into the lake of fire. Chapter 12 of Revelation makes it clear that this war is between Satan and those who follow God.

When the promised Seed was about to be born so He could do His work of redemption, Satan tried to kill Him. We see this in the gospels. Herod wanted to kill baby Jesus, but when Herod could not find the Child, he ordered that all the male children under two years of age be killed. This was fulfilment of prophecy found in Jeremiah 31:15 and repeated in the gospel of Matthew: "In Rama was there a voice heard, lamentation, and weeping, and great mourning, Rachel weeping for her children, and would not be comforted, because they are not" (Matt. 2:18).

Like Herod, when the dragon of Revelation found that he could not kill the Seed, he turned on those who followed Him. The Bible states, "And the dragon was wroth with the woman, and went to make war with the remnant of her seed, which keep the commandments of God, and have the testimony of Jesus Christ" (Rev. 12:17). By the way, if you are following Jesus Christ and you are persecuted, you are in good company. Do not be surprised, because it is to be expected.

As one strives to keep a sound mind and to follow God, it may seem the Enemy is getting the upper hand. He parades around, particularly after he has scored what may seem to be a victory over God's elect, as though he is the heavyweight champion of the world. But let us be cognizant that we are more than conquerors (Rom. 8:37). In the end, God is going to silence Satan, humble him, and trample him under our feet. The day we recognize that the power within us is greater than anything the Enemy can bring against us, our churches will become great and powerful, both in numerical and spiritual terms. The Devil will have been put in his rightful place: under our feet (Rom. 16:20).

In a real sense, our victory over Satan is already assured, because Jesus Christ defeated him two thousand years ago. Jesus's death took away our sin and guilt, and His bodily resurrection from the dead was for our justification (Rom. 4:25). At Lazarus's graveside, Jesus said, "I am the resurrection, and the life: he that believeth in me, though he were dead, yet shall he live: And whosoever liveth and believeth in me shall never die" (John 11:25–26). Jesus has Himself risen from the dead so that we also can have victory over Satan, death, and hell.

Since this is the case, why does the Devil have such a great hold on us? If Jesus Christ has defeated him, from where is he getting his power? I believe we overestimate the Enemy's strength and give him too much power over us. If we compare him with any of us, clearly he seems to have more power. But that is the wrong comparison. We should not compare the Devil with ourselves. Rather, we must compare him to the God we serve, who now resides in us in the person of the Holy Ghost. When we do that, it becomes obvious how defeated Satan is.

We need a complete and radical mind makeover. This is what the Bible terms a transformed mind (Rom. 12:2). As our minds are renewed, it becomes easier for us to embrace this often-repeated benediction in our churches: "Now unto him that is able to do exceeding abundantly above all that we ask or think, according to the power that worketh in us, Unto him be glory in the church by Christ Jesus throughout all ages, world without end. Amen" (Eph. 3:20–21).

Let us examine ourselves and ask, "Does the Devil have power over me when I am fully immersed in God's Word? Does the Enemy have power over me when I am Holy Ghost-filled and the Spirit is working through me?" You will find after close examination that at such times, the Devil's hold and influence on us are minimal. That describes a state of walking in the Spirit and not in the flesh.

What happens when we walk in the Spirit? The Bible tells us that those who are led by the Spirit of God are in fact the sons of God (Rom. 8:14). Paul further admonished the Galatians to "walk in the Spirit, and ye shall not fulfil the lust of the flesh" (Gal. 5:16). To walk in the Spirit means to have a renewed mind. Our thinking must be changed. We must begin to accept the fact that to truly please God, our thought lives must be informed by a kingdom worldview. When our thought lives are properly ordered around a kingdom mentality, we recognize that we are operating on a higher and purer level than the world does.

What is the kingdom of God? And what is it to have a kingdom mentality? Well, according to Scripture, "The kingdom of God is not meat and drink; but righteousness, and peace, and joy in the Holy Ghost" (Rom. 14:17). Those who are operating after the principles of a kingdom mentality are not overly concerned with the material things of this life. They are not desirous of having "an eye for an eye and a tooth for a tooth" relationships. Rather, they are focused on things above.

It is worth noting that our faulty thinking produces faulty behaviors. These maladaptive behaviors are not relegated only to the young people or those we would consider weak Christians. These behaviors represent nothing short of spiritual wickedness even in the highest of places. In other words, some believers whom we regard as strong, even recognize as leaders, behave in ways that are contrary to kingdom principles. We need to rebuke such behaviors. We must have the attitude that this is God's holy church where the Word of God rules. We must constantly renew our minds by delving into God's written Word, and take every dysfunctional thought captive to the obedience of Christ.

I believe the Enemy of our souls is too comfortable in our assemblies. When we come together as a body of believers, wherever we may be, we should make the Enemy extremely uncomfortable. We should, for example, make people who talk too much very uncomfortable in our church by not participating in their negative talk. When your friend calls to gossip about a brother or sister, you should say, "Friend, I am a sanctified child of God, and I cannot participate in this talk. I suggest that you bring all those negative thoughts captive to the obedience of Christ." If your friend insists on pursuing that line of talk, graciously excuse yourself from that conversation and hang up the telephone. If this gossiping person gets this treatment from three or four acquaintances, before long that person will get the point.

Why is it sinful to talk negatively about God's people? Because we are all God's children and are all subject to mistakes. Renewed thinking recognizes that we must learn to cover each other in love. The Bible tells us that love covers a multitude of sins (1 Pet. 4:8). Even if my brother has sinned, if he is willing to acknowledge the wrong he did, my job is to embrace him and to forgive him.

Some believers are purveyors of bad news. They need not witness the word or deed. All they need is to hear it through the grapevine, and they immediately begin to spread the bad news. The sad part is that they never once ask their target, "Did you do it, and if so, why did you do it?" Sadder still, gossipers never pray for their target. Instead, they set out to assassinate a character on a rumor. That kind of a slanderous thought must be brought captive to the obedience of Christ.

When we run with a rumor, are we not doing things just like the political world does it? Politicians will run with any rumor, however slight, and use it as a means of destroying their rivals. As believers, we should not engage in such behaviors. Remember, although we walk in the flesh, we do not wage war using worldly weapons (2 Cor. 10:3). We should love and protect each other in the body of Christ, even if at times we hurt each other. The Bible says, "Therefore if thine enemy hunger, feed him; if he thirst, give him drink: for in so doing thou shalt heap coals of fire on his head" (Rom. 12:20). If we are required to treat even our enemies that way, how should we treat those who are our brothers and sisters in the Lord?

I will do a bit of self-disclosure here because I do not wish you to believe that I am perfect in this matter. Many of us struggle with it. My late wife took ill, and despite our prayers and the cancer treatments, she died. This left me devastated. I was unprepared. There were things I needed to do. There were conversations I needed to have with her. In retrospect, although I may not have realized it at time, I needed to make confessions to her and to ask her forgiveness. I was left empty, confused, and deeply pained.

At such times of bereavement, we need all the comfort we can get. In addition, like most people affected by the passing of a loved one, I needed much attention. A fellow minister, whom I expected to reach out and embrace me, did not do so. In my time of self-pity, I concluded that it was because I had confronted him about something not long before. Frankly, I was hurt and disappointed.

Not long after that, he had a crisis in his life, and I decided that I was not going to reach out to him either. I wanted him to see how he liked the abandonment. However, in a moment of godly clarity, I said to myself, "No, I am a child of God. I know better than that." I defied that feeling of revenge and reached out to him because he needed the support of a brother.

I call this a moment of godly clarity because I am convinced that God intervened. God would not allow me to wallow in self-pity and bask in my revenge, and as a result render a slight for a slight.

As we strive to become mature Christians, we need to behave in a loving and godly way to our brethren, even if they hurt us. This requires a change in our thinking. We must reject the desire to get even. Our best example is Jesus. They spat on Him and they beat Him, yet He loved them with an everlasting love. We must do what He did. The Bible tells us, "Forasmuch then as Christ hath suffered for us in the flesh, arm yourselves likewise with the same mind: for he that hath suffered in the flesh hath ceased from sin" (1 Pet. 4:1). We must be prepared to suffer for righteousness's sake.

How is that possible? Because we are guided by a different principle. Remember our theme passage from Scripture: "For though we walk in the flesh, we do not war after the flesh" (2 Cor. 10:3). We need to change our thinking. If we think pure thoughts, we will act pure acts.

I have devoted a considerable amount of time and space to the understanding of the sphere of battle in which we are engaged. I did this because I believe that if we are going to win this fight, we must, as a matter of first principles, know the type of fight that we are in. Now that we know the type of warfare we are dealing with, it will be worth our while to examine the weapons, offensive and defensive, we must use, as well as the appropriate clothing that we must have on, if we intend to win. That will be the subject of the next chapter.

A Prayer

Heavenly Father, please help us to properly understand the sphere of warfare in which we are engaged, so that we will not be ignorant of the Devil's strategies. In Jesus's name. Amen!

CHAPTER 2

Understand the Weapons of Our Warfare

For my thoughts are not your thoughts, neither are your ways my ways, saith the Lord. *For as the heavens are higher than the earth, so are my ways higher than your ways, and my thoughts than your thoughts.*

—Isaiah 55:8–9

In the previous chapter, I talked about the need to understand the sphere of the battle in which we are engaged. It is a spiritual battle that we must fight in the spiritual realm, using spiritual weapons. Spiritual weapons are available to us.

At the heart of every sin that we commit is a thought. People do act and speak without forethought, but often before they do or say anything, they are aware of a thought behind it. It is very rare that we act thoughtlessly. The mind, therefore, must be appropriately clad so that it will produce positive results. If we were good at monitoring our thoughts, we would readily recognize that the things we say and do germinate in our thought process. The Bible tells us, "As a man thinks in the heart so is he" (Prov. 23:7). That is why the Word says we should guard our hearts with all diligence, for out of our hearts are the wellsprings of life (Prov. 4:23).

In the 1970s, there was a popular comedian named Flip Wilson who played a character called Geraldine. Whenever Geraldine did something naughty, she would say, "The Devil made me do it." Like Geraldine, many of us blame the Devil. Sometimes we blame others, and we even blame God for our thoughtless words and deeds. Is that really appropriate? I argue that it is not!

James tells us that when we are tempted, we should never say that it was God who tempted us. God is not responsible for our individual acts of wrongdoing. That is up to us, really. James wrote, "Let no man say when he is tempted, I am tempted of God: for God cannot be tempted with evil, neither tempteth he any man: But every man is tempted, when he is drawn away of his own lust, and enticed. Then when lust hath conceived, it bringeth forth sin: and sin, when it is finished, bringeth forth death" (James 1:13–15).

James seems to be teaching that the roots of evil lie within our desires. We must conceive of that desire in our minds before we can act upon or achieve it. One who controls one's mind controls one's emotions and behaviors. God made us with the ability to think and to make choices, so we must wisely exercise those abilities by properly regulating our thought lives.

The mind is a powerful thing. If you think you are strong, then you are. If you think you are weak, then you are. If you think you can change things around you by your individual actions, then you can. Start thinking good thoughts, and you will start creating good things.

The opposite, of course, is also true. There are some folks who have all the potential in the world, but they think so negatively of themselves that they cannot accomplish anything worthwhile. By their negative thinking, they constantly live defeated lives although victory was within reach.

I wish the opposite to be true of us. We want to be able to snatch victory out of the mouth of defeat. When you are down on your face, people write you off, saying, "You are done. You are finished!" You can rise like the phoenix out of the ashes of despair, give God the glory, and claim your victory. For as a person thinks in their heart, so they become.

We come again to our theme passage: "For though we walk in the flesh, we do not war after the flesh: For the weapons of our warfare are not carnal, but mighty through God to the pulling down of strong holds; Casting down imaginations, and every high thing that exalteth itself against the knowledge of God, and bringing into captivity every thought to the obedience of Christ" (2 Cor. 10:3–5). The battle for our souls did not start with us, but in the garden of Eden. It is between

Satan and the Seed of the woman, who is Christ, and all those who put their faith in Him. The Bible says, "I will put enmity between thee and the woman, and between thy seed and her seed. It shall bruise thy head and thou shall bruise his heel" (Gen. 3:15). After the Devil inveigled Eve and subsequently Adam to sin against God, there would ever exist animosity between the seed of the serpent and the seed of the woman.

Although the battle is fierce, we know from God's Word how it turns out. This is the advantage we have as Christians as we fight the good fight of faith: we know how the war ends. Because of Christ's work on the cross and His subsequent triumphant bodily resurrection from the dead, we know we have total victory.

When countries wage war, we can never know for sure how the conflict will turn out, even in cases when one side seems to have the advantage. Upon its entry in the Vietnam War, not many experts thought that the United States would lose. After all, the United States' armed forces certainly outnumbered and outclassed those of the Vietnamese. We know from history, however, that America left Vietnam in shame. Not only did the American government not achieve its military or political objectives, its soldiers returned home only to be rejected by the people in whose name they had fought. Whatever spin the military and civilian leadership may have put on the outcome, it was no success.

The Vietnam conflict changed America in important ways, not least of which was that Americans became more cautious in how we wage war. There are still many adventurists, in and out of the government and the military, who would not mind intervening in the internal affairs of other nations. But thankfully, because of our experience in Vietnam, those responsible for waging wars tend to be more deliberate. There have been notable exceptions, but those are in the minority.

This is not the case when it comes to the war in which we are engaged. The Bible tells us, "For this purpose the Son of God was manifested, that he might destroy the works of the devil" (1 John 3:8). This should give us ample reason to be hopeful. We know the outcome of this battle. In this war, the Devil's defeat is not partial. There are no accommodations with him. There are no peace treaties with him. The war ends in complete and unqualified defeat and destruction for the Devil and his minions.

In this chapter, the emphasis is on the need to understand the weapons of our warfare. We need to employ the right weapons for the right fight.

Back in era of World War I, the horse was an indispensable resource in prosecuting warfare. The horse was probably the swiftest way to advance against the enemy then. Although battle tanks saw their debut in that war, they were too crude and slow to have a significant impact on the outcome.

By the advent of World War II, although horses were still being used, armies that employed horses as their main means of advancing the fight were at a distinct disadvantage. Tanks and airplanes ruled the day.

Change continues. If an army today attempted to use World War II-era airplanes and tanks, it would lose miserably.

Similarly, Christians today cannot use weapons of the world to fight their spiritual battle. We are told in Scripture, "The weapons of our warfare are not carnal, but mighty through God to the pulling down of strong holds" (2 Cor. 10:4). We must fight the battle with spiritual weapons.

In natural armies, we have offensive weapons as deterrents to aggression, and defensive weapons against the offensive weapons of our enemies. Why do we need these weapons in our spiritual arsenals? Because we are threatened every day. If we had no threats, we would not need weapons.

The former Soviet Union and the United States of America avoided a direct or "hot" war for over fifty years for one reason: they each knew the destructive potential of the weapons the other possessed. They each had weapons that could destroy themselves and the world repeatedly. They declared a military doctrine called *mutually assured destruction* (MAD). MAD assured each side that if the other attacked, this would mean all-out war in which both sides would face destruction by nuclear weapons. For the duration of the Cold War, the world remained relatively safe because the superpowers knew the potential for destruction. Though the United States and the Soviet Union were rivals at best and enemies at worst, one could argue that the world was a lot safer during the Cold War than it is today, because each side understood their weapons.

In the battle for our souls, if we follow God's prescription, there is no defeat for us. The battle continues in the spiritual realm, and we must employ spiritual implements of war if we hope to succeed. What are those implements of war? The apostle Paul provides us a list: loins girt about with truth, the breastplate of righteousness, feet shod with the preparation of the gospel of peace, the shield of faith, the helmet of salvation, and the sword of the Spirit, which is the word of God. Paul added praying always to that list (Eph. 6:10–18).

The proper employment of these implements of warfare assures our victory. We may seek to find some other set of equipment if we choose, but none will be as effective as these. I encourage you to consider putting these in your toolbox. You will need them soon.

As believers, we should not to be surprised when we face wars and strife in our lives, or even in the church. The children of God who have not experienced conflicts in their lives are the exception rather than the rule. The church that is trouble-free is most unusual indeed. We recall Jesus's words to His disciples: "These things I have spoken unto you, that in me ye might have peace. In the world ye shall have tribulation: but be of good cheer; I have overcome the world" (John 16:33). Although the battle is bloody and painful, it ends in victory for the Christian. The Bible says, "And the God of peace shall bruise Satan under your feet shortly" (Rom. 16:20).

What is the reason that the apostle Paul, through the inspiration of the Holy Ghost, provided the armaments prescribed in Ephesians? "That ye may be able to stand against the wiles of the devil" (v. 10). The Devil is strategic. He does not come at us in an unplanned manner. The Lord has plans for our lives (Jer. 29:11). Likewise the Devil has plans for us—only his plans are sinister and designed to destroy us.

How strategic is the Devil in tempting us? He will study us and bring to us the things that he knows will appeal to us most. Take the example of Jesus's encounter with him in the wilderness. Jesus had been fasting for forty days and nights. Scripture observes that afterward, Jesus was hungry. The Devil did not come to him and say, "If you are the son of God, fast one more day." I imagine if one has fasted for forty days, one could fast another day.

No, the Devil did not say that. He brought to Jesus what he thought would be most appealing from a human perspective: food. More than that, he challenged Jesus's very identity. If Jesus Christ were not the Son of God, His ministry would have been a fraud. His willingness to bring glory to the Father would have failed. The work that He did to demonstrate that He was from the Father would have all been for nothing. The works that He performed were to reveal the Father. He told Philip, "Believe me that I am in the Father, and the Father in me: or else believe me for the very works' sake" (John 14:11).

What was the Devil's strategy in tempting Jesus? He thought that Jesus was so keen to show that He was the Son of the Father, He would naturally seize the opportunity to prove as much to the Devil. The Devil calculated that if Jesus were to turn stone into bread at the Devil's prompting, He would effectively be obeying the Devil. Such an action would have had far-reaching implications, not only for God's redemptive program, but also for God's sovereignty. Jesus understood that God's divine prerogative, glory, dignity, and majesty proscribed any action on Jesus's part that would aid and abet the Devil in his long-standing campaign to usurp God's power.

The Devil's plan for Jesus, therefore, was not haphazard. It was strategic, designed to unseat God, robbing Him of His glory. The Devil also miscalculated, supposing that since Jesus was human, perhaps the Devil could appeal to Jesus's human vanity, and thereby get Jesus to prove that He was indeed God's Son. That act of turning stone to bread would have been most ungodlike, and would have represented a failure of the highest order. God would have been obeying the Devil, and that would have brought to a screeching halt God's plan of redemption.

Paul also defines for his audience the nature of their warfare: "For we wrestle not against flesh and blood, but against principalities, against powers, against the rulers of the darkness of this world, against spiritual wickedness in high places" (Eph. 6:12). The apostle made it clear that this is not a carnal battle, and therefore cannot be fought with carnal weapons. Like the Ephesians, we are dealing with supernatural forces. We must meet those forces with supernatural weapons.

Most of this armament is defensive in nature. Only one, the sword of the Spirit, which is God's Word, is an offensive weapon. Each piece of this armament must be present, or we will be vulnerable.

I will now take a closer look at each piece of the prescribed armor for the Christian soldier. While I will not provide an exhaustive explication, what I offer will, I hope, give the reader a sense of their importance.

Loins Girt About with Truth

I am not sure whether the apostle listed the items of the armament in order of importance, but it strikes me as interesting that he listed truth first. It matters not what else we do; if it is not clothed in truth, it amounts to nothing. David rightly observes that God desires truth in the inward part (Ps. 51:6).

Paul admonished the Ephesians to gird their loins with truth, or, as the NIV puts it, "with the belt of truth buckled around your waist." How are we to understand Paul's instruction? What is truth? Whose truth? Is it the truth of God, or is it living a life of truthfulness?

Klyne Snodgrass argues that in the context of Ephesians, "truth is used in this letter both with reference to God's truth revealed in the gospel (1: 13; 4: 21) and to truth as right living and speaking in the new being (4: 15, 24–25; 5: 9). To belt on truth means to be strengthened by God's truth in the gospel and to resolve to live truth."[8]

The instruction to gird the loins with truth conveys the idea of a soldier readying himself for battle in the ancient world. Back then, men did not wear pants as we do today. They wore long robes. You can observe this even today among Middle Eastern men. Going to battle in long robes would certainly hinder the soldier's mobility, and therefore his effectiveness. Securing the robe under the belt was an essential preparation for battle. In addition, the belt provided some covering and protection of the lower abdomen, according to Snodgrass. Having the robe secured and the abdomen covered signaled that the soldier was ready for battle.

Paul instructs them and us to secure whatever may hinder them and to protect the vulnerable area of the abdomen with the belt of truth. What truth? The truth about who God is and the manner in which Christians should conduct their lives. Girded with truth, we have no deficiencies. Truth's essential nature is pure and without flaws. We do not want any flawed material covering our tender areas. The belt of

God's truth forms this covering for us and protects from the Enemy's attacks.

Charles Hodge, many years ago, observed that truth about God as revealed in the gospel is:

> ... the first and indispensable qualification for a Christian soldier. To enter on this spiritual conflict ignorant or doubting would be to enter battle blind and lame. As the belt gives strength and freedom of action, and therefore confidence, so does the truth when spiritually apprehended and believed. Truth alone, as abiding in the mind in the form of divine knowledge, can give strength of confidence even in the ordinary conflicts of the Christian life, much more in any really evil day.[9]

Let us not start in the fight unless we know we have on truth.

Breastplate of Righteousness

As the proper protection of the loins with truth is important for our survival, so is the breastplate of righteousness necessary to protect our upper torsos. The breastplate is another piece of defensive weaponry with which the soldier must be equipped in this fight. The breastplate was armor that covered the body from the neck to the thighs. It was made up of two parts: one part to protect the soldier's front and the other his back. Charles Hodge writes, "A warrior without his breastplate was naked, exposed to every thrust of his enemy, and even to every random spear. In such a state, flight or death is inevitable. Isaiah 59:17 describes Jehovah as putting on "*righteousness like a breastplate, and a helmet of salvation on his head.*"[10]

Under no circumstances should the Christian go into this warfare naked. That would be an invitation to disaster. Christians are not defeated because they do not love the Lord. Their defeat is not an indication that they are not saved. Very often it boils down to being unprepared for the fight. Sometimes they think they are prepared, but their armor is not suitable. Having the loins girt with truth, and having the breastplate of righteousness to protect front and back, the believer is well on the way to being ready for battle.

Feet Shod with the Preparation of the Gospel of Peace

Paul next instructs the Ephesians, "and with your feet fitted with the readiness that comes from the gospel of peace" (Eph. 6:4, NIV). It is hardly necessary for me to remark that going to war without shoes or with the wrong shoes is a very ill-advised move. Max Anders observes that the shoes to which Paul refers were "hobnailed shoes which kept the soldiers['] footing sure in battle."[11]

One of my sons is a member of the armed forces of the United States. When he comes home from his drills, I am always impressed with the boots he wears. He has told me that they go out on long runs with these boots, because the boots provide the necessary support for their feet. The boots are comfortable and sturdy and protective.

Having shoes fitted to the feet harkens to Isaiah's words: "How beautiful upon the mountains are the feet of him that bringeth good tidings, that publisheth peace; that bringeth good tidings of good, that publisheth salvation; that saith unto Zion, Thy God reigneth" (Isa. 52:7). It should be obvious that the apostle Paul was speaking metaphorically. In Isaiah, the Lord describes those who bring good news of salvation. Snodgrass argues that having feet shod with the good news is indicative of someone who is willing and ready to share the gospel of salvation. This readiness is not reserved to the spreading of the gospel, but also pertains to life in all aspects. He states: "Knowledge of the gospel should make people alert and ready for life. They are careful about their speech and actions. They do not live in the dark. They live wisely, redeeming the time and understanding the will of the Lord. Such people not only share the good news, but they are also agents of peace and love, ready to do the whole will of God."[12]

When faced with life's challenges, when hurt by the Enemy, when the hosts of hell are arrayed against you and there is no way out, the Lord says to put on the gospel shoes and share your faith with a dying world. Wearing the armament is the only way you are going to stand against the schemes of the Devil.

Shield of Faith

With girded loins, a breastplate, and shod feet, we are getting closer to being fully armed, but we are not there yet. We need another defensive weapon: a shield, the shield of faith. Because we are clad as we are does not mean that Satan will not throw his darts at us. Far from it. He will do his best to test your belt, breastplate, and shoes. The darts and sharp objects will come. The stones and bricks will come. We therefore need a shield.

That shield is faith. Faith brings into reality the things for which we hope (Heb. 11:1), and without which it is impossible to please God (Heb. 11:6). The shield of faith is not merely human faith in God, because unfortunately our faith fails sometimes. Human faith is important, but even more important is God's faithfulness.

In other words, it is not that our faith in God is so strong that we get His protection from the fire darts. Rather, it is the faithfulness of God, who promised that He would never leave us or forsake us, that forms the bedrock of our protection. Paul was encouraging the Ephesians—and us—to be shielded with the knowledge of God's faithfulness that never fails. It is certainly important for Christians to exercise their faith in God, but we can rest securely in the knowledge that even when our faith grows weak, God's faithfulness remains immutable.

Snodgrass cogently observes, "To speak of faith is not to focus on human belief, but on the faithfulness of God. What protects us from the arrows of the evil one is our relationship with God."[13] Faced with our difficulties, we can afford not to fight the Devil's fight when we are shielded by God's faithfulness toward us. Our relationship with Him is seen in our exercise of our faith in Him. Such faith envisions our ultimate deliverance through Christ.

Helmet of Salvation

Next, Paul instructs his audience to put on the helmet of salvation. Our heads contain our brains, which govern our corporal motions. Our brains are also the centers of our cognition and emotions. If we expose our heads to an enemy's attack, we might as well just give up the fight. A traumatic brain injury will put us out of commission or even kill us.

I write this chapter in the aftermath of a tragedy that occurred to one of our church members. He was in good health and went out daily, doing general contractual work. Over the years, he had taken his share of minor injuries. Not long ago, he was helping a relative move some household furniture down a flight of stairs, and an accident occurred. The furniture slipped from their grasp and tumbled down the stairs. As he was the lead man, it hit him in the front of his head, and knocked him on his back, where he hit the back of his head on a hard object. It took only a few hours before he lost consciousness, from which he never recovered. Some three weeks after the accident, he died. All his other vital organs were working just fine. It was only his head that was not protected, and so he is no more. Many of us asked why. We call his death untimely. But if he had had on a helmet of some sort, might he still be alive?

Snodgrass offers that the believer puts on the helmet to do righteousness and to receive salvation. God's salvation is the ultimate assurance of protection.[14]

Anders disagrees and writes that the helmet of salvation pictures the Roman soldier's metal protective headgear. It does not refer to our salvation in Christ. Taking the helmet of salvation can be understood as resting our hope in the future and living in this world according to the value system of the next.[15]

Charles Hodges states, "Salvation is itself the helmet. What adorns and protects the Christian, which enables him to hold up his head with confidence and joy, is the fact that he is saved. He is one of the redeemed, translated from the kingdom of darkness into the kingdom of God's dear Son. If still under condemnation, if still estranged from God, a foreigner, and alien, without God and without Christ, he could have no courage to enter into this conflict."[16]

These differences among the apologists may be splitting hairs. The reality is that we are not going to have hope in Christ, now or in the future, if we are not saved. The assurance of salvation protects the Christian, even in the most difficult binds. One cannot fight this war with any degree of confidence if one is uncertain of one's salvation. Moreover, if one is not saved—that is, if one does not have on the helmet of salvation—it stands to reason that one is possessed with an earthly perspective, and therefore that one is fighting using carnal weapons.

The reverse is likewise true. When Christians are saved, their minds are transformed, and they no longer fit into the mold of the world (Rom. 12:1–2). They therefore engage in this fight with a heavenly mind-set.

Sword of the Spirit, which Is the Word of God

Up to this point, the apostle Paul described defensive weapons that are required to take on this fight. If we are thus clad, we are almost ready to defend against the strategies of Satan. Having a good defensive posture is always a good plan for victory, but the soldier must do more than be defensive. Sometimes a soldier must attack the stronghold of the enemy. To do that, he needs offensive weapons. With the sword of the Spirit, which is God's Word, the soldier is completely prepared for both defensive and offensive warfare.

Every country must have defensive as well as offensive weapons to keep its people safe. Back in 1983, the president of the United States, Ronald Reagan, proposed a defense system against nuclear attack. The system was mounted on intercontinental ballistic missiles. It was named the Strategic Defense Initiative (SDI), which some called Star Wars. As conceived, the system was to combine ground-based units and orbital deployment platforms, which would change the nation's nuclear posture from offensive to defensive. The underlying philosophy was that if the United States protected itself from potential attacks, its people would be safer. Eventually the country could spend less on stockpiling and maintaining offensive nuclear weapons. Even given the sanguinity and boundless optimism of Reagan, no one around him, including himself, proposed giving up offensive nuclear weapons.

Our offensive weapon in this fight is not our words, education, family attachments, political alliances, or offices in ministry. Rather, it is the sword of the Spirit, which Paul says is the God's Word. Snodgrass observes that the "Spirit is the one who empowers the sword. Throughout Scripture God's Word is the instrument by which His power is shown."[17]

Joseph Wang states that Paul may have intended the term *word* (*rhema*) to mean the sacred Scripture of Judaism. However, Ephesians 5:26 uses the same word to connote words spoken at the time of baptism.

"If the latter is the intended sense, then the word of God is any helpful word from God in the moment of need."[18] I believe that the sword of the Spirit encompasses the written Word (both Testaments) and the spoken word of exhortation inspired by the Holy Spirit.

On this battlefield, Christians must have God's Word, which Jesus characterizes as "Spirit" and "life" (John 6:63). The Christian, be they a lay person or a pastor, has the right to go on the offensive using God's Word, as for example when sin is being tolerated in the church. Paul reminded Timothy of the various usefulness of God's Word. He wrote, "All scripture is given by inspiration of God, and is profitable for doctrine, for reproof, for correction, for instruction in righteousness: That the man of God may be perfect, thoroughly furnished unto all good works" (2 Tim. 3:16–17). God's Word is a two-edged sword that must be skillfully used to remove sin (Heb. 4:12).

Being thus accoutered with the various defensive armaments and the offensive weapon, Christians are ready to do battle God's way. Following this prescription, there is no defeat for the believer. God strictly prohibits the use of carnal weapons in spiritual warfare (2 Cor. 10:3–5).

Praying and Watching

Undergirding all of this is an active and vibrant prayer life. Paul instructs his audience, "praying always with all prayer and supplication in the Spirit, and watching thereunto with all perseverance and supplication for all saints" (Eph. 6:18).

Observe the imperatives: "praying always" with "all prayer," watching "with all perseverance," and supplication for "all saints." While prayer does not fit the metaphor of bodily armor described in Ephesians 6, it is nevertheless an indispensable tool for the Christian soldier engaged in battle against the ruler of the darkness of this world. The soldier ignores prayer at his peril and certainly invites defeat. Prayer is a defensive as well as an offensive weapon.

As we choose the right weapons with which to fight, I really want each of us to think about our thought lives. That's right! We must think about what we think about. I think we get defeated many times because we do not think about our thought lives. As we think, we become.

In the 2008 US presidential election, we had two candidates: seventy-two-year-old John McCain, the Republican candidate, and forty-seven-year-old Barack Obama, his Democratic counterpart. We watched with fascination the energy of these two men. Whatever one may think of John McCain's politics and ideology, one must admire him for the grit and persistence he demonstrated throughout the campaign.

What about McCain convinced him that he could become the president of the United States at his age? If he had been elected, he would have been the oldest presidents to take office. The odds seemed to be against him in the spring and summer, during the Republican primary elections. The press virtually wrote him off. Somehow, he pulled out of that slump and became the Republican nominee. How was that possible? Because he thought in his mind that he could do it. For him, age was never a factor.

There is something transformative about that kind of optimism. The mind can generate an optimism that sees no barriers. Such a mind sees what others would regard as insurmountable obstacles, and perceives opportunities to grow and expand.

And how about Barack Obama? Prior to the election, who would have thought that a Black man and a rookie senator would have had a chance of becoming the president of the United States? When he announced his improbable candidacy to become the leader of the free world, I for one thought that he was just an egomaniac who wanted to make headlines. Like millions of Americans, I did not give him a chance. History has shown that we were all wrong. His positive thinking proved transformative for the country and, indeed, the world. You do not get to be the president as a Black man without possessing a strong mind. Any defeatist attitude on his part would have meant certain failure. He had to choose the right political weapons to defeat the Democratic establishment, and then to win in the general election.

Not only are we to understand the weapons of our warfare, we must always be at the ready. To further the analogy, if the United States during the Cold War had decided to unilaterally disarm itself of nuclear weapons and go back to bayonets and horses, it would have ceased to exist.

I remain convinced that if the Devil thought that we were armed with the right spiritual weapons, he would be less inclined to attack us. He is a strategic thinker, and he is not going to attack us at our strong points. If he knows that we have the right weapon in our homes and churches—the weapons of prayer and reading the Word—he would not bother our households or churches with the petty arguments in which we seem embroiled. The reason the Devil is in our homes and in our churches is that we arm ourselves with the wrong, ineffective weapons. He surmises that his chances of success are greatly enhanced when we are so ill-equipped.

Think. If we use slander as a weapon against the brethren, this delights the Devil, because he is the biggest slanderer. The Bible says, "He is the accuser of the brethren" (Rev. 12:10). If we use lies as a weapon in our arsenal, the Devil will always be the bigger liar. The Bible says he is the father of lies (John 8:44).

It would be ridiculous for Russia to attack the United States with machetes in this time when the United States has advanced technological weapons of war. It is equally ridiculous for us to respond to the Devil's attack using his weapons. He can build bigger ones than we can, and he is better capable of using those weapons than we are. Moreover, be assured that the Enemy has no constraints with regard to the weapons he uses against us. He will simply use whatever means are available to him, and he knows no scruples. In other words, the Devil will not regard any means as being too painful or too destructive for us. If he has the means, he will use them!

We are talking about controlling the thought life. The battle is primarily a battle for the mind. When faced with a battle, let us first think what weapon is suitable for the situation. Reading the Word, it seems very easy to understand the weapons that we have. But how often do we lose our contests because we are ill-prepared to face the Enemy? We each know our challenges. Therefore, we must know how to strengthen ourselves by prayer and the Word.

For some, their weakness is lying. If it were not for the Holy Spirit in them, they would be expert liars. For some men, their weakness is chasing women. If it were not for the Word of God in such men, we would be all over the place. However, those of us who are sober Christians know how to employ the appropriate weapons in our fight against these impulses and habits. Whenever I have failed in my walk with the Lord, I have always traced it to being unprepared to fight, or to fighting with the wrong weapons.

We can take heart that we were not given the task to fight our battles without the appropriate weapons. God has given us some powerful weapons that, when used as intended, will lead us into total victory. Let us take fasting and prayer as an example. The Enemy has no chance of overcoming the believer who is truly praying and fasting. No matter what the challenge is, we need to start with these tools if we are to be successful. I assure you that God's power will be released in us, so we can fight and win over the Enemy. We also have the written Word as a weapon in our arsenal, and should use the Word to maximum our advantage.

I want you to understand that we are not puny Christians. We have the whole armor of God, the power of prayer and fasting, the Holy Ghost, and the written Word of God to get us over whatever challenges we face. So choose your weapon and choose well. Luckily, we do not have to figure out which weapons to choose, for Bible provides us the answer.

Begin by rejecting the attitude that we are weak and helpless. We are not simply passive, helpless victims of circumstance. We are more than conquerors (Rom. 8:37). Even if we feel weak, we need to confess that we are strong (Joel 3:10; 2 Cor. 12:10). We are not deluding ourselves when we affirm that we are strong when we feel weak. When we affirm our strength, we are following the Bible's prescription for total victory. The Bible says, "Let the weak say I am strong" (Joel 3:10). We also learn from Scripture that we "overcome by the word our testimony and by the blood of the Lamb" (Rev. 12:11).

If the Devil hears you say, "I'm strong," he knows no differently. As far as he is concerned, you are strong. The Devil is not a mind reader. He hears our confession, and he forms a strategy based upon what we have confessed. If you confess that you are strong, he must think twice about attacking you. If he does, you have the confidence to fight him with spiritual weapons and win.

In this warfare, we must be careful to stay with people of like Christian minds. Sometimes we, the community of Christian believers, are our own greatest critics. Sadly, we even criticize the church before the unbelievers. We occasionally conceive of church folks as the worst people in the world, but I would argue that if you think it is bad in the church, try the workplace. There is no dearth of people on your secular jobs who will betray you to get a promotion over your head. At least in the church, we are among people who are guided by a godly compass. Although we make mistakes at times because we are human beings, at least we have the Holy Ghost as our guide. He gives us direction and convicts us when we do wrong.

Using the wrong weapons will get us in trouble most of the time. How did David fight Goliath? Goliath was a big person; he was about nine feet nine inches tall, and was an expert in the use of the implements of warfare in his day. Goliath presented himself before the armies of Israel for forty days, defying them and challenging them to a battle. He thought that the fight was fixed in his favor. He wanted to face Israel's best fighter. The challenge was this: if Goliath won this one-on-one fight, then Israel would serve his people. On the other hand, if Israel's champion won, then Goliath's people, the Philistines, would serve Israel (see 1 Sam. 17). Given his military prowess, Goliath believed that there was no way in the world that he would lose this fight. He was full of confidence in his abilities and weapons.

David, a boy of about fifteen or sixteen years old, went by the camp of Israel on a mission: to bring food from his father to his brothers, who were fighters in Israel's army. He evidently was not old enough to go to war. Furthermore, his father, Jesse, needed David to tend to the sheep in the field.

When David arrived on the scene, it so happened that Goliath was just emerging from the Philistines' camp to utter his daily threats to King Saul and Israel's army. It became clear to David that no one in the camp of Israel was prepared to take up this challenge. Fear crippled them all at the sight of this giant.

Having heard this, and seeing that no one was prepared to answer the challenge, David indicated that he would go. No doubt King Saul was appreciative of the spunk of this young man, but he did not think that

David stood a chance against this proven warrior. Saul observed, "Thou art not able to go against this Philistine to fight with him: for thou art but a youth, and he a man of war from his youth" (1 Sam. 17:33).

At this stage, Saul was not thinking rationally. Listen to his reason: David cannot fight Goliath, because David is but a youth, and Goliath is a man of war from his youth. However, David's age did not bother David. To him, youth was the best time to start. David must have reasoned, "If he started as a youth, maybe I should start as a youth." It is clear that even at that early age, David recognized that the weapon with which he would fight Goliath was not carnal, but mighty through the power of God.

His brothers were not too thrilled with the brashness of this kid. They told him frankly that he was an out of order and naughty fellow, and in effect told him to go back home. They suggested that he was derelict in his duties as a shepherd: "And with whom hast thou left those few sheep in the wilderness?" (1 Sam. 17:28).

When it became clear that David's brothers were not going to deter him by their disparagement, the king relented, but told David that he was not properly suited for battle. The king rightly surmised that a shepherd's normal clothing was not meant for war. Therefore, the king put on his own armor on David, supposing that it would provide him some protection against Goliath.

David realized that Saul's armor was not suitable for the work he had in hand. If this fight were to be fought only on the human sphere, then Saul's war clothing and weapons would have been just fine. But this fight was on a spiritual level. David needed more than a sword. Saul's armor and weapons were not suited for this fight. David realized that he needed something better. He needed to be nimble. He did not need to be weighed down by Saul's heavy gear.

He needed a weapon that was proven. Though it may have appeared inappropriate for the fight, when placed in the hands of one anointed by God, it was just the right weapon. A donkey's jawbone in the hand of an anointed servant could kill a thousand men (see Judg. 15). David needed something to use that would bring glory to God. Therefore, he discarded Saul's armor. The logical question was "What armor and what weapon will you use against this skilled and experienced fighter?"

David did not have a second thought. To him, a sling and a few stones were just what the situation called for.

On his way to meet Goliath, David stopped by a brook, picked up five smooth stones, and placed them in his bag. Nearing Goliath, he reached into the bag, took one of those stones out, placed it in his sling, and ran to the encounter with the giant. David released the sling, and the stone found its mark in Goliath's forehead. Down Goliath went!

Now, what happened here? Was a stone thrown by a teenage boy sufficient to floor a giant? Perhaps so. Here is what I am convinced about: the right weapon in the hand of God's anointed servant can do the impossible. Reliance upon God to fight for us always results in triumph. I believe that the moment the stone left the sling, the power of the Holy Spirt accelerated it to its intended target.

When Goliath saw David coming toward him with a slingshot, he was most indignant. "And the Philistine said unto David, am I a dog that thou comest to me with staves? And the Philistine cursed David by his gods. And the Philistine said to David, come to me and I will give thy flesh unto the fowls of the air, and to the beasts of the field" (1 Sam. 17:43–44). Goliath was so sure of himself and his implements of war that he had no doubt he would make quick work of David.

The Devil is still breathing out all sorts of threats against God's people. He thinks he has you pinned down. He thinks he has you under his control. But when you go in the name of Jesus Christ, wearing the right armor and carrying the right weapon, you can say, like David, "Though I walk through the valley of the shadow of death, I will fear no evil" (Ps. 23:4). It does not matter how the Devil threatens you. Just stay with God, arm yourselves with the right tools of war, and see how God is going to deliver.

Goliath cursed David and assured him that he would give his flesh to the fowls of the air and to the beasts of the field. Armed as he was with the right weapon, David was not intimidated with that talk. When you are confident that you are fighting the right fight with the right weapons, you can afford to be confident. David's response was that he would face Goliath in the name of the Lord of hosts, and would make an end of him that day (see 1 Sam. 17:45–46).

When you go to do your battle, do so in the name of the Lord. When you face your troubles, face them in the name of Jesus. For at the name of Jesus, the Bible says, "every knee shall bow and every tongue must confess that Jesus Christ is Lord to the glory of God the Father" (Phil. 2:10–11). The troubles we face are no match for us when we engage the Enemy with the right weapons.

When David released that stone from his sling, Goliath had no idea what hit him. Can you imagine the amazement on both sides?

"Is that Goliath?"

"He must be faking!"

"He is just probably trying to lull David into a false sense of security."

Can you imagine their surprise when David ran upon him, took out Goliath's own sword, and chopped off Goliath's head? That sword was probably so heavy that David had to use both hands to lift it. Can you imagine the shock and consternation among the Philistines? Can you imagine their awe when they saw what happened when the name of God and the right spiritual weapon were used in combination?

Stop fighting your battles using carnal weapons. Rather, let God fight for you. If we trust in the natural, carnal implements of war, we will fail. The horse at one time was the most important resource in war. However, to trust in horses was always vain. The psalmist says, "An horse is a vain thing for safety: neither shall he deliver any by his great strength" (Ps. 33:17). These things do not deliver us. We must remember, "The weapons of our warfare are not carnal but mighty through God to the pulling down of strong holds" (2 Cor. 6:4).

We need to understand the weapons of our warfare, and to realize that they are not carnal weapons. The psalmist wrote, "Some trust in chariots and some in horses, but we will remember the name of the Lord our God. They are brought down and fallen, but we are risen and stand upright" (Ps. 20:7–8). Let the people of the world threaten you if they wish. Let them bring out their big guns against you. When you have on the whole armor of God, you will know for sure that the weapons formed against you will fail (Isa. 54:17).

Underlying the spiritual weaponry is a robust prayer life. The apostle Paul wrote, "Praying always with all prayer and supplication in the Spirit, and watching thereunto with all perseverance and supplication for all saints" (Eph. 6:18). Nothing will substitute for a rich prayer life.

No matter how many spiritual weapons we believe we have, they are of no use if we are not prayed up.

In fact, it seems doubtful whether one could even acquire these spiritual weapons without a contemplative, deliberate, and volitional prayer life. Remember that the weapons of our warfare are not carnal but mighty through God to the pulling down of strongholds. These strongholds will not come down unless we get on our knees in earnest prayer and supplication before God. Jesus told His disciples that people should always pray and not faint, or not give up, according to the NIV (Luke 18:1).

In the final analysis, only when we understand the weapons of our warfare can we hope to be truly successful. Then and only then will our thought lives be brought captive to the obedience of Christ. Only then will our emotions and behavior honor God.

A Prayer

Dear Lord, help us today, not just to become acquainted with the various spiritual weapons in this warfare, but to receive the skills to use them effectively for your glory. In Jesus's name. Amen!

CHAPTER 3

Demolish Arguments and Every Pretension that Sets Itself Up against the Knowledge of God

Casting down imaginations, and every high thing that exalteth itself against the knowledge of God, and bringing into captivity every thought to the obedience of Christ.

—2 Corinthians 10:5

I have asserted that we win or lose our battles in the province of the mind. The person who controls their mind controls the way they feel and behave. Consequently, we must take care to guard our minds with all diligence. The Bible tells us, "Keep thy heart with all diligence; for out of it are the issues of life" (Prov. 4:23). The Hebrew word used here for heart is *Leb*. It is translated as the heart, feelings, or intellect. God's Word admonishes us to keep our intellect, our mind, our thinking, and our emotions with all diligence—that is, with all carefulness. Take time to protect your mind, for how you think will affect the quality of your life.

What you think is what you become. The Bible says as a man thinks, so is he (Prov. 23:7). Barack Obama became the president of the United States, despite the obvious disadvantages faced by an African American living in a not-so-postracial society, because he thought in his heart that he could become the president. Every objective political and social indicator argued that an African American male could not become president. Nevertheless, he, like the little engine, thought that he could—and did. His pursuit of the presidency started with a positive thought.

Our minds at times play tricks on us. We think that we see or hear something bad, and it upsets us terribly. But when we take the time to investigate the matter, we often find that if we calm down, there is no need to react negatively. Given the right amount of time and thought, we will find out that the situation is not exactly the way we had perceived it in the first place.

I counseled a couple some years ago. Among their many presenting problems was the wife's undue jealousy. She got really worked up over any and every contact the husband had with the opposite sex, no matter how unlikely it was that her husband could be engaged in an inappropriate relationship. If he said hello to another woman, even the sales clerk in a shoes store, she interpreted that to mean that he was having an affair or looking to have an affair with her.

On one occasion she, her husband, and their baby were out in the shopping mall, and a young woman commented to the husband that the baby was cute. The wife confronted the young woman and told her, "I am the mother, and I am right here. Why are you talking to my husband?" When I asked her why she had done that, she indicated that she felt that the clerk was trying to "talk" to her husband. In her mind, this was brazen and rude. That wife admitted that to the best of her knowledge, she had no reason to suspect that her husband was not being faithful to her.

Now, all the husband did was say hello to the clerk and thank her for her kind comment about their child. The wife's faulty thinking led her down a path that was altogether unnecessary, not to mention embarrassing and distressing for all involved. Her thinking affected not just her emotions and behavior, but also her husband's.

In attempting to change our thinking, we must assume an optimistic and positive outlook on life. Some folks could walk into the sanctuary, see a hundred people, and say the church building was half-empty. Other people could see the same number of people and say the building was half-full. It is a matter of your perspective; it is a matter of how you think.

That wife could have thought, "What a friendly clerk. And how caring she is to see how beautiful our child is." She could have thanked the clerk, and that would have been the end of that encounter. Instead, because of her pessimistic and jaded thinking, she immediately jumped to the worst possible conclusion.

Some folks could have a headache and say, "I need to take two aspirins to get rid of this pain. This headache is due to the fact that I am stressed."

Another person could say, "Oh dear, I believe I have a brain tumor."

It is a matter of how we think. Our thinking makes all the difference in the world. Do I just take the aspirin and go to sleep, or do I stay up all night dealing with anxiety about a brain tumor? It is not difficult to see how the quality of one's life, short term and long term, can be tremendously affected by one's thinking.

I once treated a patient who suffered from anxiety over his health. His father had died from a heart attack at around age forty. His uncle on his father's side had died at age forty-five from the same malady. This patient was now forty-one and had convinced himself that he was going to die from a heart attack, just like his father and uncle.

This man frequented the emergency room of his local hospital on an almost biweekly basis, complaining of symptoms of heart disease. Several tests for coronary disease came back negative, yet the patient kept frequenting the emergency room. Eventually, they referred him to the outpatient mental health clinic, where he became my patient.

During one particularly difficult session, he insisted that he needed to go to the emergency room because he felt he was having a heart attack. Despite my attempts to persuade him otherwise, I did not prevail. I eventually acceded and summoned an ambulance for him. I then called a contact in the emergency room and asked her to admit him to the psychiatric ward and to perform a battery of physical tests on him, just to set him at ease.

As the reader may suspect, the physical tests came back negative. Upon the next visit to my office, the patient was baffled, almost disappointed that there was nothing wrong with him except a sinus infection. He calmed down for a few sessions but soon reverted to his old way of thinking. It was obvious to all, even the least skilled clinician, that this patient's problem was not physiological but rather psychological; his pains had their origin in his faulty thinking.

By contrast we have the example of the apostle Paul, who, although he was imprisoned, met shipwreck, suffered hunger, endured shame, and was subjected to the severest criticisms and physical punishment, was a free man in his mind. He was a man who had achieved the highest level of self-actualization. This was not a self-actualization based upon self-delusion; rather, it was based on his belief that the hand of the Lord was guiding him. His mind was clear, and he had the ability to put things in their proper perspective. Even when he was afflicted, he could write, "For our light affliction, which is but for a moment, worketh for us a far more exceeding and eternal weight of glory" (2 Cor. 4:17).

We know indeed that Paul's afflictions were not light. His afflictions led to the loss of his freedom and eventually to his death. To him it was fine, for his thinking was right. He knew that there was something ahead far better than what he was experiencing in this present life. He saw a glimmer of hope in all his affliction, because his mind was sound.

During one of his imprisonments, Paul saw reasons to rejoice. He wrote to the Philippians that his imprisonment was a good thing, in the final analysis, for because of it, others were emboldened to preach the gospel. Some of these others were insincere in their preaching, while others were sincere, but in either case, Paul rejoiced, because the gospel was being preached (see Phil. 1:12–18). What a perspective! Although his circumstance was dire and he had lost his physical freedom, he was quite free in his mind.

How could Paul maintain this equilibrium? Because his thought life was sound. Who has ever rejoiced in imprisonment? It was not so much that Paul was rejoicing because of being in prison. He rejoiced because his imprisonment served to promote the spread of the gospel. Instead of choosing to focus on the negative (the imprisonment), he chose to focus on the positive (the spreading of the gospel).

The late president of Egypt, Anwar El Sadat, was one of my heroes, because of his ability to look at the glass as being half-full. In his book *In Search of Identity: An Autobiography,* he related how he was locked up in cell 54 of a prison. At first, he thought and felt like a prisoner, but after a while he released himself from the prison of his mind. His freedom came not when he was released from prison, but while he was still here. Although physically incarcerated, his mind became free, so that his physical prison became a place of freedom and reflection. He not only knew that he would be free, but that his nation would also be free from colonial rule.

How did Mr. Sadat arrive at that existential place of freedom and resolution? He got there because his thought life was well ordered.

The main point of this chapter is that we must challenge every faulty thought and bring it captive to the obedience of Christ. Instead of entertaining and encouraging faulty thinking, we should arrest those thoughts and make them obedient to the Word of God. Paul instructs, "We demolish arguments and every pretension that sets itself up against the knowledge of God, and we take captive every thought to make it obedient to Christ" (2 Cor. 10:5 NIV). He gives the distinct impression that we are in a war, and there are forces attacking our thinking that must be demolished, conquered, and brought to the feet of Jesus Christ in total obedience.

As a practical matter, how does this work? How do we bring these thoughts captive to the obedience of Christ? Well, we do this by knowing what God's Word says about our thinking. When, for example, the thought comes in our minds to hate someone, we must remember what Christ said about loving each other: "A new commandment I give unto you, That ye love one another; as I have loved you, that ye also love one another. By this shall all men know that ye are my disciples, if ye have love one to another" (John 13:34–35). To love each other is a command of Jesus Christ. Therefore, when a thought invades our minds and tells us to do something contrary to what Jesus commanded, we must take that thought and make it obedient to Christ's command.

We could say something like this to a hateful thought: "I will not hate my brother or sister, because God's Word tells me to love one another."

Elsewhere we are told that all the law is fulfilled in one word: "Thou shalt love thy neighbour as thyself" (Gal. 5:14). When faced with these instructions from God's Word, our only viable option is to capture every thought that is contrary to God's Word for our lives and make it obedient to Christ.

Of ourselves, we cannot subdue negative thoughts. Our own efforts to combat these thoughts will be met with only limited success, if any success at all. Our success lies in our obedience in bringing these thoughts and making them obedient to Christ. It is Christ who wins the victory on our behalf.

In the following chapters, I will identify several debilitating thoughts with which Christians over the years have struggled. I will discuss such issues as:

- unforgiving thought
- slandering thought
- angry thought
- hateful thought
- lying thought
- discouraging thought
- fearful thought
- doubtful thought
- disobedient thought
- defeatist thought
- proud thought
- murmuring thought

I will view these dysfunctional thoughts through the lens of God's Word. My interest is to discover what the Bible says about each of these. My view is toward getting the reader to commit to bringing each of these thoughts captive to obey Christ's Word, so that we can live wholesome lives in this present world.

A Prayer

Heavenly Father, please grant us divine anointing to demolish all arguments and all pretensions that set themselves up against the knowledge of God, that we may bring such to obey Christ. In Jesus's name. Amen!

CHAPTER 4

Bring Every Unforgiving Thought Captive to the Obedience of Christ

The weak can never forgive. Forgiveness is the attribute of the strong.

—Mahatma Gandhi

Having lived for a while, and being a keen observer of humanity, I have noticed that one of the most difficult things for humans to do is forgive someone who hurts them. Our natural tendency is to hurt someone who hurts us. If someone talks about us in a negative way, we are tempted to return the favor.

While that is the world's way of responding, that is not God's way. Let us keep in mind that a different set of rules govern us. We are in the world but not of the world. We are ultimately accountable to God, not to our bruised feelings. You will recall that the underlying thesis of this book is that we fight with spiritual weapons. According to the apostle Paul: "The weapons of our warfare are not carnal, but mighty through God to the pulling down of strong holds" (2 Cor. 10:4).

Since we know that as humans we are prone to unforgiveness, as Christians we must bring thoughts of unforgiveness captive to the obedience of Christ. Unforgiveness is a product of faulty thinking. It is informed by "an eye for an eye" cognition. We decide not to forgive a person who has hurt us, because we think that such a person does not deserve our forgiveness.

The fact of the matter is that no one deserves forgiveness. One who stands in need of forgiveness has transgressed some law or moral code for which there are just punishments. Forgiveness is based on grace, a gift given and not a merit earned. When someone hurts us, we forgive because God has forgiven us many times. We who are the recipients of grace must in turn offer grace.

Sometimes the decision is conscious, and at other times it is subconscious. Either way, unforgiveness is a function of our thinking. If we can control our thinking, then we will learn how to forgive those who have hurt us.

When you fail to forgive somebody, it hurts you more than it hurts them. While you are harboring up the hurt and pain in your heart, they are going about their business and having a great time. You cannot sleep, while your "enemy" is sleeping just fine. You cannot eat because you have acid indigestion and acid reflux, and they are feasting every day. When the object of your unforgiveness goes to their doctor, they get a wonderful report, while your health is falling apart because you are holding on to the thing they did five years ago.

Many years ago, two brothers parted ways due to a dispute over some matter that could have been resolved with prayer, forgiveness, and application of the Word. The Christian fellowship they had shared broke, and for over thirty years, they did not speak to each other in any meaningful way.

They both grew old, and one of the brothers developed memory loss. Near the end of this brother's life, someone close to him asked why that fellowship had broken. He confessed that he did not remember. To the best of my knowledge, the two brothers never resolved their differences.

These men had made a choice not to forgive or to fellowship with each other, and that decision stood for over thirty years, never to be resolved in this life. I make no judgment here as to the fate of their souls, but I do wonder how they will get along in heaven.

There is a strong relationship between forgiveness and health. Alex Harris and Carl Thoresen stated, "The core components of unforgiveness (e.g., anger, hostility, blame, fear) have been associated with health and disease outcomes."[19] They found that although the research linking unforgiveness and forgiveness and health was inconclusive they nevertheless indicated that it provides a basis from which we can reasonably hypothesize some correlations.

After being hurt, a person's feelings of anger, suffering loss, envy, and unforgiveness profoundly affect the way their body functions, with a negative effect on their health. Unforgiveness can disrupt the harmony of the brain waves, making one less able to think clearly or to make good decisions. Unforgiveness distresses the musculoskeletal system by increasing muscle tension, and producing headaches and other physiological symptoms such as stomachaches, muscle tension, and joint pain, among others. To the extent that unforgiveness disrupts sleep patterns, the chances of inadequate repair during sleep increases. This negatively impacts recovery from an injury. The lack of adequate sleep is also known to have negative impacts on the management of diabetes. Erika Gebel reports that sleep affects blood glucose levels in people with diabetes. She stated, "A 2006 study in the *Archives of Internal Medicine* found that those who report poor sleep quality have higher A1Cs (average blood glucose over two to three months)."[20]

Kathi Norman found that, "Failing to forgive, or unforgiveness, is the practice of engaging in ruminative thoughts of anger, vengeance, hate, and resentment that have unproductive outcomes for the ruminator, such as increased anxiety, depression, elevated blood pressure, vascular resistance, decreased immune response, and worse outcomes in coronary artery disease."[21] Christie Hunter stated that in extreme cases unforgiveness causes some people to develop suicidal tendencies. She found also that in addition to causing cardiovascular issues and high blood pressure, the chronic stress that results from unforgiveness can also cause brain hemorrhage. Hunter reports that, "According to the study of Bauer (2002), short-term unforgiveness provokes a person to respond intensely which ultimately impacts the social and cognitive behavior of a person."[22] While unforgiveness may not be the sole cause of all these biological or psychological problems, it increases one's vulnerability to them. We become more susceptible to illness when we possess an unforgiving heart.

The unfortunate thing about an unforgiving heart is that it takes on a life of its own. I have observed that often when a person has not received or given forgiveness, that person gets stuck in a bad place for a long time, if not forever. Faced with a similar set of circumstances in the future, that person responds in a similar way.

Dr. George O. Wood, in an article titled *The High Cost of Unforgiveness: Healing Life's Hurts,* argues that life has a way of programming us so that we keep repeating the same mistakes, expressing the same attitudes, and engaging in the same situations. The question is, why do we—humans, believers—repeat ourselves this way? To quote Dr. Wood, "Why is it that we can't be more imaginative and free to break out of this confining thing in our life? The computer is telling us, 'Bad sector.' And you need to reprogram."[23]

Child of God, this reprogramming that we so desperately need will never come using the same carnal weapons. Unforgiveness emanates for our cognitive selves—our thought lives. If we want to change our attitude toward forgiveness, we must change our thinking. This requires the application of God's Word through the power of the Holy Spirit. When you think a brother or a sister has wronged you one time too many, and forgiveness is the last thing on your mind, you must take that thought captive to obey what Christ has to say about forgiveness.

Let us now examine what the Bible teaches about forgiveness. In Matthew, we read, "Then came Peter to him, and said, Lord, how oft shall my brother sin against me, and I forgive him? Till seven times? Jesus saith unto him, I say not unto thee, until seven times: but, until seventy times seven" (Matt. 18:21, 22). That is four hundred and ninety (490) times. Peter came to Jesus fully expecting Jesus to say, "No, not seven times, just three or four." In Peter's mind, seven times was way over the top as far as a person's obligation to forgive was concerned.

Nevertheless, Jesus Christ responded, "Not seven times—rather, 490 times." Christ's teaching boils down to this: our obligation to forgive each other is without limit.

I believe that the 490 number was arbitrary and hyperbolic, meant to communicate that our obligation to forgive is a serious matter. It is doubtful if anyone we know would or could seriously sin against us 490 times in a lifetime. Most of us have a built-in guidance system or survival instinct that helps us to avoid a person who could possibly sin against us that many times. So when Jesus responded this way to Peter, we know, as I am sure Peter did, that it was highly improbable he would ever encounter such a scenario.

Nevertheless, if someone could offend us that many times, it would still not give us the right to withhold forgiveness. The context of Scripture suggests that there is no limit as to the number of times we are obligated to forgive our brother or sister.

In the Lord's Prayer, Jesus taught us to pray for forgiveness of our own sins (debt) as we forgive the sins of others. He ties our own forgiveness with our willingness to forgive others. He says, "For if ye forgive men their trespasses, your heavenly Father will also forgive you: But if ye forgive not men their trespasses, neither will your Father forgive your trespasses" (Matt. 6:14–15; see also Mark 11:26; Luke 6:37, 17:3–4).

Our model for forgiveness is God. The question we must ask ourselves is, "How many times has God forgiven me?" If we are brutally honest with ourselves, we will find that we have sinned against God a lot more than that.

Unfortunately, we sin every day. Let us assume that a person becomes aware of sin at age ten. Let us assume further that that person sinned only once per day for ten years. How many sins will that person have committed by age twenty? Since there are 365 days in a year, that person would have sinned 3,650 times.

If you are forty, fifty, sixty, seventy, or eighty years old, you can see how many times you have potentially sinned against God. You know what the beautiful truth is. As many times as we have sinned, if we ask forgiveness of God, He is faithful and just to forgive us of all our sins.

Are we required to forgive people for every wrong they have done us? Yes! Jesus said, "But if ye forgive not men their trespasses, neither will your Father forgive your trespasses" (Matt. 6:15).

The apostle Paul, who, like us, had received God's forgiveness, had something to say on the subject. Under the inspiration of the Holy Spirit, he wrote, "And be ye kind one to another, tenderhearted, forgiving one another, even as God for Christ's sake hath forgiven you" (Eph. 4:32). Also, "Put on therefore, as the elect of God, holy and beloved, bowels of mercies, kindness, humbleness of mind, meekness, longsuffering; Forbearing one another, and forgiving one another, if any man have a quarrel against any: even as Christ forgave you, so also do ye" (Col. 3:12–13). In the same manner that God, for Christ's sake, has forgiven us, we must also forgive others.

That kind of forgiveness needs one of the fruits of the Spirit, which is longsuffering. It should come as no surprise that this forgiveness business is not easy, and I am not trying to tell you that it is easy. From the human perspective, it is difficult to forgive someone whom you suspect or have reason to believe is talking about you, disrespecting you, and slandering your name. However, it is something that we are going to have to do. If we want to please God, there are no other options. It is the only way. Jesus is our example. He forgave those who mocked Him and those who crucified Him. On the cross, He prayed to His Father to forgive them, for they did not know what they were doing.

Longsuffering means to suffer long. Even if our suffering is brought upon us by our enemies or some well-meaning church member, we must endure it and offer forgiveness. Longsuffering as it relates to forgiveness means that we forgive those who wrong us repeatedly, even when we do not feel that we should.

The Bible teaches that God's forgiveness of us is contingent upon our willingness to forgive others. "But if you do not forgive others their sins, your Father will not forgive your sins" (Matt. 6:15). Each of us stands in need of forgiveness from God every day. We sin daily, sometimes without even realizing it. It may not be cursing, stealing, committing adultery, or any of the "big" sins, but living in sinful flesh as we do, we make mistakes. We may embrace the thought of holding a grudge and be unwilling to forgive. As innocuous as those actions may seem, they constitute sin. In the final analysis, we need forgiveness from God for those sins, just as we do for the so-called "big sins."

We can confidently approach God because we know that the Bible teaches if a person sins, that person "has an advocate with the Father, Jesus Christ the righteous" (1 John 2:1). Because of Jesus's advocacy, "if we confess our sins, he is faithful and just to forgive us our sins, and to cleanse us from all unrighteousness" (1 John 1:9). Since we all stand in need of forgiveness, and we freely receive it when we ask God, He wants us to be quick to forgive others.

By the way, forgiveness is liberating for both the forgiver and the one receiving forgiveness. To hold a grudge truly enslaves one to negative emotions. Therefore, when we take the liberating act of forgiving others, we are making a declaration of independence from that which had previously enslaved us.

I find it extraordinary that many of us, who have been the recipients of God's forgiveness on so many occasions, fail to forgive others when they sin against us. The Lord told a parable about a man who owed a creditor a huge amount of money. When the time arrived that he should pay his creditor, he could not. The legal remedy was that this man should go to prison.

The man approached his creditor and asked for forbearance. He begged for an extension of time to repay him. Graciously, the creditor extended the time he required. He left the presence of his creditor with relief, rejoicing that he had been granted grace.

This man went out and found another man who owed him, by comparison, a very small sum. Like his creditor, the man demanded payment because payment was due him. The man who owed a small sum appealed to him using words similar to the ones the man had used when making an appeal to his creditor.

The Bible says the man grabbed the small debtor by the throat and demanded payment. Notwithstanding his debtor's earnest pleas, this man would not forgive or relent, and so he commanded the debtor's arrest.

A witness, observing this, went to his creditor and related the story of this unforgiving man. His creditor's response was predictably harsh. He pointed out to this wicked man that after he had received forgiveness of his large debt, he should have done likewise to someone who owed him a lot less. The creditor turned him over to tormentors until he paid everything that he owed (Matt. 18:32–35). Verse 35 contains an ominous warning, "So likewise shall my heavenly Father do also unto you, if ye from your hearts forgive not everyone his brother their trespasses."

Those who stand every moment in need of forgiveness are at times the most reluctant to offer forgiveness. Our own need for forgiveness should prompt us to graciously offer forgiveness to others. Sadly, we act against our own self-interest when we do not forgive others, since God indicates that if we are not willing to forgive others, neither will He forgive us.

An unforgiving heart is antithetical to the holiness of God. If we truly understand what God has done for us, if we see how bad we really are and how many times God has forgiven us, then we will be able to forgive others. It is rather a self-righteous person who fails to forgive someone else. They have forgotten what God has done for them, and perhaps think that they merit God's favor.

As I write this today, I am cognizant of the fact that I stand redeemed not because I was good. I have been graciously forgiven for all my trespasses because God is a merciful and forgiving God. I am forgiven not because I deserve it, but because of God's grace. When we come to realize that we were pitiful sinners on our way to hell, but God forgave us, we should rejoice and be willing to forgive others also.

Where does unforgiveness come from? It starts in the thought life. Someone does something to offend us, and we immediately begin to think of all the reasons he or she may have done so. Many times, our assumptions are wrong, but we convince ourselves that the offender meant us evil. Our natural reaction then is to pay them back. Our anger level rises. Our anxiety level also rises. Before long, we back ourselves into an emotional place from which it becomes very difficult to move. We then decide that we are done with the person and will not forgive them.

So what are we to do with such thoughts? We must bring them captive to the obedience of Christ. How does that work? It simply means that we must examine Scripture to see what the Bible says about forgiveness.

For example, we read, "Judge not, and ye shall not be judged: condemn not, and ye shall not be condemned: forgive, and ye shall be forgiven" (Luke 6: 37). If we follow God's Word on this matter, we will be quick to forgive. First, Jesus says we should not judge. Moreover, what are we doing when we assume what the person meant by their gesture? We are judging their motives. When we do that, we often arrive at faulty conclusions.

I have repeatedly made the point that our own forgiveness rests on our willingness to forgive others. Jesus said if we forgive not men their trespasses, neither will our heavenly Father forgive us. It is not easy, but we really do not have a viable choice as far as Jesus is concerned. The path to perfection is never easy, but it is expedient at times to take the difficult path. It is not always pleasant, but it is necessary.

The mandate to forgive is profound and carries with it our

responsibility as children of God. As God's elect, we assume certain privileges and responsibilities. Here is how the apostle Paul put it: "Put on therefore, as the elect of God, holy and beloved, bowels of mercies, kindness, humbleness of mind, meekness, longsuffering. Forbearing one another and forgiving one another, if any man have a quarrel against any: even as Christ forgave you, so also do ye" (Col. 3: 12–13).

Forgiving and forbearing with each other mean you must put up with me and I must put up with you. We all have our idiosyncrasies and behavior quirks that aggravate others. However, the Bible mandates that we put up (forebear) with one another. I like the words of the song by James Cleveland, "Please be patient with me, God is not through with me yet. When God gets through with me, I shall come forth as pure gold." We are not yet as pure as gold, so we need to be patient with each other and forgive each other.

Why is it such a difficult thing for Christian believers to forgive? There are people in the world who may not be Christians by our standards, yet who show a tremendous capacity to forgive. Mahatma Gandhi, rejecting the urge to take revenge, once observed, "An eye for an eye would make the whole world blind."[24] I am afraid that if the church of Jesus Christ does not bring unforgiving thoughts captive to the obedience of Christ, soon we will have a church full of blind and toothless Christians.

There are others who likewise have demonstrated a tremendous ability to forgive others for egregious wrongs. I think of the late Nelson Mandela, who was incarcerated for some twenty-seven years for fighting against the system of apartheid in South Africa. That diabolical system was responsible for over 600,000 displacements of Black Africans. They were forced to leave their homes. In addition, thousands of Africans died in the struggle.

After Mandela's release, he became the president of South Africa. The world would not have been surprised if he had called for reprisals against his former oppressors. Instead, the president called for the creation of the Truth and Reconciliation Commission, before which those who were responsible for the evil of apartheid were given an opportunity to cleanse their souls. All they were required to do was confess their sins and there would be no revenge. How godly that was!

If the world can do that, what about God's people who are washed in the blood of Jesus Christ?

The New Testament amply demonstrates Jesus's attitude toward forgiveness. I think of His treatment of Peter, who had denied Him three times. When Peter realized what he had done, he wept bitterly. Jesus was crucified and buried. On the third day, He rose again. He called for His disciples and in particular for Peter. Why was it necessary to ask for Peter by name? Peter was probably so ashamed and sad over his denial of the Lord that he migh not have presumed to join the other disciples if Jesus had not mentioned him by name. He may have felt that he had forfeited his right to be Jesus's disciple. In his mind, his denial of the Lord had disqualified him from being a disciple.

Jesus surprised and delighted Peter by that special invitation. Did Peter deserve such? No! His denial was a very grave sin, but Jesus forgave him. Jesus knew that although Peter had sinned, there was something redeemable in him. Jesus knew that there was ministry in Peter. To hold this sin against Peter forever would mean that a powerful, effective ministry would be lost. It was as though Jesus were saying to Peter, "Now go out there and preach my gospel. I am not going to judge you because you denied me. I am not going to judge you because you abandoned me when I needed you most." To Jesus it was time to heal and get on with the work of the ministry, and the best place to start was to wipe Peter's slate clean.

Why are we so reluctant to forgive? I believe it is because of self. We need to get over self and release the person who hurts us. We need to follow the Lord's example and be quick to forgive. We need to bring the unforgiving thought captive to the obedience of Jesus Christ.

There are spouses who never forgive their wives or husbands for one mistake made twenty years ago. These couples have the potential to have beautiful relationships, but miss it because of one mistake. I say, get over it and get over yourself. Begin to forgive each other in love, and enjoy the bliss of a loving forgiving, and nurturing relationship. Certainly, if the sin committed is grave, and the offended party cannot handle this forgiveness thing alone, then they should find a pastor or godly counselor to help them through the forgiveness process. But to leave this matter unresolved is spiritually deadly.

If we were to follow God's direction on this, we would be better able to bring unforgiving thoughts captive to the obedience of Christ. Listen to God's Word: "Forbearing one another and forgiving one another, if any man have a quarrel against any: even as Christ forgave you, so also do ye" (Col. 3:13). What the apostle Paul is instructing his readers here is to get a stomach of mercy. When we are merciful, we are quicker to forgive. In addition, in extending mercy to others, we will obtain mercy when we need it. Jesus said, "Blessed are the merciful, for they shall obtain mercy" (Matt. 5:7).

Why is it expedient for us to forgive those who hurt us? Because when we do, we release ourselves. The anger, resentment, and pain we have carried hurt us more than they hurt the object of our anger.

It is time to move on and let love prevail in order for you to attain the next level of ministry. You are denying yourself the blessings of God by having an unforgiving heart. In the context of our discussion, it is okay if someone hurts you and gets away with it. If "getting away with it" brings peace to the body of Christ, it is okay. If it releases you from your resentment, hurt, and pain, it is okay.

I believe the apostle Paul was arguing for forgiveness and taking the wrong when he wrote this to the saints at Corinth: "Now therefore there is utterly a fault among you, because ye go to law one with another. Why do ye not rather take wrong? Why do ye not rather suffer yourselves to be defrauded?" (1 Cor. 6:7). It appears that those believers were taking other believers to court to settle matters. Instead of judging matters among themselves and forgiving one another, they were taking their business before secular judges, who were unbelievers.

My late wife Erica and I met when we were teenagers. We fell in love, and as unworthy as I was, when I asked her to marry me, she consented. (Well, it was not that easy, but she eventually said yes.) We were married for thirty years and four months. In that time, we naturally disagreed. We had to disagree because, after all, she married a very imperfect person. I suppose she had some imperfections too, but I believe that most of the disagreements were my own fault.

Being young, arrogant, and a know-it-all, I made life difficult for my wife in the early years of our marriage. What saved the marriage was the fact that Erica possessed a forgiving heart from God Himself.

Her ability to love me and forgive me afforded me the requisite time I needed to grow up and mature in love. Her forgiving heart forged a strong bond between us.

I will never forget that at the end of her life, while she was in the hospital, her doctor asked me what I wanted to do about a living will for Erica. A living will is a written statement detailing a person's desires regarding medical treatment in circumstances in which the person is no longer able to make such decisions.

I naturally conferred with Erica as to what her wishes were. She looked up at me with those forgiving, trusting eyes, with which she had always looked at me even in my most insufferable moments, and said, "B, I'm in your hands. Whatever you think is right, do it. I trust your judgment."

That was a woman who understood forgiveness. If she had judged me for all the wrong words I spoke or wrong things I did in those thirty years, her response might not have been the same. However, she forgave her flawed husband and loved him. Despite his issues, she was able to see him grow to the point where she could express total trust. I think that God demands this kind of love and forgiveness from us.

When you grow to that level of maturity, you can look at a church brother who hurt you yesterday, and perhaps repeatedly in the past, and you can still forgive him. Perhaps the thought has come to you that you should not forgive him. But for Christ's sake, you can and must forgive. This becomes easier when you bring that thought of unforgiveness captive to obey God's Word. The Bible says to forgive such a one not because he is right, not because he deserves it, not because he is perfect, but because God says we must do it, and we must be obedient to Christ.

A Prayer

Dear heavenly Father, we have often sinned because of our failure to forgive others their trespasses against us, although we expect You to forgive us. Please forgive us this wrong, and place within us hearts that freely and quickly forgive those who have wronged us. In Jesus's name, we pray. Amen!

CHAPTER 5

Bring Every Slandering Thought Captive to the Obedience of Christ

Slander slays three persons: the speaker, the spoken to, and the spoken of.

—Hebrew proverb

We now turn to another difficulty that the body of Christ faces: slander. Let us face it, bad news sells! If it were not for bad news, we would have no news at all on CNN or any of the news media. People seem to relish passing on bad news, and the more salacious and slanderous, the faster it spreads.

The great playwright William Shakespeare once observed, "The evil that men do lives after them; the good is oft interred with their bones" (Julius Caesar, Act 3 Scene 2). Is it not a sad commentary on the nature of humanity? When something good happens, news of it usually does not spread very fast or last very long. However, have you ever noticed the ease and speed at which bad news travels? Whenever we are tempted to spread slander, let us bring that thought captive to the obedience of Christ.

I am convinced that when people slander others, they do not usually consider that what they are doing is slander. It would therefore be helpful to define the word *slander*. Slander is a malicious, false, and defamatory statement or report, designed to ruin the reputation of another person. The legal definition of slander is an "oral defamation, in which someone tells one or more persons an untruth about another, which untruth will harm the reputation of the person defamed."[25]

A person's action in committing slander does not have to be intentional. If you thought the story was true and you passed it on and then found out later that it was not true, you were still guilty of slander. In some states, even if the story is true but the disclosure of it constitutes an invasion of privacy, it is considered slander, and the slanderer may be sued. In our relationships as Christians, therefore, the guiding principle should be to protect the reputation of our fellow Christians.

What is it about human nature that relishes in the spreading and hearing of bad news? Have you ever turned on the television and heard the meteorologist say, "Today is going to be a nice, sunny day all over your city," and then spend three hours talking about how sunny and nice it is going to be? Of course not! That would be rather boring to most listeners. However, let there be a threat of a hurricane or tornado, and see how many news outlets carry it and how much time they devote to it. If the storm destroys some houses and many people became homeless, the media are all over it—because it is bad news, and it captures our imagination.

Who among us has not seen the unfortunate stories of mass school shootings in the United States? Is it not nauseating the amount of footage that television media allots to this type of story? It is bad news, and bad news sells!

One could argue that of course the media cover bad news, because it is more remarkable than good news. After all, there are many more nice weather days during the year than there are bad weather days. I concede that point. However, how about the many remarkable good deeds done on a daily basis by many people all over the world? These are newsworthy but are not covered. The bottom line is that bad news sells more newspapers and is better for TV ratings than good news.

While negative news is more sensational and grabs most of the media attention, as Christians, we are governed by a different mind-set. Whenever the thought to slander each other arises, let us consider its full implications. It seems difficult for people to remember the good things others do, but very easy to keep in mind the bad things. As Christians, we should not be adding to the bad memories. Let us bury a person's bad deeds and instead recall the good, redeemable things about them.

Generally, a person is never as bad as other people make them out to be. Moreover, we are never as good as some may esteem us to be. On balance, most of us reside somewhere between those two poles. In the best of us, there is some evil. In the worst of us, there is some good. We must seek to find the good in one another and encourage and nurture it.

Christians should be governed by a principle of talking about the good things that others do instead of focusing on the bad things. Love covers a multitude of sins (1 Pet. 4:8). We should possess the heart of a mother toward her child. No matter how bad the child is, the mother always finds some good. In fact, a mother may totally overlook the bad her son does, and even blame others for his bad deeds, because in her mind, her son is a good boy. The boy could be an ax murderer, but the mother will find a way to excuse his behavior. "He didn't mean to murder the man with the ax. He was just frustrated. He threw the ax and it accidentally flew off the handle and split the man's head open." I am not saying that she is right; I am just stating what a loving mother does.

I am not arguing here that we should cover the sins of others at the expense of their souls, or of the reputation of the church. We must not gloss over the deeds that bring disrepute to the name of our God. What I am arguing for is that we not seek to find ways to hold things against others that perhaps they have repented of, and then slander them in a reckless manner. Instead of slandering others, we must find ways to restore and repair them when they have fallen into sin.

The apostle Paul wrote to the church at Corinth about a man in the church who was living a life of sexual immorality. The church's attitude toward the matter was lax. Paul rebuked the leaders for not handling this in a godly manner. His instruction to them was unmistakable. They were to take action: "Hand this man over to Satan for the destruction of the flesh, so that his spirit may be saved on the day of the Lord" (1 Cor. 1:4–5 NIV). Sexual immorality is such a grave sin that the proposed punishment seems appropriate.

It appears that the Corinthian church took Paul seriously and went at this man with a will. Paul, having heard of their actions and the man's evident repentance, wanted them to relent and forgive. Paul knew instinctively, or perhaps from experience, that a relentless barrage of punishment could discourage a person. So in his second epistle, Paul asked for forbearance on this brother's behalf. He told them that the punishment inflicted on this man was sufficient. He appealed to them to forgive and comfort him so that his excessive sorrow did not become overwhelming (see 2 Cor. 2:5–11).

Our heavenly Father made provisions in Jesus Christ to forgive us even when we do not deserve it. He knew that there was nothing good in us, but based on our faith in Jesus Christ, He considers us as being in good standing with Him. When we sin against God, He does not jump up and say, "Ah! I got you now!" Instead, He forgives when we come to Him and ask Him for forgiveness. He offers forgiveness and does not slander us.

The Devil accuses and slanders us before God day and night, for he is the slanderer in chief (Rev. 12:10). When we slander our brothers and sisters, we are not doing God's work. We are unwittingly doing the Devil's work. The Devil actively accuses us before the Lord. Thank God for the blood of Jesus Christ that paid for all my sins and yours.

We need to be careful when we slander others that we ourselves are not destroyed in the process. I read a story of a woman who lived alone in a small town. Let us call her Jane. She was the town's slanderer. She took it upon herself to be the gatekeeper of morality. Anyone who did not conform to her standard of right and wrong was subject to her gossip.

There was a brother in the same town—let us call him John—who was a carpenter. He was frequently called to do repairs at homes and businesses. One day, he was called to do some work at a bar. For several days, Brother John parked his car in the driveway of that drinking establishment.

One day Sister Jane happened by and saw Brother John's car parked in that driveway. Sister Jane became very curious. On the next day, she drove by for the express purpose of ascertaining whether Brother John's car was there. Indeed it was. She concluded that Brother John was a drunkard.

Sister Jane immediately spread the news. Everyone in that town became aware of this by Sister Jane's ingenuity. Brother John could not go anywhere without being regarded as a drunkard and an outcast.

Brother John soon had enough of this, and thought of a way to put an end to it once and for all. One night, Brother John drove to Sister Jane's home well after midnight, parked his truck in her driveway, and walked home. The next day, all who passed by could see Brother John's car in Sister Jane's driveway. Sister Jane too observed his car when she got up.

The upshot of the story is obvious. Should the passersby have concluded that since John's car was in her driveway, Jane was having an affair with John?

If we follow Scripture in governing our interpersonal relationships, we will not err in the matter of slander. The Bible is clear as to how we should operate with each other: "Let us therefore follow after the things which make for peace, and things wherewith one may edify another" (Rom. 14:19). The word *edify* means to build up.

Now, we know when we are engaged in slander that we are not building up the person. In fact, we are not building up ourselves, or anyone else who hears the slander. Keeping fidelity to this verse to edify each other precludes slandering them. If we truly understand God's instruction, we are required to say good things about one another, and to cover others for the sake of Christ.

It is worth repeating that sin in the lives of believers must be handled in a godly way. The offending party must be lovingly confronted and allowed to repent and make amends for the wrongs done. This is particularly true when the sin is public knowledge. However, even in dealing with the sinner, we have an obligation not to slander them. Philippians provides an excellent way to avoid spreading negative information: "Finally, brethren, whatsoever things are true, whatsoever things are honest, whatsoever things are just, whatsoever things are pure, whatsoever things are lovely, whatsoever things are of good report; if there be any virtue, and if there be any praise, think on these things" (Phil. 4:8).

How would we apply this verse in a practical way? Let us say Brother Doe is given a project to manage. After observing him, we see that he does two or three things well, but he is not so good at a few other things. We now have a choice as to how we report on Brother Doe's performance. We can, if we choose, publish how lousy a project manager he is, and we would be partially right. But in focusing on the negative aspects of his performance, we would overlook all the things he does well. Our other choice is to focus on the positive aspects of his performance. This encourages him and builds up his efficacy. If we allow ourselves to accentuate the positive, and lovingly coach Brother Doe on his poor performance, we may find that he improves in those areas in which he is now weak.

When I worked in a corporate setting, I learned several important lessons as to how to deal with people. In one firm, they taught us that when we gave feedback, we should resist the temptation to say, "You did such and such right, *but*—" For when you put a "but" in the feedback, immediately the listener's defenses go up.

Here is how they taught us to give good and constructive feedback: "Mary, when you did *XYZ* yesterday, you were good at it. I particularly liked it when you said or did *X*. I believe that you would be even more effective if next time you did *Z* this way." Find something good to say.

Let us endeavor to look for the lovely things in each other. Too often, we seem to want to catch another person doing the wrong things. Let us try to catch them doing something right for a change, and then applaud them for it. God's Word is our best guide on this subject, as on all other subjects affecting our interpersonal relationships.

The Bible says, "As cold waters to a thirsty soul, so is good news from a far country" (Prov. 25:25). Is that not something to think about? Some of you who have never traveled or have not had anyone in your family travel may not readily grasp the truth of this verse. But those of us who have experienced this can identify.

In Jamaica and many other countries, back in the old days, our parents would leave for England or the United States or some other faraway country. They took ship and traveled for weeks before they reached their destination. These were the days before e-mail, text messages, or social media. You had to wait until they landed and wrote a letter, which would then take another two weeks to get back to Jamaica. You waited for what seemed like an eternity to hear news of your loved ones. When you finally got their letter, what good news! At Christmastime, they would send a parcel with clothes and other goodies, and you could not wait to see what was in that parcel. That was good news from a far country, and it came to us as cold water to a thirsty soul, in a manner of speaking!

All of us, at some point in our lives, need some cold water to quench our thirst. Many of us are thirsty, and we need to hear some good news in a world bereft of good news. We should do our part to spread good news. That can begin among us when we stop slandering each other. Please consider that when you make a phone call, the person on the other end may be dying spiritually. They may have missed the service on Sunday because they were thirsty, tired, and depressed. They did not have the strength to venture into the house the Lord. Have we considered how awful a disservice we would do to this soul if we gave them bad news to compound their depression? Slanderous bad news would make them thirstier and more depressed.

We must practice bringing every thought of slander captive to the obedience of Christ. Again, in doing this, we must know what God's Word says. If we want to be the person to bring good news and avoid slander, we must turn to Scripture for guidance. The Bible says, "How beautiful upon the mountains are the feet of him that bringeth good tidings, that publisheth peace; that bringeth good tidings of good, that publisheth salvation; that saith unto Zion, thy God reigneth" (Isa. 52: 7). I have told our church members that they should strive to have beautiful feet by bringing good news. When folks see us coming, they should be happy and say, "Here come beautiful feet. Their coming must mean good news!" Even when the bearer does not have good news, the delivery of the news at hand must be so considerate and loving that it leaves the receiver informed, not incensed.

I believe that slander comes from impure thinking. For example, an impure person sees a brother at church talking to a woman, perhaps shaking her hand or giving her a godly hug. An impure person may conclude that something impure is taking place between them, when nothing of the sort is going on. It is not bad enough that the impure person thinks this; they will go one step further to make slandering statements about the situation.

To be safe, we must operate on the assumption that our eyes and ears can deceive us. Let us recognize that when we think to slander a person, our thinking is at its worst. Before we start slandering, we must consider that it may not be the other person's action that is corrupt. Rather, it may be our thinking that is corrupt. We should consider that we are seeing things through the prism of our own experiences. That is why we draw the conclusions we make.

I have a friend whom I met some years ago in Canada. This was before e-mails and all the social media options. We wrote letters by hand and mailed them to each other. Over time, I got married and so did she. My wife was fine with our friendship, and so was her husband. They both knew that things were pure between us. However, several people on both sides of the border began to raise questions as to the nature of this relationship. This went on until her husband, unbeknown to me, started to get jealous.

One day my friend went to a church convention in England. Her husband, who had stayed home to watch the children, went into her things and read every letter I ever wrote to her, looking for evidence that there was something amiss. When she returned from her trip, he confessed that, having been convinced by others that he needed to watch us, he had taken the liberty of reading her letters. He further confessed that he was shocked to find nothing in those letters but talk of the goodness of God. His socialization had groomed him to believe that it was not possible to have a wholesome friendship with a person of the opposite sex. His own experience was that all his female relationships naturally led to sexual intimacy. From his experience and socialization, and from the input of slandering people, he had developed a mistrust that was hurting him.

Indeed, as members of the body of Christ, we must avoid the very appearance of evil, and not give anyone occasion to suspect our motives (1 Thess. 5:22). And before we start sharing suspicions, we must consider how this may affect, not just the person, but also the church. I have repeated the Bible truth that "to the pure all things are pure" (Titus 1:15). When we are tempted to possess slanderous thoughts, we must remember to bring those thoughts captive to the obedience of Christ. We do that by applying God's Word.

The thought to slander comes from thinking that is jaded by the fall of Adam. Slander is dangerous and hurtful to the body of Christ. Christians must therefore apply God's Word to their thinking and ensure that every word that comes out of our mouths will serve to edify each other and not hurt others. Remember: slander slays three people—the slanderer, the one slandered, and those who hear the slander.

A Prayer

Heavenly Father, sometimes we sin with our tongues by slandering others. We do this at times in defense of ourselves and at times out of malice. When we do this, we forget that we are injuring people for whom Christ died. Please forgive us this wrong and help us to bring every slandering thought captive to the obedience of Christ. In Jesus's name. Amen.

CHAPTER 6

Bring Every Angry Thought Captive to the Obedience of Christ

> *Anger will never disappear so long as thoughts of resentment are cherished in the mind. Anger will disappear just as soon as thoughts of resentment are forgotten.*
>
> —Buddha

The operating principle of our discussion is that many of the issues we face and the emotions we feel as human beings are generated in our minds. If we can control our thought lives, then we will be better able to manage our feelings and actions. Since the battle for our emotions, our behaviors, and even our very souls are fought in the sphere of the mind, we must control our thinking. We must bring every dysfunctional thought captive to the obedience of Christ. "For though we walk in the flesh, we do not war after the flesh. For the weapons of our warfare are not carnal, but mighty through God to the pulling down of strong holds; Casting down imaginations, and every high thing that exalteth itself against the knowledge of God, and bringing into captivity every thought to the obedience of Christ." (2 Cor. 10:3–5).

We now turn our attention to the issue of anger. Our angry feelings and reactions come from within our thought lives. If we hope to master anger, we must master the thinking behind why we are angry. Once we have explored and understood the thought behind our anger, we must bring those angry thoughts and feelings captive to the obedience of Christ. The point to remember is we need to examine what the Word of God says about anger. The Bible tells us, "Be ye angry, and sin not: let not the sun go down upon your wrath" (Eph. 4:26).

Some have argued that the apostle Paul was instructing his audience never to be angry and never to sin. I do not support that interpretation. To demand that a human being never be angry is not realistic. As humans, we are emotional beings, and anger is as natural to us as love is. No one would seriously argue that we should not feel love or sadness or happiness, because these are natural emotional reactions to stimuli in our environments. To place an injunction against anger, therefore, is a prescription for failure.

If we were never to become angry, then Jesus would have failed in this particular, because He got angry. The Bible contains several instances where God's servants and even God Himself displayed anger. After reading several versions of the Bible, I am convinced that the apostle Paul was simply telling his intended audience not to let anger cause them to sin. The NIV renders that verse, "In your anger do not sin. Do not let the sun go down while you are still angry." The weight of biblical evidence argues against a denial of a perfectly legitimate and natural human reaction.

However, even as we recognize that anger is natural, we must admit that it is a significant problem in our society today. Research has shown that anger has a significant impact on cognitive development and mental health.[26] If your children see anger in your home, they will become angry as well, and it will distort or slow down their cognitive development. Research also shows that anger plays an active role in the commission of crimes.[27] On a sociological level, our anger must be put in check in order for us to think right, live in a balanced mental state, and avoid committing crimes.

Anger is not just a spiritual issue. It is also a sociological problem that needs to be carefully looked at and managed. One of the things that counselors must deal with a lot is the anger of the people who come to see us. Some anger is justified. However, anger that consumes us and causes us to lose control of our reactions is dangerous and needs to be managed.

What is anger? A 2012 article on the American Psychological Association's website, titled "Controlling Anger before It Controls You," states that we are all acquainted with anger. At times we experience it as a fleeting annoyance, and at other times as full-fledged rage. Anger is normal in all human beings, and when controlled it is a healthy emotion. But when it gets out of control and turns destructive, it can lead to problems that affect work and personal relationships, and that impact negatively the overall quality of one's life. Anger can make you feel as though you are at its mercy.

The article quotes Dr. Charles Spielberger, a psychologist who specializes in the study of anger. He states that anger is "an emotional state that varies in intensity from mild irritation to intense fury and rage."[28] Like other emotions, anger is accompanied by physiological and biological changes. When you get angry, your heart rate and blood pressure go up, as do the levels of your energy, hormones, adrenaline, and noradrenaline. External and internal events can evoke anger. You could be angry with a specific person or event, or your anger could be caused by brooding about your personal problems. Memories of traumatic or enraging events can also trigger angry feelings.

As bad as the sociological and biological implications of anger are, when it comes to our spiritual lives and our future with God, anger is even worse. Let me be clear: we all get angry at times. The question is, how do we handle our anger? Remember, we must bring every angry thought captive to the obedience of Christ. Here are some Bible verses about anger:

- "He that is soon angry dealeth foolishly: and a man of wicked devices is hated" (Prov. 14:17). An angry person does not have many friends. As a matter of fact, according to this verse, an angry person is hated.
- "It is better to dwell in the wilderness, than with a contentious and an angry woman" (Prov. 21:19).
- "Make no friendship with an angry man; and with a furious man thou shalt not go: Lest thou learn his ways, and get a snare to thy soul" (Prov. 22:24–25). If you hang around an angry person, his angry ways will rub off on you, and you will become as ensnared as he is.
- "An angry man stirreth up strife, and a furious man aboundeth in transgression" (Prov. 29:22). In other words, an angry person is a catalyst for strife and war.

I have seen men who otherwise were good providers, hardworking, and in some ways loving toward their families—but when they got angry, they physically assaulted their wives and children. In some of these cases, when the anger subsided, these men experienced tremendous guilt and shame. Why did they act this way? They did it because they were so angry. Anger consumes an individual and causes them to act in ways that they could not imagine when they are calm.

I am convinced that there is nothing impossible with God. If we allow God's Word to be our guide, we can overcome the thoughts that give birth to explosive anger. Christ died to save us. I believe that in that atonement is healing for our out-of-control emotions, including anger. Approaching anger from a biblical perspective, we can manage it and function better.

Readers who struggle with anger problems that you cannot handle by yourself: you need help. Sit down with a godly counselor who understands both the psychology of anger and the power of the Word to transform minds. It is a good first step.

I have often heard people affirm, "That's the way I was born; I can't help it," when dealing with difficult emotions. They seem resigned to the notion that their situation cannot be helped. I reject such a notion. If Jesus Christ can save them from sin, He can also help them to control their anger. Maybe we cannot change ourselves, but God certainly can, when we are ready to change. If we bring ourselves under the covering of God's Word and submit ourselves to it, we can bring angry thoughts and feelings captive to the obedience of Christ.

The implications of uncontrolled anger are far-reaching. We must consider the broken relationships and missed opportunities that result from acting in ways that break the law, among them having to pay the penalty. There are the other economic issues associated with anger, because not only are there the criminal elements to it, but resources that must be spent to defend the perpetrators and compensate victims.

As bad as the sociological and economic implications of anger are, when it comes to our spiritual lives and future with God, anger is even more costly. One could be angry and go to prison, but if one repents and turns to Christ, one will go to heaven. However, if anger consumes one, and one disrupts lives and then dies angry, I think one is lost.

We all get angry sometimes. It is not a sin to be angry at some things. Some reasonable and measured anger is appropriate. I heard a preacher on television argue that at times anger is good. He said if you send your young teenage boy to a community choir as a heterosexual person, and he comes home homosexual, it is time to be angry. He termed this a righteous anger. If the Devil comes into your family and takes your son or daughter out of the church, hooking them on drugs, it is time to get angry.

Such anger should not drive us to get a gun and shoot someone. Instead, it should drive us to our knees, pouring out our souls to God for relief. While on our knees, if we feel angry and hurt, we should tell God exactly how we feel.

If someone goes on a deliberate mission of maligning your good name, it is appropriate to be angry and sad. Such anger should send you into the Word of God. "If thine enemy hunger, feed him; if he thirst, give him drink: for in so doing thou shalt heap coals of fire on his head" (Rom. 12:20). You must bring that anger captive to obey what Christ has to say about the matter.

We must not let anger consume us. Rather, we must control anger before it controls us.

Remember another thing the Bible says about anger? "He that is soon angry dealeth foolishly: and a man of wicked devices is hated" (Prov. 14:17). Is that clear enough? If you are soon angry, you deal foolishly. How does that affect you, if you are an angry person? How is that a problem? Well, do you really believe that a fool has any part in God's kingdom? If a person could be considered foolish when God saves them, He changes them from that foolish state to be wise. God's laws (the Word) make the simple wise (Ps. 19:7). Many of us, when we were unsaved, were foolish people, but when God saved us and we absorbed His Word, we became wise people.

Because we are all susceptible to angry reactions, we must learn to conquer things that have the potential to conquer us. Even if you are friends with an angry person, anger does not regard friendship. Anger has no respect for anybody. When that angry person is in the middle of an explosive episode, he will tell you anything that comes to his mind. He will injure you and only later may apologize for his actions. Of course, by then the damage is already done.

What are some practical ways to curb our anger? As I have been saying, we need to apply God's Word to this problem. There are also some things we can do ourselves to calm down.

Let us look at an easy example: you are a Black male driving in a White neighborhood, and a White police officer stops you. You have a couple of choices as to how to handle this situation. One choice is to conclude that this White police officer stopped you only because you are Black. With that thinking, you will immediately get angry.

Sometimes, unfortunately, it is true that the police stop Black people because of the color of our skin. Racial profiling is real because we live in a racially divided society, notwithstanding the progress made over the last fifty years.

Be that as it may, your attitude toward that White police officer could mean that you get several tickets or even get dragged down to the police station. Arguing with a police officer who has a gun strapped to their waist and a ticket pad in hand is not a good idea. Responses such as "Why did you stop me?" or "I wasn't doing anything" or "A White man just passed me and you did not stop him" are probably not good things to say to an officer who may have been on duty for eight hours and is fed up with hearing smart talk all day.

In response, the officer may say something back to you, perhaps rude and uncalled for. You react in an angry manner. At the end of such an encounter, you will be lucky if all you get are tickets. You could find yourself needing bail and a lawyer. You could even end up dead, as we have too often observed in our society.

There is an alternative. Say the police officer stops you and asks, "Do you know why I stopped you?"

Instead of telling him that it is because you are Black in a White neighborhood, you can calmly say, "Officer, I don't know, but I am sure you will tell me." If he tells you that you were speeding, and you were not aware, you could say, "Officer, I was not aware of that." You can then follow his instructions and give him what he needs to do his job. You may be convinced that this is a racial profiling case, but will it be helpful to throw that in the police officer's face? No. When he asks you for your papers, just hand them over to him. And do not shove them at him either—do it gently.

One day a police officer stopped me. After asking me why I thought he stopped me, he asked for my papers. My papers were in my wallet, which was in my briefcase in the backseat of my car. I looked at the officer with a smile on my face and said, "Officer, my papers are in my wallet in the backseat. I'm now going to turn around and get my wallet. I am not making any sudden moves, so please be careful what you do. I would hate to give you the wrong impression and then you make a mistake that could not be corrected in my lifetime."

He looked at me, and I saw a smile come over his face. Instead of getting angry that he stopped me, I had disarmed him. After looking over my papers, he said, "Okay, Mr. Hibbert, I am not going to give you a ticket today. Please be careful." I thanked him and was on my way.

One night I was stopped because one of my car's headlights was out, I did not properly signal, I was speeding, and I was zigzagging all over the road. I was tired and sleepy.

The officer asked me, "Do you know why I stopped you?"

I said, "No sir."

He then told me all the violations that I was facing. I said, "I'm in trouble now. By the time you get done writing me these tickets tonight, I will probably need to take out a second mortgage to pay them."

He laughed and struck up a conversation with me. In the end, he let me go without a ticket.

Why did I get off these two times, and several other times before those, without tickets? I learned to curb my anger and then to treat the police officers with the dignity that their office deserves. I have found that if I treat people with respect and in a nonconfrontational manner, I get respect in return.

We will never win over another person when we deal with them in an angry manner. Even when under stress, we need not get angry. If we do get angry, we need to learn how to curb our anger. We can defuse it by bringing it captive to the obedience of God's Word. The Bible tells us, "A soft answer turneth away wrath: but grievous words stir up anger" (Prov. 15:1).

Anger can make a simple situation complicated. Instead of defusing a situation, anger makes a mountain out of a molehill. If we practice the biblical principle of turning away wrath, we will find that we can get out of situations that would otherwise cause us much trouble.

Anger causes us to become wrong even when we were right, because when we are angry, we lose our cool and say and do inappropriate things. Christians ought not to be caught like that. We are in Christ, and the Bible says, "Therefore if any man be in Christ, he is a new creature: old things are passed away; behold, all things are become new" (2 Cor. 5:17). Even if you grew up in an angry family, now that you are grown and saved, you must find ways to deal with anger appropriately.

If you find that you have an anger problem, another way to manage it is to have forethought. Understanding your own capacity to get angry goes a long way in dealing with anger. Understanding what makes you really upset and thinking before you speak or act will enable you to manage your angry responses better. In addition to using God's Word and applying it to our situation, you must also practice anger management skills.

It may seem that the explosive anger that we experience is out of control, and that there is nothing we can do about it, but I remain convinced that if we apply the Word of God to our situation, and if we practice sensible anger management techniques, we will be able to overcome anger.

In the gospel of Matthew, Jesus, speaking to his disciples, said, "But I say unto you, that whosoever is angry with his brother without a cause shall be in danger of the judgment: and whosoever shall say to his brother, Raca, shall be in danger of the council: and whosoever shall say, thou fool, shall be in danger of hell fire" (Matt. 5:22). This passage is quite instructive. Think about this. Jesus says if you are angry with your brother, you shall be in danger of the judgment.

I do not believe that Jesus meant simply if you are annoyed, you could be tried before the judgment seat. Rather, I think Jesus is teaching that if our anger causes us to treat our brothers in ways that are sinful, then we are in danger of the judgment. The lesson is that we should take care how we think about someone else, how we talk about them, and what we say to them.

Jesus used the word *raca* for angry. We need to investigate that a little bit further. The word *raca* is an Aramaic word, and it means a few things. It says to somebody, "You are an empty person. You are useless. You are worthless." It is a term that vilifies a person. In other words, *raca* is a curse word because it belittles a person.

When we, in our anger, tell our children that they are no good, we are using the *raca* word to them. Children who hear that word repeated consistently begin to believe indeed that they are no good. Although we said this in our anger and did not really mean to communicate to them that they were no good, because we said those words, our speech had unintended consequences.

My mother did not study psychology, but she had learned this principle. She believed that if she spoke positive things to her children, they would do positive things. She believed that when she told me I was a good child, I would act in accordance with that affirmation. She told me often, "You are my child, and more importantly, you are a child of God. I expect you to act as such, and I believe that you will act as such. I am not afraid to send you anywhere, because I know that you will act like a Christian."

Many, many times as a teenager, I was tempted to do stuff that young people do. But I could not, because I kept hearing my mother's voice saying, "I trust you. You are a child of God. You are filled with the Holy Ghost, and you will not do such and such."

If, in your anger, you accuse your children or your spouse of a deed that they did not do, they may become discouraged. If they are suffering the consequences just as though they had done the deed, they may in fact do the deed, because they are suffering the pain anyhow. They might at least get the pleasure.

If, in your anger, you are accusing me as a thief, and I know I am not a thief, I nevertheless cannot sleep or eat, because every time I look around, you angrily tell me that I am a thief. So I may just as well go ahead and steal. When you pound that into my head that I am a thief, it gives me the idea. The next time I am somewhere where I may be tempted to steal, I may just get discouraged and say, "What difference does it really make?" If I steal, I will not be treated any differently than I was when I did not steal. Yours is a self-fulfilling prophecy. If you prophesy that I am thief, you should not be surprised if I end up a thief.

When our children or our spouses or people with whom we work do things that make us angry, let us pause and take some time to think through our responses. When we respond in anger, we are likely to say things that we will later regret. We need to step back, take a deep breath, perhaps go for a walk, perhaps count to ten, or do any combination of those things before we speak.

Moreover, as Christians, we need to read God's Word and ask ourselves what Jesus would do if faced with a similar situation. Jesus says that if you say unto your brother *raca*—that is, if you vilify him, denigrate him, and dehumanize him—you are in danger of the judgment. Jesus further stated that if you get that angry to call your brother a fool, you are in danger of hell fire.

If the truth were known, many of us are guilty of that. How often have we referred to our brothers and sisters in belittling ways that, in the final analysis, serve to diminish their mental abilities in our eyes? We say those things in our anger, not thinking of the consequences to them and to ourselves.

Do you think anger is a slight matter? It is not. Christ died to save us, and one of the things He did was give us the ability to bridle our tongues and control our anger. This will come only insofar as we allow Him to control our emotions. That will only happen when we bring angry thoughts captive to the obedience of Christ.

Many people reading this book will not commit adultery. Thank God for that! They will not commit fornication. Nevertheless, when it comes to their tongues, it is as though their behavior is beyond the reach of the blood of Christ. There are people who go to the house of God to worship God, but something upsets them, and they cannot wait to get home and vent their anger. With social media, they do not even have to wait to get home. They just angrily text from the pews. They Facebook from the basement. They rat out the preacher and malign the brother just to assuage their anger.

The preacher may be in the pulpit, preaching out his soul, doing his best to bring you God's Word. Perhaps he makes a mistake. Should we not pray for him? Should we not intercede on his behalf? Should we not cover him if he makes a mistake? If what he says makes us angry, should we not perhaps examine ourselves to see if we are guilty? Instead of responding in anger, should we not go to God in humility and ask Him to forgive us and to help the preacher to declare to us the unadulterated Word of God?

The Word of God tells us, "Be ye angry, and sin not: let not the sun go down upon your wrath" (Eph. 4:26). I read a story some years ago about a couple who lived together. Their kids had grown up and left home. They were together, but they were angry at each other constantly and would not speak to each other.

The man would come home and go directly into the study without speaking to his wife. She would go off to sleep without speaking to him. He would then take a shower and go off to sleep in another room. The anger between them had gotten deeper for years.

The man came home one night, went into his study, and stayed there—because he had died in his chair. His wife found him four days later, only because his body had begun to decompose and stink up the house.

That is a sad story. Factual or not, it depicts the potential of living in a state of anger. This is the reason the apostle Paul tells us that we should not let the sun go down upon our wrath.

Perhaps in your anger, you storm out of the house in the morning without kissing your spouse or saying goodbye to your children. What if a car hits you and you died? What would happen to your soul? What if you got mad at your spouse and had a heart attack in the middle of your rage? What would be the state of your soul?

The people around you are the folks God has given you as helpful mechanisms in your life, to make your life better. When you abuse them in your anger, yet you need them to help you out, it makes it a lot more difficult for them to come to your aid. Anger pushes people away from you. People who have been abused by it cannot really do what they want to do for you, because they are afraid.

I was told a story about two Christian women who lived together as roommates. One of them was of angry disposition. In her anger, she would fuss with her roommate, yell at her, and make her life generally miserable. One day before she left the house, the angry woman yelled at and cursed out her roommate. The episode left the roommate shaken and nervous.

No sooner had the angry roommate returned home that evening, than she resumed her angry tirade. The abused woman looked up at the angry roommate and sighed. Then her head fell into her dinner plate. She had evidently died from a heart attack.

The angry roommate was terrified and filled with guilt. She lived with the belief that she had contributed to the death of her roommate. It may have been a coincidence that her roommate died during her emotional rampage. Maybe the roommate would have died on that day anyway. But in her mind, she had killed her roommate by constant anger and nagging.

What a thing to live with! Can you imagine the guilt trip? We need to be very careful lest we cause others to stumble and lose their way because of our anger.

The Bible tells us, "Let all bitterness, and wrath, and anger, and clamour, and evil speaking, be put away from you, with all malice. And be kind one to another, tenderhearted, forgiving one another, even as God for Christ's sake hath forgiven you" (Eph. 4:31–32). Sometimes people hurt us and we want to be angry and bitter with them, because we are human beings. As human beings, we feel the pain when others hurt us. But our response to such things must be measured and governed by God's Word, not from a place of anger. When your brother or your sister hurts you and you are tempted to act in anger, remember what the Bible says: "And be kind one to another, tenderhearted, forgiving one another, even as God for Christ's sake hath forgiven you" (Eph. 4:32).

If Jesus Christ got angry every time I made a mistake, I would have been dead a long time ago. Many of us who become so angry with others for their wrong deeds would be ashamed if our own sins were ever revealed. If we are tenderhearted and forgiving as the Bible demands, we have no place for uncontrolled anger.

Because we are born with emotions, we respond to things in emotional ways. There are conditions that we face that will make us angry. That is natural, and it is okay for us to respond based upon our feelings, but such response should be considered, godly, measured, and controlled by God's Word. The question "What would Jesus do?" is a very good question to ask when we experience angry emotions. We should ask the question, and if the answer is not readily apparent to us, we should take time out and consult the Word of God. Consulting God's Word is a way to postpone responding when we are angry. If we discipline ourselves and delay our responses until we consult with God's Word, we make a lot fewer mistakes.

As believers we operate on a different plane. The sphere of our battle is not worldly. We are fighting a spiritual battle, and we must therefore use spiritual weapons to fight. There is nothing that God cannot do. If He can save you, He certainly can help you control your angry thoughts and reactions.

A Prayer

Lord, sometimes our anger gets the best of us. As a result, we say and do things that are injurious to others and to ourselves, and that dishonor Your name. Please forgive us this fault and help us to learn the principles of being angry and not sinning. In Jesus's name. Amen.

CHAPTER 7

Bring Every Hateful Thought Captive to the Obedience of Christ

I have decided to stick with love. Hate is too great a burden to bear.

—Martin Luther King Jr.

We now turn our attention to the matter of hateful thoughts. There should be no such thing as a hateful Christian. Since the Christian serves the God of love, who is Love, and since the Christian, by the miracle of regeneration, has become a partaker of the divine nature, there should be no room for hate (2 Pet. 1:4). Unfortunately, since we still live in the flesh, hate becomes problematic for us. We must deal with it in the context of God's Word.

I have repeatedly observed that our behaviors and feelings are controlled by the way we think. Those of you who have studied psychology understand that there is school of counseling known as cognitive behavioral therapy (CBT). The philosophical premise of this construct is that a person's feelings and behaviors are controlled in large measure by how the person thinks.

The thinkers who came up with this theoretical postulation tell us in large volumes what the Bible teaches in a few words. The Bible tells us that as a man thinks in his heart, so is he (Prov. 23:7). What this boils down to is that if you think hateful thoughts, you are likely to turn out to be a hateful person.

Hate starts in the recesses of the mind. It is a conscious decision that we make. We tell ourselves that so-and-so has hurt us one time too many, and we will not forgive them. We decide that we hate them, and we will have nothing to do with them again. We may not go so far as to say that we hate the person, although we may admit that we dislike their ways. There is, however, a thin line between dislike and hate, and the Christian must be careful not to take the chance of falling into a state of hate.

Let us continue to remember that in dealing with hateful thoughts, as with all negative thoughts, we are not doing this by our own strength. Hate is a strong emotion, and it is very difficult to control by ourselves. However, when we apply God's Word to it, like any other emotion, we can control it. Keep in mind our controlling Scripture passage, reminding us that we are fighting with spiritual weapons as we bring every thought captive to the obedience of Christ.

When I think about that verse, I see in my mind's eye the scene that was often played out in the rural areas of Jamaica where I lived as a child. Back then we were used to roping animals. When we wanted to capture them and make them obedient to us, we would grab a rope, make a noose, and throw it around their necks. When we caught them, we could lead them where we wanted them to go. We brought those animals bound and captive to obey us. They had little choice but to follow where we led them.

In a manner of speaking, there are things that we have to "rope" and drag before Christ. This says to me that such habits, thoughts, and feelings will not surrender easily. They have to be compelled and brought captive, involuntarily dragged to the foot of the cross. You can say to those thoughts and feelings, "I know you do not want to come to the obedience of Christ, but I'm going to rope you in, drag you, bring you to the cross, and say, 'The blood of Jesus prevails against you.'" We need to rope in our hateful thoughts, whether we like it or not.

If we were left to our own devices, we would do much damage to ourselves. If I followed my feelings, I would let hate kill others and me. When you really hate somebody, you are hurting yourself more than you are hurting them. It takes more energy to hate than to love.

I have been in love once or twice in my life, and I know how uplifting and rewarding that feeling is. Sadly, I have also felt the emotions of dislike, resentment, and hate. Believe me, it is painful to maintain a psychological posture of dislike, resentment, or hate for long without it taking a psychological, physiological, and spiritual toll.

There was one episode in my life when I felt hate. I could not sleep well, and when I saw the person I hated, it felt to me as though my blood pressure went up. I recognized that I was in a dire situation. I needed help. I needed divine intervention to help me overcome a feeling that was almost consuming me. I had to cry and pray for deliverance.

How did I overcome this? For one year straight, I had to pray every single day, "God, create in me a clean heart," because I knew that my heart was not right. I had convinced myself that I did not hate this person. I intellectualized my emotion as being careful and cautious. I told myself that I did not hurt him; he was the one who inflicted pain on me, and therefore it was his responsibility to make it right. However, I found that the longer I waited, the more the feelings of resentment boiled in me. Until I began to pray to God to create in me a clean heart, I was not happy, and I was very uncomfortable around the person I hated.

To be sure, this person was as culpable as I was. This person had behaved in a way that could only be characterized as ungodly. The competitive nature of our relationship had ballooned into a rivalry that gave birth to resentment. I knew I had to do something about it, and I knew it would destroy me if I did not seek God for His divine help. Therefore, I had to keep on saying, "Dear Lord, please fix this."

Thank God, He hears and answers prayer. I remembered the day when I reconciled with this person. It was as if a great burden had been lifted from my shoulders. It was like a ball and chain had been loosed from my feet. The weight of hate had burdened me down and shackled me. I could not soar like an eagle because the quagmire called hate had pinned me down.

So what is hate? Merriam-Webster's online dictionary says that hate is (1) "an intense hostility and aversion usually deriving from fear, anger, or a sense of injury. (2) Extreme dislike and antipathy." Sometimes you hear some folks say, "I do not hate him. I just do not like him much." But at what point does dislike turn to hate? We need to examine that, because we understand as Christians that hate is a bad thing. That's why we substitute the word *hate* for *dislike*.

We need to be real. If it feels like hate and responds like hate, then it is hate. Someone once observed if a thing walks like a duck, looks like a duck, quacks like a duck, and has webbed feet like a duck, then it is a duck.

Dictionary.com defines hate as to "dislike intensely or passionately; feel extreme aversion for or extreme hostility toward; detest." When one says, "I can't stand him," is that not detestation? You know it is hate when you see them coming and something in you rises up. Call it dislike if you want, call it just avoiding him if you please—call it whatever you want, but it comes down to hate. Let us call it what it is.

The first step in dealing with hate is to recognize that we do have that emotion. Hiding it or using more pleasant euphemisms may be convenient, but the result is the same. Who would argue that resentment and intense dislike could not possibly result in deep-seated hatred? Since the possibility exists that what we consider dislike could turn to hate, let us bring those thoughts and feelings captive to the obedience of Christ.

I have not done any scholarly research on the impact of hate on the physical health of the one who hates, but from anecdotal information, there seems to be a consensus that when a person hates, their blood pressure goes up when they see the object of their hate. That would be a good study for a research project: "To what extent does hate impact one's physical and mental health on objective measures such as hypertension?" I am willing to bet that hate has a negative impact on both physical and psychological well-being. I am also willing to theorize that when we practice love, it has a positive impact on those same objective measures. There is a degree of stress in love, but it is a positive stress.

Hate is incompatible with the God of love. The Bible teaches, "He that loveth not knoweth not God; for God is love" (1 John 4:8). If we are the children of God and we hate each other, we are disharmonious with God. If we claim that we have the love of God in us, it is impossible to hate at the same time. Love and hate are at opposite end of the spectrum. They are antithetical to each other. The apostle John writes, "If a man say, I love God, and hateth his brother, he is a liar: for he that loveth not his brother whom he hath seen, how can he love God whom he hath not seen?" (1 John 4:20). It is hard to love the invisible God if we do not love the visible person. God has given us His image bearers—other human beings—to love, so that we can truly love Him.

We cannot say that we love God and hate our brothers, yet call ourselves the children of God. That is a contradiction in terms. You cannot do both. It does not matter how clever you are. It does not matter how ingenious and creative you are. If you hate your brother, you cannot love God, for God is love.

Is it ever appropriate to hate anything? Yes. The Bible teaches that we must hate sin. Sin is of the Devil. We should have an abhorrence of sin. Sin is a reproach to any people. It destroys the fabric of our societies. Sin destroys the foundations of a home and our families. Therefore, we should hate sin in all its manifestations. As born-again believers, we should have nothing to do with sin. We should avoid sin as we would avoid a plague. In a manner of speaking, sin is the worst plague the world has ever known. God's Word mandates that His people reject sin and be separate from the world (2 Cor. 6:17).

We should also hate injustice. For those of us who lived in the United States in the days of blatant and sanctioned segregation, when African Americans had to sit in the back of the bus, that was something we should hate. Whenever injustice raises its ugly head, we should hate it, for injustice is an affront to God. We should hate the injustice, but not the unjust person.

We can safely hate child abuse, incest, and the desecration of houses of worship. The Bible tells us, "The fear of the Lord is to hate evil: pride, and arrogancy, and the evil way, and the forward mouth, do I hate" (Prov. 8:13). It is safe to hate these things, for when we hate them, it is not the person we hate. Rather, it is their deeds that we hate. It is never okay to hate the sinner, but it is always okay to hate the sin that the sinner commits. The Bible teaches, "Hate the evil, and love the good, and establish judgment in the gate: it may be that the Lord God of hosts will be gracious unto the remnant of Joseph" (Amos 5:15).

I may be belaboring the point, but it is necessary to reiterate here that it is never okay to hate a brother or a sister. When the thought of hate comes in our minds, we must always consult God's Word on the subject. Again, the Bible tells us, "Thou shalt not hate thy brother in thine heart: thou shalt in any wise rebuke thy neighbor, and not suffer sin upon him" (Lev. 19:17). The NIV version renders this verse, "Do not hate your brother in your heart: rebuke your neighbor frankly so you will not share in his guilt."

It is worth noting that loving somebody, or not hating them, does not mean you cannot correct them. Because we love each other, we are obligated to correct each other. When as believers we observe wrongdoing in the lives of fellow believers, we have an obligation to point out such wrongs in a godly manner. That might be difficult at times, because people may reject and resent us for presuming to correct them. Nevertheless, for the love of God, we must do it. In doing godly correction, we demonstrate the love of God. It is God's way. The Bible teaches, "For whom the Lord loveth he chasteneth, and scourgeth every son whom he receiveth" (Heb. 12:6).

I believe that hate comes because of fear, hurt, perceived or real danger, or injustice done to us. When hate comes, which is a natural reaction to these things, we must say, "No, no, no, I can't afford to hate." The Bible has some very harsh words for people who hate others: "The blood thirsty hate the upright: but the just seek his soul" (Prov. 29:10). Anytime you see somebody who really hates another person, according to Scripture, that hater is bloodthirsty.

Some people get very upset when others do great things. If your children are more successful than theirs are, these folks become very upset. They may even go so far as to develop resentment over something you had nothing to do with. Instead of loving you and rejoicing with you in your triumph, they develop hatred in their hearts.

Is that not what Cain did? His brother Abel offered a more acceptable sacrifice than he did. The Bible said that God accepted Abel's sacrifice, but God rejected Cain's. Instead of seeking to find out what sacrifice would have been acceptable to God, hatred consumed Cain, and he murdered his own brother. Abel did nothing against Cain. He simply obeyed God. That act of pleasing God should have delighted his brother. It should have been instructive to Cain. But it had the opposite effect. It resulted in murder. (See Gen. 4.)

Here is the attitude that some assume, when they see a brother or sister advancing in ministry and apparently close to the pastor: "She is showing off. She is trying to get close to the pastor. He is trying to get a name for himself. He is trying to take over my job." They develop hate in their hearts for this person, while all this person is doing is genuinely working hard for God and trying to please God. Every time they try to take a step for God, others attempt to block them. They are hated for the good they are trying to do.

If we find in ourselves any such feelings of resentment or hate when someone is advancing in ministry, in their careers, or in their personal lives, we should rebuke the thought that gave rise to such a feeling. We should recognize it for what it is, for such thoughts are not of God. They are from the Enemy. We must rebuke them and bring such thoughts captive to the obedience of Christ.

Let us understand that it is easy at times to fall into a resentment mode. Let us recognize our ability to be resentful and hateful. Let us understand that sometimes our thoughts run away with us. Let us recognize when, for no good reason, we feel a sense of discomfort as others are just going about their own business. Let us be aware and manage those thoughts. The thoughts come from our hearts. The Bible says the heart is "deceitful above all things and desperately wicked" (Jer. 17:9). Let us not pretend that we are exempt from such feelings, for we are not. It is in understanding our potential to fall into the hate mode that we can plan against it and respond when it first emerges.

Hate is a very dangerous thing. Jesus Christ makes no provision for us ever to hate our brothers. He teaches us to love even our enemies, to bless those who curse us, and to render good deeds to those who hate us (Matt. 5:43–44). Mosaic Law had something else to say about this. Under that law, it was okay to love your neighbor and to hate your enemies. However, Jesus came and established the New Testament. He has given us a new commandment. His commandment is that we love everybody, even those who hate us and despitefully use us.

I believe some Christians are operating under the old covenant. That will not do! Jesus has made a new covenant. Is it easy? No, it is not. The first reaction we naturally have when somebody is cursing us out is to curse back. We must hold our tongues and let the Holy Spirit guide us.

Like many of you reading this book, I struggle to love someone who I know or believe does not love me. It is particularly difficult when I have reason to believe they speak evil against me without a cause. I am tempted to confront them at the very least, or to hate them in return. I therefore must be very cognizant of the fact that I am prone to hate. I must bring all thoughts of hate and resentment captive to the obedience of Christ. I must know what the Bible says about hate and how destructive hate is to my own spiritual walk. I must not let hate get the better of me.

Instead of giving place to the feelings and thoughts of hate, I must practice loving my enemies. Yes, I must practice loving those who hate me, because agape love (the God kind of love) is not an emotional love. Rather, it is volitional, deliberate, and willful. As Christians, we must develop a will to love even those whom we do not like very much.

The Christian's responsibility in this is not easy at all. I submit to you that, like most other people, when I believe that my character is being maligned, I do not find it easy to overcome. However, if I expect an easy life on earth, perhaps I do not quite understand the nature of the Christian faith.

It is no wonder that the symbol of Christianity is a cross, because the cross represents suffering, pain, and ignominy. It is no wonder Jesus Christ said, "Whosoever will come after me, let him deny himself, and take up his cross, and follow me" (Mark 8:34). Maybe your cross is to love people who hate you. Maybe your cross is to understand that although they do not really like you very much, you are still going to love them. It is not so much about us; it is about what God is doing in us. By loving the person who hates you, you can bring them to Jesus. Because when they see that you did not respond the way you could have, but instead responded in love, they just may be drawn to the God of love whom you represent.

Let us think about some consequences of hate. The Bible teaches that if we hate our brother, we are still in darkness, and we do not know where we are going because darkness blinds our eyes (1 John 2:9–11). It does not matter how educated or how enlightened we think we are; if we hate, we are blind. It is of little significance that we believe we are street smart and know the ways of the world. If we hate our brothers or our sisters, we are in darkness. That means that we are ignorant. We are walking around not knowing where we are going, because the darkness has so blinded our eyes that we cannot see.

The Bible teaches that God is light and there is no darkness in Him (1 John 1:15). If we are walking in darkness, we are not walking in Christ, for in God there is no darkness at all. If we are in darkness, it is safe to say that we are not in Him.

The Devil hates the people of God. That is the reason he accuses us day and night before the Father. If we hate our brothers, are we not squarely on the side of the Devil? The Devil goes before God and brings up the smallest infractions that you have ever done. With his hateful heart, the Devil says to God, "Kill this person! Put them in hell! They are not worthy of you. They have violated your holy standard of righteousness and must be punished." The Devil says this as if he had any regard for God's standards of righteousness. The truth is that the Devil hates righteousness—but that does not stop him from accusing us before God, because he simply hates us. The Devil is so hateful, he convinces you that your actions of yesterday preclude you from going to heaven, because God must hate you for what you have done.

As Christians, we often face a moral and spiritual dilemma. This dilemma arises from a belief that we can love God and hate our brothers. That is inconsistent with God's Word. Hating our brothers and loving God at the same time are mutually exclusive concepts. The Bible is quite clear on this: "If a man say, I love God, and hateth his brother, he is a liar" (1 John 4:20). He tells us to love each other and never to hate one another. In the context of Scripture, God tells us that if we love our brother, we show ourselves to be His disciples (John 13:35).

As far as learning to love each other is concerned, we need cognitive restructuring. By this, I mean that we need to change our thinking about others in our lives. If we expect great things from them, placing all our hopes and aspirations on their goodness, we will most likely be disappointed. We need to rethink who we, as humans, really are. The people whom God places in our lives are just like us; flawed, broken, and in need of a whole lot of help. Therefore, when we are tempted to hate somebody who hurts us, we need to look in the mirror and examine ourselves. Are we capable of doing the very same things to them that they have done to us? When we consider that we share in the same humanity and are beset on every side by human frailties, we should rather have compassion on them than hate them.

When we are tempted to hate someone who hurts us, we must consider God's attitude toward that emotion called hate. He uses the strongest terms to describe hate. The Bible tells us, "Whosoever hateth his brother is a murderer, and ye know that no murderer hath eternal life abiding in him" (1 John 3:15). Generally, to murder someone, you really must hate them. I am not talking about accidentally killing someone. I believe that is called manslaughter, and as unfortunate as that crime is, it is not the same as murder. Most often murder takes forethought, and that forethought comes from a place of hate. When a person decides to kill somebody out of hate, the only consideration the person has is how to do this without leaving any evidence. A murder that comes from hate is a premeditated, considered, and deliberate act. Therefore, when God says if we hate our brothers, we are murderers, He is saying that when a heart is full of hate, the hater can kill in cold blood.

How do we rid ourselves of hate? One way is to ask God for hearts of love. When love fills our hearts, there is no place for hate. Love therefore is the antidote for hate. Love is able to embrace the unlovable, to forgive the unforgivable, and to tolerate the intolerable.

I recall a story in the Old Testament, in which God instructed a prophet to marry a prostitute. He married her, cleaned her up, made her respectable, and gave her children. In the process of time, that woman went back to her old ways. God instructed the prophet to go back, marry her again, and make her respectable again. The prophet obeyed (see the book of Hosea).

This story does not teach that God has no moral standards. Rather, it shows Israel God's undying and forgiving love. Pure love such as that can forgive our brothers and sisters when they have committed the most egregious acts against us. This is the case because, according to Paul, love "keeps no record of wrongs" (1 Cor. 13:5 NIV). Because love keeps no record of wrongs, if we have love in our hearts, it is impossible to exact a price from those who have hurt us.

If anyone had a reason to hate those who persecuted Him, it was Jesus Christ our Lord. He came to earth, and all He ever did was good. He healed the sick, turned water into wine, raised the dead, and did all sorts of wonderful things, yet His detractors hated Him without a cause. They plotted, connived, politicked, and finally crucified him.

Death by crucifixion was one of the most shameful and painful means of putting anyone to death. To hang on a cruel cross was bitter, dehumanizing, and simply shameful. The Bible says, "Cursed is everyone that hangs on a tree" (Gal. 3:13). When one was crucified, it was pure ignominy. Yet on the cross that day, not only did Jesus forgive the thief, He prayed to His Father to forgive those who crucified Him, for they knew not what they did (Luke 23:34). That was love!

So, as I have suggested before, when someone hurts us and we are tempted to hate them, we should ask this question: "What would Jesus do?" If we practice this approach, we will never go wrong. We will never give ourselves the latitude to harbor hate in our hearts. Instead, we will follow the footsteps of our Lord.

I am sure that when Jesus Christ was on the cross, it did not feel good to die. Nothing that the world did endeared itself to Christ. Everything that they did, from the day He was born until the day they crucified Him, was designed to discredit Him. Jesus was God. He knew the hearts of men, and knew that out of human jealousy and malice, He was being crucified. Yet on the cross, there was no room in His heart for hate. It was love that brought Him there in the first place.

Hate is destructive and causes all kinds of physical and emotional distress in people who hate. To have hate in our hearts is an evident token that there is something wrong with our testimony. It shows we have not experienced the love of God toward us. How many times have we wronged God? How many times have we walked outside His will? And for our sins, God is justly displeased. Yet when we come asking for His forgiveness, He forgives us willingly. He forgives us when we do not deserve it. In fact, we never deserve His forgiveness. It is by His grace, mercy, and love that we are able to stand before Him at all. If God ever takes retribution against us for the things that we have done to offend Him, not one of us will be able to stand. If God ever deals with us based on His righteous justice, we will all perish.

Happily, God forbears. He postpones His anger against our transgressions and instead looks at us through the eyes of love and compassion. In dealing with our brothers and sisters, should we not have the same attitude as God?

For all of us, there are some people who rub us the wrong way. They seem to go out of their way to inflict pain on us. There are some mean people in the world. They are inconsiderate and care very little about the feelings of others. I wish I could say that such people are relegated to the world and not the church. It's just not so. There are people in the church who, perhaps because they were hurt themselves, have grown bitter and callous toward the feelings of others. They have no problem inflicting pain on others. Some of them have personality problems, such as narcissism. If you try to point out their behavior, somehow they will turn it back on you. It seems quite justified to them to inflict pain on you.

Such people should not be hated. Instead, we should have compassion on them and pray for them that God will change their hearts. Again, I argue that love is the antidote for hate, and that a heart filled with love has no room for hate. Therefore, if we find hate in our hearts, we need to examine ourselves and ask God to wash out those hate impulses and fill us with His love.

It is the premise of this book that the emotions we feel, the impulses we express, germinate in our thought lives. We cannot really hate people unless we conceive of them in a negative way. I learned that when armies train to go to war, they have to prepare themselves to kill their opponents. It is difficult to kill somebody whom you love; therefore, the soldiers are trained to conceive of their opponents as somehow less than they are and deserving of death. A soldier must see the enemy as not being worthy to live. In other words, they must develop some measure of hate in their hearts, so that when they see the enemy, they can justify shooting him and not have any remorse about it.

That ability to hate our enemy comes from the thinking that he or she is less than we are and does not deserve our love. We must recognize, however, that in our walk with Christ, we are not fighting with worldly weapons. The Bible tells us that the weapons of our warfare are not carnal, but they are mighty through God to the pulling down of strongholds. Having a heart full of hate represents a stronghold, against which we must apply God's love. When the thought of hate emerges, we must bring such thoughts captive to the obedience of Christ.

A Prayer

Father, often when others hurt us, we harbor resentment in our hearts that borders on hate, although we may not admit it. Help us, dear Lord, to bring every hateful thought captive to the obedience of Christ. In Jesus's name. Amen.

CHAPTER 8

Bring Every Lying Thought Captive to the Obedience of Christ

A liar begins with making falsehood appear like truth, and ends with making truth itself appear like falsehood.
—William Shenstone

We now turn our attention to the problem of lying in our society—and, sadly, also among believers. Lying is a problem that must be dealt with in a godly way. The origin of lying is not with us. Although it is as old as the human race, it did not start with us; it came from the Devil himself. The Devil is rightly called the father of lies (John 8:44). When we find ourselves prone to lie, we must reckon that we are after the order of Satan, and not after Christ, who is "the way, the *truth*, and the life" (John 14:6, emphasis added).

Most "good" liars are practiced. They have made a conscious decision to deceive, because lying takes forethought. A liar must first deceive himself as to the veracity of his own story before he can convince others of it. This, I think, is the reason David affirmed that God desires truth in the "innermost being" (Ps. 51:6 NASB).

Lying is endemic in the human race. It comes so naturally that it seems to me that our first line of defense when we are cornered is the lie our way out of it. It is amazing to watch even the youngest child, who can barely speak, lie. You can observe a child picking up an object. The child knows they are observed. Yet, when you ask that child, "Did you do it?" that child will say no.

When I was a child, my grandmother would tell us that if we told the truth, she would not spank us. Yet somehow, when she confronted us about something that we did, we either did not believe her or simply could not help ourselves; we would lie. We took the chance of getting an even more severe spanking if we were discovered to be liars, and we lied anyway. I believe that we reasoned that if we lied about the deed, we had a better chance of getting off. That perhaps is true with humans, but never with God. God knows the intentions of our hearts (Heb. 4:12).

One time a friend of mine and I observed a duck's nest with about a dozen eggs. We said to each other, "Nobody really eats duck eggs, so let us break them." We picked up stones, threw them in the nest, and broke every egg.

We went home thinking, "No harm, no foul." But when the owner of the duck came home and discovered that his eggs were destroyed, he caught a fit. He screamed and cursed. He asked us whether we knew who did this, and we solemnly swore that we did not know. My grandmother asked me if I had any idea who had perpetrated this awful deed, and again I solemnly swore that I had no idea.

We lied because that is what human beings do when they are cornered. However, as Christians, we are governed by a different set of rules. Back in those days, our parents taught us, "Speak the truth and speak it ever, cost what it will. He who hides the wrongs he did, does the wrong thing still." That is a wonderful principle to go by, but I suppose it is easier said than done. Nevertheless, as believers we must find a way to bring every lying thought captive to the obedience of Christ.

Let us identify lying for what it is. It is a pathological problem that must be dealt with from God's Word or it will destroy us. Why would I call it a pathological problem? It is pathological because it is a disease of the character. Merriam-Webster defines *pathological* as "relating to pathology, being such to a degree that is extreme, excessive, or markedly abnormal." You often hear, "He is a pathological liar" or "She has a pathological fear of things that crawl." *Pathology* itself is defined as "the structural and functional deviations from the normal, that constitute disease or characterize a particular disease." When a person practices lying, therefore, this is not a casual matter. It is a disease of one's character and if not handled, it could mean the doom of one's soul.

Like all the issues that we deal with in this book, lying has its foundation in our cognition. To be a good liar, one must think through the process and be very astute in order not to be caught. I once had a patient who boasted on her ability to lie. She said that her husband was jealous, but in her mind, she needed to do what she had to do. She wanted to be free to live a certain lifestyle without being caught. To keep her lies straight, she maintained a book in which she recorded her responses to questions her husband asked. She indicated that when he asked her a question again in the future, she would postpone answering if she was not sure what her original response was. She would then consult her little book and respond to him in a way consistent with her previous answer. She was a practiced and accomplished liar. You could call her a pathological liar.

A male patient told me that his mother had taught him how to lie and cheat. This young man had a proclivity for cheating on his girlfriends. In order to disguise his behavior when he went by another girl's house and did his business, he would take a shower before going home to his live-in girlfriend. Yet his girlfriend always knew that he had cheated on her.

He could not figure out how she knew, and so he confided in his mother. His mother told him that he was going about this all wrong; if he wanted to cheat, he needed to know how to disguise his actions. She told him that his girlfriend probably knew that he had cheated because the soap he was using in the other woman's apartment was different from the soap in his apartment. To ensure that he not get caught, his mother recommended that he purchase the same soap he had at home and bring it to his other girlfriend's apartment.

Then his mother told him one more thing: when he leaves his other girlfriend's apartment, he should not go home directly, but take a walk for about an hour. That way, he would not smell as though he had recently taken a shower.

Now that is a pathological liar. Lying as instructed by this young man's mother did not have to be with words. Instead, she taught him that he could deceive his girlfriend by disguising his actions. She set him up so that if his live-in girlfriend were to ask him, "Where have you been?" he could say he had been with friends or some other story. Such is the nature and modus operandi of a pathological liar.

According to Merriam-Webster, "lying is speech marked by or containing falsehood. *Lie* is a verb, and it designed to (1) make a blatant deliberate untrue statement with the intent to deceive, (2) create a false or misleading impression." This second form of lie is not a blatant verbal or written statement, but it is equally deadly. It is a verbal circumlocution or an action designed to create a maze of confusion. Recall the story that I just related of the mother who taught her son how to deceive his girlfriend. He did not have to say a word; his actions were designed to deceive.

Years ago, my then-pastor, who is now with the Lord, did not like it when too many of the members of the church were absent to visit other churches on a Sunday. He maintained that parishioners had an obligation to be in their own church. He felt it was particularly incumbent upon those who were ministers to be present at every service possible.

As an evangelist, I loved to travel, and would get his permission to do so. One weekend, however, I wanted to attend church in Toronto, Canada. I felt that if I asked him again to let me go, he would not consent. So I decided not to tell him the truth about where I was going. Instead, I told him that I would be out of town. That was truthful in a way, for, after all, I lived in New Jersey, and going to Toronto was going out of town. So what was wrong with that statement?

Well, at that time, I was working for a large telecommunications firm. My job required that I travel out of town sometimes, and he knew that to be the case. I thought, and correctly so, that when I told him that I was going out of town, he would assume that I was going on a business trip. When I arrived in Toronto, I felt a sense of guilt that I had misled my pastor, so I called him and confessed my deception.

Sometimes the act of lying takes the form of verbal roundaboutness—or, as we say, beating around the bush. Politicians do this very well. You ask a question and they go around and around, issuing statements designed to confuse people. Lying is a threat to the moral fabric of society. If you cannot believe what your leaders tell you, then nothing is sacred anymore. There was a time in the United States when you could look another person in the eye and enter into a contract without putting down anything on paper. Back then, a handshake was all that was needed. People remained true to their word.

I have argued that to tell a lie, we must first conceive it in our thought process. How is it possible that a young child knows how to lie? All forms of lies, deceits, and deceptions come from the Devil, whom the Bible refers to as the father of lies: "Ye are of your father the devil, and the lusts of your father ye will do. He was a murderer from the beginning, and abode not in the truth, because there is no truth in him. When he speaketh a lie, he speaketh of his own: for he is a liar, and the father of it." (John 8:44). If we lie, are we not the children of the father of lies? That is very tough to acknowledge, but it is true.

The Bible says when the Devil speaks a lie, he speaks of his own—or as the NIV puts it, "when he lies, he speaks his natural language." Sometimes we speak what we call "a little fib" or "a little white lie," thinking that there is no harm in that. Please understand this: there is no difference between the "little white lie" and a big black lie. Lying is simply lying.

Lying takes on another subtle form that manifests itself in the way some people project their family relationships. I have known couples who have awful relationships at home. They live in pain and suffer tremendously. Yet when they come out in public, they put on a facade and pretend everything is just wonderful. The sad thing is that they do not leave it at that. When they comment about other people's relationships, they condemn those relationships. They comment negatively about others' broken relationships, although their own relationships are even more broken. They leave the impression in the minds of observers that there is nothing wrong with them. Then they go home and resume their most dysfunctional and painful relationships.

I do not advocate that couples who are involved in broken relationships come out in public and make a big deal about it. There are some private pains that should remain private. These couples should seek counseling in a private setting to deal with their problems. But to put on a public front that everything is just beautiful, and then to condemn others, is the height of hypocrisy and deception. A good principle to follow in such cases is that if a couple does not have anything positive to say, it is best if they just say nothing.

I have read somewhere that lying refers to the act by which one deliberately makes a false statement with the intent to instill false beliefs in the minds of recipients. Is that not what the Devil does all the time? Do you remember the unfortunate dialogue the Devil held with Eve in the garden of Eden? God had told Adam that he should not eat of the tree of the knowledge of good and evil, for in the day he ate of that tree, he would surely die (Gen. 2:17). The Devil entered, and listen to his twist on God's injunction:

> Now the serpent was more subtil than any beast of the field which the LORD God had made. And he said unto the woman, Yea, hath God said, Ye shall not eat of every tree of the garden? And the woman said unto the serpent, We may eat of the fruit of the trees of the garden: But of the fruit of the tree which is in the midst of the garden, God hath said, Ye shall not eat of it, neither shall ye touch it, lest ye die. And the serpent said unto the woman, Ye shall not surely die: For God doth know that in the day ye eat thereof, then your eyes shall be opened, and ye shall be as gods, knowing good and evil. (Gen. 3:1–5)

Did you notice the Devil's strategy? His first order of business was to create a question mark in Eve's mind. In Genesis 3:1, he posed this cynical question: "Yea, hath God said, ye shall not eat of every tree of the garden?" Now why was the question necessary? The Devil knew what God had said. The fact that he posed that question in the first place presupposes that he had the information. His question, therefore, was not designed to get him any new information. Rather, the question was designed to create doubt in Eve's mind.

Once the Devil succeeded in creating doubt in her mind, Eve became confused. Because of this confusion, in her response to the Devil, she added a requirement to God's injunction that was not initially there. God had told them not to eat of the tree of the knowledge of good and evil. But when Eve responded to the Devil, she said, "We may eat of the fruit of the trees of the garden: But of the fruit of the tree which is in the midst of the garden, God hath said, Ye shall not eat of it." Crucially, she added, "*neither shall ye touch it*, lest ye die" (emphasis added).

Adding this seemingly innocuous phrase led Eve down the wrong path. If Eve had simply touched that tree, she would in fact not have died, for that was not the prohibition. The prohibition was that they should not *eat* of it.

After the Devil placed this doubt as to God's Word in Eve's mind, he then said, "Ye shall not surely die: For God doth know that in the day ye eat thereof, then your eyes shall be opened, and ye shall be as gods, knowing good and evil." Maybe he even said something to the effect of "Let me prove this to you. Go ahead and touch the tree. Touch it. You won't die. Go ahead touch it." Let us assume that was the way it went.

Let us continue this assumption. After she touched the tree and was not struck down dead, the Devil may have said, "See, God lied. You touched it and you are very much alive. The reason God does not want you to touch this tree or to eat of it is because He knows that when you do, you will be just as wise as Himself. So pick a fruit and eat it. You'll be just fine."

And so Eve was deceived and ate of the forbidden fruit. Then she gave it to Adam, and from that instant, they and all of us died spiritually. By that disobedience, physical death was also introduced. This all started with a lie from the Devil.

Another aspect to the Devil's deception is that he failed to tell humanity of the true consequences of eating: that it would not only introduce physical death, but more importantly, spiritual death. Sometimes people lie to give false information, and sometimes they withhold important details, but either way, the intent is to mislead and manipulate the mind of the hearer. It is very dangerous.

To lie successfully, liars must have an assessment of their own and the recipient's mental state. When a person looks another person in the eyes and tells a blatant lie, the liar is basically saying, "I'm smarter than you. I am going to deceive you, and you are not smart enough to figure it out."

What else goes on in the mind of a liar? When liars tell a lie, they must construct and produce false statements that differ from their true belief about the issue at hand. In truth, when a liar lies, they must first convince themselves so that they may be able to convince and deceive another person. Liars must necessarily be the first consumer of their product. False statements must be carefully constructed and plausible, so they will not arouse suspicion. If the lie is not convincing to the liar, the liar cannot credibly purvey it to others.

Liars are very creative people. It takes a very intelligent person to lie successfully. People who are less intellectually endowed trip themselves up and are found out easily. I once had a client, a student in the fifth or sixth grade, who was not doing all that well academically. One of her problems was that she would not complete her homework assignments. One marking period, her grades were pretty bad, so her teacher sent home a note with the report card, requesting a parent's signature on the report card.

The student, not knowing how to face her mother with this poor report card, decided to forge her mother's signature. She wrote a note to the teacher as if she were the mother: "Dear Miss X, I am sorry that I could not sign the report card because I was too busy." She then signed her mother's name to the note.

I told her and her mother that she should be punished—not for the bad grade, nor even for the bogus note, but for the illogical lie she told. That note took a lot more time than a simple signature. Clearly, the student had not yet developed a proficiency in telling lies, and one hopes she proceeded no further in that line of work.

A person who is a proper liar takes steps to cover their lies and to ensure consistency. A professional pathological liar can really work this thing for a long time. It is hard to maintain a pattern of lies, so the liar must keep track of all previous lies in order not to contradict themselves. Lying betrays a deep character flaw.

Usha Sutliff states that a University of Southern California study found that the brains of people who lie habitually, cheat, and manipulate others are structurally different from a normal, (mostly) honest brain. Whether a liar is born with an abnormal predisposition to lie, or simply lies until it changes their brain, is not known. These researchers reported that pathological liars have more white matter than gray matter in their prefrontal cortex—the area of the brain that enables individuals to feel remorse. When a person is a habitual liar, something happens in the structure of the brain that causes them not to have remorse about things in the way that "ordinary" people do.[29]

Lying, then, has at least two components: the physiological and the spiritual. I believe it is safe to conclude that lying results from satanic activities. I say this because the Devil is the father or originator of all lies. If it comes from the Devil, it is demonic. Since it is demonic, we must rebuke the spirit of lying, in the name of Jesus Christ. We must bring the thought that gives rise to the practice of lying captive to the obedience of Christ.

As believers, we must come to a place where we can trust the authenticity of each other's words. I have what some would call a very naive sense of trust, for when I ask a Christian a direct question, I tend to accept the response as truthful. Notwithstanding what my heart tells me to the contrary at times, I accept the response. I am sure some folks think I am naive because I do not say to them, "You are lying." I just let it go.

It is not naivete. I am looking at the Christian believer and saying, in effect, that if they are born again, washed in the blood of Christ, and God is their Father, then when they speak, I should believe in the veracity of their words.

When I argued that lying comes from a demonic spirit, I was not speculating. The Bible backs up this conclusion. We find in 1 Kings the following statement: "Now therefore, behold, the Lord hath put a lying spirit in the mouth of all these thy prophets, and the Lord hath spoken evil concerning thee" (1 Kings 22:23). Here God indicates that He would put a lying spirit in the mouths of certain prophets. We observe something similar in 2 Chronicles 18:20–22.

Lying is an evil spirit. If a Christian finds themselves incapable of telling the truth, this is a very serious matter that requires the power of the Holy Spirit and the application of God's Word to expel that spirit.

When the Enemy tempts us to lie, he shows us the benefits of lying. We rationalize and say, "If I tell them this, if I lead them down that path, it may advantage me. I may get out of trouble, so no harm, no foul." What does it really hurt to tell a little white lie?

What the Enemy does not tell us is the long-term, even everlasting consequences of lying. When we lie, we may get out of trouble temporarily, but there is long-term erosion of character too. He neglects to tell us that when we practice lies, we become the children of the

Devil. He fails to tell us that God hates lies, and that every liar who remains a liar until death has a part in the lake of fire. The Bible tells us, "But the fearful, and unbelieving, and the abominable, and murderers, and whoremongers, and sorcerers, and idolaters, and all *liars*, shall have their part in the lake which burneth with fire and brimstone: which is the second death." (Rev. 21:8, emphasis added). On the judgment day, liars will be thrown in the lake of fire along with murderers, whoremongers, and all sorts of bad people. Instead of pointing to the long-term consequence of lying, the Devil shows us the expediency of lying and the short-term benefits we may gain from not telling the truth.

There are those who take a relativistic view of lying. The relativistic view is that the end justifies the means. In other words, if the lie enables us to avoid certain pain, or if it brings financial advantage, then it is okay. They say, "It does not hurt anyone, so why not?"

Some years ago, my wife and I were in the process of refinancing the mortgage on our primary residence. The bank's representative came to our home and filled out the forms with us. He asked us how much we made combined, and we told him the truth.

Those were the days when the banks were a lot looser in their approval process and did not necessarily verify income. The bank representative said to me, "With your income, you may qualify, but if you represent on the application that you make $20,000 more per year, this will be a slam-dunk transaction." I told him I could not do that because it would bother my conscience. He said, "I see no problem with it." I said that to lie violated my standards of morality, which were grounded in my religious beliefs. I told him that as a Christian, I could not do that. He said to me, "That seems strange to me, because in my religion and culture, if I lie and that lie benefits my family, then it is quite acceptable." I told him I could not do that, and that he should let the application stand or fall on its merits.

As it turned out, we did get the refinancing done without having to lie. Bu the point is that in the practice of doing business, many of us stretch the truth a bit because, in our minds, the end justifies the means. This situational ethics cannot work with God. In the Bible, which shows us the heart of God, there is an objective standard of right and wrong.

In God's eyes, the truth is not situational, it is not relative, and the end does not justify the means if the means are unscrupulous.

I know it is tempting to focus on the immediate benefits of lying in some cases. But what we need to be concerned about are not so much the immediate benefits but the outcomes of our becoming practicing liars. We must understand that God will judge us according to the deeds done in our bodies, whether they be good or bad (2 Cor. 5:10). And so we must understand that, while we may get out of a situation right now by lying, in the end we will face some serious consequences for lying.

The Bible is replete with descriptions of God's attitude toward lying. "These six things doth the Lord hate: yea, seven are an abomination unto him: A proud look, *a lying tongue,* and hands that shed innocent blood" (Prov. 6:16–17, emphasis added). God put lying there with murderers, and he hates them both.

Why does God hate lies so much? I believe God hates lies because lies kill. I have not done the research, but I am willing to wager that lies have sent many people to prison and even to their deaths. Lies have caused many people to lose their reputations, if not their characters. Lies can result in one losing a job.

Some years ago, I worked for a large firm and lost my job for a year over a lie. My bosses received a written communication containing an allegation about me. They allegedly conducted an investigation and concluded that I was guilty as charged. They fired me on the spot, two days before Christmas. In my heart, I believed that the people who did the investigation knew that I was not guilty. But whether to protect themselves or perhaps due to racial bias, they fired me. Upon my departure, I told them that I would see them again.

To make a long story short, the truth did prevail, and I was reinstated after a year. I was the blessed one, for there are many others who have been fired on false accusations and never were able to prove their innocence.

When people are tempted to lie, they must understand this: "the lip of truth shall be established for ever: but a lying tongue is but for a moment" (Prov. 12:19). The lie may stand for a while. It may prevail for the moment. But in the end, it shall not endure. On the other hand, when we engage in truth-telling, it will last forever. The truth lasts forever because it is not alterable. What was truth a thousand years ago will be truth a thousand years hence.

I believe this is the reason Jesus said, "And you shall know the truth and the truth shall make you free" (John 8:32). Once a person tells the truth, they do not have to look over their shoulder, nor do they have to fear. They face the consequences then and there, and let the chips fall where they may. When a person lies, they must continually wonder whether they will be discovered.

"Lying lips are abomination to the Lord: but they that deal truly are his delight" (Prov. 12:22). The word *abomination* is an extremely strong word, but it tells us in an unmistakable way God's attitude toward liars. According to the Merriam-Webster's online dictionary, *abomination* is defined as "to regard with extreme disgust and hatred." It is to loathe something or someone. Imagine that—if we practice telling lies, God loathes us and looks at us with extreme disgust and hatred. That is a dangerous position to be in. This is the reason the Bible tells us that all liars shall have their part in the lake of fire (Rev. 21:8).

The opposite of this is God's attitude toward those who tell the truth. According to the same verse, "they that deal truly are his delight." According to the NIV, God "delights in people who are trustworthy." A liar is an untrustworthy person, and it is very difficult to deal with such a person. You can never rely on anything they say. Even their very gestures are designed to mislead and confuse the observer.

Frankly, although I am not thrilled about having thieves around me, I believe it is easier to safeguard against a thief than against a liar. If I live among people who I know will steal from me, I can lock up my stuff. I can alarm my house. I can have somebody on watch. But a liar is more difficult to defend against. Why? Because a liar can lie their way into your confidence. Through deception and conniving ways, a liar can endear themselves to you, and once in your confidence, can take advantage of you. I can take reasonable steps to prevent a thief from ripping me off, but I cannot prevent a liar from lying to me. In the final analysis, the result of lying is costlier to me than the taking my material goods. When a thief takes my material goods, I may be able to replace them, but when a liar succeeds in tarnishing my reputation, the cost is immeasurable.

The problem of lying is so pervasive that the church needs to emphasize it and deal with it in a godly way. There is an organization called Alcoholics Anonymous (AA) for alcoholics. There needs to be a similar organization named Liars Anonymous (LA) to help compulsive liars deal with this pathology. Many of our political figures would be great candidates for admittance in such a program.

As a pastor, I have had to deal with people who at times do not tell me the truth. I find it frustrating and upsetting. Thankfully, there are some I must deal with who will speak the truth even though it makes them look bad. When they tell the truth about what they have done, it may upset me that they did the deed, but I am left with a clear sense of direction as to what my next steps will be. When you are dealing with the truth, you can be clear in your thinking about what punishment, encouragement, or instruction that you should offer. Ordinarily when a person becomes transparent and tells the truth, there is nothing more for me to do but pray for them, because they have told the truth and cleared their souls.

The psalmist posed the question in Psalm 15:

> Lord, who shall abide in thy tabernacle?
> who shall dwell in thy holy hill?
> He that walketh uprightly,
> and worketh righteousness,
> and Speaketh the truth in his heart (Ps. 15:1-2).

According to the psalmist, the person who speaks the truth will live with God. So if we want to live with God, we have to practice telling the truth in this present world. That is how important it is.

I posited earlier that sometimes lying is blatant, but at other times it is subtle. Frankly, all of us are susceptible to lying if we are not careful. We must therefore be watchful and be aware of our responses, as well as of the impressions we leave with others.

Although I write so strongly against lying, this does not mean that I am altogether perfect in this matter. My history shows that, like most human beings, if the conditions are right, I can be tempted to lie.

Lying is contrary to God's standard of justice. In the Old Testament,

God carefully laid out the process by which a person could be a witness in a court of law against another person. Do you know what happen in the Old Testament when a person brought a false accusation against another person in the courts? If John falsely accused Bob of murder, and if the penalty for murder was death, then John, the false accuser, would be put to death instead of Bob (see Deut. 9:16–19).

That's one way to stop folks from bringing false reports against other people. If one knew that by bringing a false report, one would bear a cost in economic terms or in freedom, perhaps one would not be so quick to bring an accusation. By God's standard, even if we believed that the report was true, we would seek to prove it before we spread that bad news. I believe that if the Old Testament process were applicable today, it would certainly prevent or at least diminish the start of vicious rumors.

While it should hardly be necessary for me to say that I am not advocating the death penalty for lying, I will say it anyway to avoid misunderstanding: I am not advocating the death penalty for lying.

When God's Word tells us to have no fellowship with the unfruitful works of darkness, we need to add lying to the list of unfruitful works of darkness (see Eph. 5:11). "All liars shall have their part in the lake with burneth with fire and brimstone" (Rev. 21:8). According to Ephesians, not only are we not to have fellowship with the unfruitful works of darkness, we should reprove them. According to Today's New International Version, we should "rather expose them."

Some years ago, I met a brother who was quite affable, well-spoken, and endearing. We were on our way to forging a friendship when I discovered that I could not rely on the authenticity of anything he said. The more I listened to this person speak, the more I became uncomfortable with him. Several things he said proved to be gross exaggerations at best, and blatant lies at worst. I concluded that I could not be friends with this man. I thought that if he were prepared to say those things about himself and others, what would he not say about me? The only safe thing to do was to distance myself from him. Have no fellowship with the unfruitful works of darkness.

In dealing with a liar, we need to be firm. The practiced liar is not content only to lie to get out of trouble. They lie because it has now become a part of their behavior pattern as well as their cognitive point of reference. Furthermore, they often want to get others involved in their deeds. They will call, text, e-mail, and tweet others to recruit them in their mission.

We must be watchful and guard against this. When a liar calls you to talk, challenge them. Do not embrace them. A liar may befriend you while slandering others, but you are never safe in the company of a liar. When you fail to please a liar, they will turn the same sword on your own heart.

I believe some Christians practice a form of "plausible deniability." The concept of plausible deniability is not new. It was practiced extensively by the Nazi party in Germany during World War II. Plausible deniability means you do something that you can believably deny, and that denial will be taken as the truth by most people. For example, the president of the United States could give an off-the-record order to someone in the Central Intelligence Agency to commit a particular act. The president's operatives would know that if such an act were made public, it could embarrass the president or have even more far-reaching ramifications. The order is still given, but there exists no evidence that the president knew about it. Absence of evidence gives him cover. Should things go wrong, the president could deny any knowledge of the matter.

As practiced by some Christians, here is how plausible deniability works. Let's say I am in a room with several other people, and I say in the hearing of all, "Brother Brown, I am going to Jamaica tomorrow." Everyone, including a man I'll call Brother John, hears me when I make that statement.

A few hours later, someone asks Brother John, "Where is the pastor going tomorrow?" Brother John wants to reserve the right to deny that he knows where I am going, so he responds that he does not know anything about it. Brother John feels safe in saying this because, though I spoke in his hearing, I was not directly addressing Brother John.

The fact is that Brother John does know, but he feels that it is not his business to tell. Is this right? No! Brother John does know, and therefore he is telling a lie. Do not say you do not know. Rather, say what you heard. If it is information that you do not think that you can divulge, say that.

Someone reading this may say that I am splitting hairs, that I am being picky. Perhaps so, but if we err, let us err on the side of telling the truth. The Bible says, "Let your yea be yea; and your nay, nay" (James 5:12).

The world wages war with lying words. As God's people, we are governed by a different set of rules. The Word tells us that we do not wage war with carnal weapons (2 Cor. 10:3–5). Lying is a carnal weapon. If you find yourself coloring the truth a bit, I ask you to repent of it and change your ways. If you find you are unable to tell the truth, ask God to help you be healed from this sickness.

One of the greatest things counselors must face when people come to talk to us about their problems is to figure out what the truth is. Let us say a couple comes to my office with a problem. When I hear each of them describe the problem, I may think, "How could these two stories be so vastly different? Are these two people in the same house talking about the same event?" Sometimes it is difficult to decipher what is true from what is false. Believe me, it is not a rarity; it goes on more often than not.

But this should he different for those of us who have put on the name of Christ. We need to be able to go into a room, sit down with Christians, and say, "Tell me the story." It should be easy. When the thought to lie comes, let us be careful to bring that thought captive to the obedience of Christ.

A Prayer

Dear Father, sometimes we lie to escape trouble, or to make ourselves look good in the eyes of others. Please help us to bring every lying thought captive to obey Your Word. Help us, dear Father, to always remember that "lying lips are abomination to the Lord: but they that deal truly are his delight" (Prov. 12:22). In Jesus's name. Amen.

CHAPTER 9

Bring Every Discouraging Thought Captive to the Obedience of Christ

Edison failed 10,000 times before he made the electric light. Do not be discouraged if you fail a few times.

—Napoleon Hill

We now turn our attention to another phenomenon that, as Christians, we face more often than perhaps we would wish to admit. I refer to thoughts of discouragement. I believe that discouragement is the enemy of progress. Many times we have great ideas that truly could make a difference in the lives of others, but because of discouragement, we abandon those ideas before they can come to fruition.

I am not exempt from this issue. From the earliest stages of my life, I can remember getting discouraged when things began to get difficult. This became a real problem for me when my fifth-grade teacher wrote in my report card that I was a good student but that I was easily discouraged. My grandmother read that report to me. She concluded, as did the teacher, that I might not finish things I started because I got discouraged easily.

That negative thought followed me through the years. When I left high school, I truly doubted whether I could finish college. That haunting thought was still plaguing me. I believe it is for that reason that it took me over fifteen years to get my first degree.

You may suspect by now that I am going to argue that discouragement begins in the thought life. We need to remember that we must apply God's Word even when we feel discouraged. I believe discouragement is a tool the Enemy uses to distract us and to defeat us ultimately. A new believer accepts the Lord Jesus Christ as their Savior with joy and gladness, but in the process of time, sometimes they fade away. When you inquire, you find that they were discouraged because something happened in their lives that brought on discomfort or emotional pain.

We must recognize discouragement for what it really is. It is a weapon that the Enemy uses to defeat us. Recognizing that, we must apply God's Word as the only effective weapon against discouragement. We must remember that discouragement is a spiritual problem that can be solved only by applying spiritual remedy.

Discouragement will happen at times to just about all of us. These are difficult times in which we live. When you consider the economic and political situations in which we find ourselves, it appears that some of us are walking in reverse, in a manner of speaking. It never seems that we are getting ahead. Some people are unemployed and have looked for jobs so long that they have become discouraged and stop looking. The statisticians account for this when they calculate the unemployment rate. In recessions, sometimes the number of people looking for work falls, and the unemployment rate drops, even though there is not a corresponding number of jobs being added. Statisticians tell us that the number of people looking for jobs has fallen because former job-seekers got discouraged and gave up looking altogether. Discouragement affects all of us, or at least many of us from various walks of life.

Christian believers become discouraged for a variety of reasons. It is not only weak or new believers who get discouraged. One has only to recall the story of Elijah, a mighty prophet of God, who did such powerful work in the name of God. He became so discouraged that he developed a death wish. When Jezebel threatened him, he asked God to take his life (1 Kings 19:3–4).

This discouragement episode followed Elijah's mighty victory over the prophets of Baal on Mount Carmel. To prove that the God of Israel was the only true God, Elijah challenged the false prophets. The terms were that after they had prayed to their false god, and Elijah had prayed to the God of Israel, the deity who answered with fire should be served as God.

Baal's prophets prayed all day to him, but he was impotent to do anything. When they were through, Elijah prayed a short prayer to the God of Israel, and immediately fire came down and consumed the sacrifice upon the altar. Elijah then had all the false prophets executed. On hearing that, Jezebel threatened Elijah's life. Instead of standing firm against this threat, the man of God became discouraged and wanted to die.

Many times we face discouraging experiences, but we can take those thoughts of discouragement captive to the obedience of Christ.

One of America's founding fathers, Thomas Paine, wrote this famous line: "These are times to try men's souls." This simple yet sobering quotation can be found in a collection of articles titled *The American Crisis*. The collection not only describes the beginnings of the American Revolution, but also the life of Paine himself. Thomas Paine had failed in many things and had been discouraged many times. He observed the crisis in America's relationship with Britain, and in response he wrote this series of articles. Those were dangerous and discouraging times. Thomas Paine reflected the feelings and realities of that time. I believe if Thomas Paine were alive today, he would probably write a sequel to the *American Crisis*, for these are indeed times to try men's souls.

Things will happen to discourage God's people. Thoughts of discouragement will permeate your very being. Discouragement hangs over believers like a dark, low, palpable cloud that dampens our spirits. Given this reality, what are we to do? Even though you have things in your life that will cause you to be discouraged, remember to look up. Just above the clouds, there is reason enough to be encouraged: the sun shines, and the Son of God, our Savior Jesus Christ, looks lovingly over you.

I flew into London some years ago. As we approached the great city, I could see absolutely nothing below but what seemed to be mountains of clouds. It had been raining in London, so clouds naturally covered the city. But above the clouds, there was nothing but beautiful sunshine peering through the windows of the aircraft. When we looked up and out, it was all pleasant, but when we looked down, all we could see was dark clouds. The pilot was experienced in these atmospheric conditions and understood how to navigate through the clouds. Those on the ground saw only clouds above, and from those clouds, rain descended. Those of us in the plane were able to appreciate the sunshine. It was all about our perspective.

I do not know how long it had been raining in London. It might have been raining for hours or for days. Maybe some on the ground were depressed as they experienced the dark clouds and rain. Perhaps they little realized that at that very moment, the sun was shining above the clouds. I encourage each of you, when you seem to be overshadowed by the clouds of life, to look up.

As a child, I was used to hearing my grandmother say, "Behind every frowning providence, there lies a smiling face." And isn't that the case? No matter what we are facing, God is always looking down on us and smiling. He loves us so, and He knows exactly what we need, and He is prepared to give us the desires of our hearts.

Discouragement comes in all forms. You may have gone to your doctor for a routine checkup and the news came back not good. You may have gotten up one morning and gone to work, and by the end of the day, you no longer had a job. It could be that your precious child who brought you so much joy became a teenager, and you can hardly recognize him, for he has turned into a real monster. That is discouraging. But even in those dire circumstances, God is still in control.

I can think of few things more devastating than when a breadwinner loses their job. The late president Ronald Reagan once observed that "Recession is when your neighbor loses his job. Depression is when you lose yours…."[30] Leave it to Ronald Reagan to coin a phrase, but it is true. It gets even more depressing and discouraging in the throes of a serious recession, when the prospect of getting another job seems very dim.

How about when the news from the doctor is that you or a loved one has a terminal disease, and the patient is expected to survive for only a very short time? I remember vividly when my late wife, Erica, was having some physical challenges. We had gone to the doctors many times, and they could not find anything wrong with her except some digestive issues. After a series of tests, we sat before the head of oncology at St. Joseph Hospital in Paterson, New Jersey, and were told in no uncertain terms that we should not worry: Erica did not have cancer.

Despite this assurance, she continued to feel sick. She underwent an eye exam, and when her eye doctor reviewed her blood test results, he suspected that there was something unusual about certain cells in her body. We went to an oncologist. Having reviewed the blood tests, he gave us a look of deep concern. We knew without him having to say a word that something was wrong.

He sat us down and explained how the bone marrow does its work. Normal counts of certain cells should be in a given proportion to others. Then he showed us the proportions of cells being produced in Erica's bone marrow. She had a form of cancer called multiple myeloma. Then, as now, there was no cure for this disease.

We kept an optimistic view. We prayed and sought a second opinion. We got a second and a third opinion, and their conclusions were the same. I must confess that I got discouraged. Although we had prayed and fasted, and we truly believed God, when I saw her body deteriorating, I felt low, confused, and helpless.

We resolved to fight this cancer with every ounce of energy and resources at our disposal. About a year after diagnosis, the cancer was in remission. We rejoiced, we testified, and we gave God thanks for His healing power. The cancer remained in remission for about a year.

One day, Erica went to her doctor for a routine monthly checkup, and he discovered that the cancer had come back. By then her kidneys had failed, and she was in real crisis. She called to tell me this, and I cannot describe my reaction. I did not have my car that day; I had dropped it off at the dealership for service. So I called my secretary for a ride. I could not sit still in my office, so I picked up my briefcase and began to walk on the street to meet her partway. Yes, I was discouraged.

Within four years of Erica being diagnosed, I lost her, on December 14, 2007. As a minister, pastor, father, and husband, I went through the motions of planning the funeral and putting on the best face possible. The funeral service having taken place, I returned to an empty home. My sons had married and left. I was, for the first time in over thirty years, going to live alone. I was fifty-one years old, a pastor, and a widower.

Shortly after Erica's death, the stock market crashed, and I lost about 40 percent of my retirement savings. The church house was almost completely destroyed by fire, her SUV was stolen, and the church van was also stolen. I was in school, working on my third master's degree.

I had no job. I was not getting any compensation from the church. I was responsible for two mortgages and the care of the church. All the while, I had the ordinary concerns about my grown children and their children. Needless to say, I had episodes of real discouragement. One could almost say that I was in depression.

One day in the winter of 2008, I was home. It was overcast and dreary. I did not feel like getting out of bed that day, so I closed the blinds and curtains, turned off the lights in my bedroom, and pulled the blanket over my head. I rolled up in the fetal position and decided that I was not leaving the house that day. I was discouraged.

There was another day when I woke up feeling down and decided that, instead of staying in the house, I would go walking. I walked that day for 9.7 miles, praying, talking to myself, singing, crying, and complaining to God. I know it was 9.7 miles because when I got home, I got in my car and drove the same route I had walked. I was discouraged and down, and I needed help. But looking back on this episode, I recognize that God was always with me, although it did not feel that way at the time.

I believe what kept me going even then was that in my mind, I believed that God was in control of everything that happened to me. If I had not had that sound mind, I would have lost this battle.

Again, as I have been saying, we fight our battles in the sphere of our minds. The extent to which we succeed or fail has a lot to do with how we condition our minds. If the Enemy can attack your mind and mess up your thinking, then he gains the victory. You need to expel him, rebuke him from your thought process, and fill your mind with good stuff. The Bible instructs us to think on the things that are honest, just, pure, lovely, and of good report (Phil. 4:8). To displace negative thoughts, we must feed our minds positive things.

If you had a bucket filled with pink lemonade and you could not overturn that bucket, but you wanted to replace the pink lemonade with pure water, how could this be accomplished? You could simply turn on a water hose, place it in the bucket, and turn on the tap. Eventually the force and volume of the clean water coming from the tap would displace the pink lemonade.

So it is with our minds. If our minds are filled with negative thoughts, we may continue to feed our minds the same negative thoughts and receive the same results. To change those outcomes, we must change what we put into our minds. If we are filled up with discouragement, we need to flush our minds with what the Bible says about God. We should simply pour the Word upon our thoughts of discouragement until the Word displaces those thoughts with the promises of God.

We need not wait until we feel better to do this. Faith does not come by feeling; it comes by acting upon God's Word. One does not have to feel victorious to act victoriously. So even if you feel so heavy that you cannot get out of bed, disregard that feeling. You are so tired, and everything tells you to stay under the blanket; do not do it. Muster the strength and say, "I'm going to get up. I shall not die here and now. I shall live, and I will declare the Word of the Lord. Amen!"

Why do we get discouraged? I believe at times we seek encouragement from those around us. That is not a bad thing. We should indeed be able to look to those who are strong and from them receive the encouragement that we need in our times of crisis. But if we rely on our friends to be our prime source of encouragement, we will be discouraged, because often they need to be encouraged. We must look to the God, who comforts us in our trials so that we can be of comfort to others (2 Cor. 1:2–3).

While there is an expectation that, as believers, we should be there for each other, other believers ought not to be our ultimate source. We must look to God. I like David's attitude. He writes, "I will lift up mine eyes unto the hills, from whence cometh my help. My help cometh from the LORD, which made heaven and earth" (Ps. 121:1–2).

Likewise, do not let your primary source of encouragement be your husband, your wife, or your children, because they will fail you. Even if they do not fail you, they might die. If Erica had been my only source of encouragement, I would be dead already. Even though I loved her dearly, God came first in my life, and my primary source of encouragement was God. So even if you have a perfect marriage, you cannot put your faith in your marriage alone. It must be in God. If your spouse disappoints you, encourage yourself in the Lord.

I have talked to many couples over the years who have become discouraged in their marriages. They had a vision of what their marriage should look like, and they had certain expectations from that union.

When things did not work out exactly as they had imagined, they got very discouraged.

You know how it is: when we were growing up, many of us had an image of the person we wanted to marry. Often what we had in mind was not what God gave to us. That reality leaves some people discouraged and disappointed.

What we must realize is that the person that you have in your life, God designed for you. Your spouse is there to support you, but your spouse must never be your primary source of encouragement. That function belongs to God. We should take whatever comes in our marriages and place it in the appropriate context. That is how we encourage ourselves when things aren't going well. Even when you have a "perfect" marriage, sometimes you are going to have bumps in the road. Stick with it and encourage yourself in it.

Some of you are not married. Perhaps you have gotten proposals already and have turned them down. Maybe your prescription and design are wrong. Follow the leading of the Lord. Find a way to accept what God has given to you. Embrace it and encourage yourself.

During periods of discouragement, if we panic and act based upon our emotions, we will be deprived of God's planned blessings for our lives. God said, "I know the plans I have for you" (Jer. 29:11 NIV). But if you stay discouraged, oppressed, and depressed, you will lose out on those blessings.

The Enemy will from time to time feed us discouraging thoughts. Those thoughts are designed to zap our energy and rob us of the joy of the Lord. But we are not helpless in this. We have the ability and the power to fight and win against thoughts of discouragement. The Word of God tells us, "Greater is he that is in you than he that is in the world" (1 John 4:4). Knowing that the power within us is greater than anything that is in the world, we should be able to encourage ourselves in the Lord. Yes, the storm clouds do threaten, but we serve the omnipotent God.

Each time I read more about the life of David, I am encouraged by the sheer strength of his will and determination to be a victor and not a victim. In 1 Samuel, we read that "David encouraged himself in the LORD his God" (1 Sam. 30:6). What occasioned this observation? The nation of Israel, under the leadership of King David, was out on the battlefield. Israel then was constantly at war, fighting for her very survival. David and his soldiers had left the women and children and had gone to fight.

When they returned, they found to their amazement that the enemy had come and taken away all their women and children. They lost everything. I imagine some of them were thinking that David was a bad leader. Indeed, they may have conjectured, "If you had planned this correctly, you would have ensured that there was an appropriate security detail in place, and we would not have suffered this great loss." The people were very upset with David, and according to Scripture, they were thinking of stoning him. In their grief and being so forlorn they had to find someone to blame, and so David was the only appropriate target.

David was now alone. All his previous victories did not mean a thing to those grieving men who had lost their families and their possessions. David had been fighting the good fight of faith and should have received their compassion and support, but instead they turned on him. His people were about to become his executioners.

We are critical of those people who wanted to kill David, but I suppose if we were in the same situation, we might not have acted any differently. And instead of running away to hide and complain about his men's behavior, the Bible says that David encouraged himself in the Lord his God.

If you are a leader and are doing the absolute best you can to guide people along the path of righteousness, do not be surprised if from time to time they turn on you. When folks are hurting and very discouraged, they need a convenient scapegoat. Those in leadership positions are the most visible, and consequently become the target. This, to be sure, is misplaced anger, but nevertheless it is the case, and we must get used to it. You may be doing everything that God has asked you to do, but folks who are discouraged will come after you, because they feel that they have no other alternative.

The Bible says that every man grieved for his sons and daughters, but David encouraged himself in the Lord his God. This by no means indicates that David was not hurt or affected by this development. What the Bible is communicating is that in the middle of our deepest grief, loss, and discouragement, we can turn to God and find encouragement in Him. Often, we may have a reasonable expectation that our closest friends will encourage us, but that does not always happen. We must encourage ourselves rather than wait for others to encourage us.

You may look for the pastor to encourage you, but maybe the pastor is away and you cannot reach him. Again, you must encourage yourself in the Lord your God. When our leaders are not available, God is always available. David wrote, "God is our refuge and strength, a very present help in trouble" (Ps. 46:1). Isn't that wonderful? When we are in trouble, when we are discouraged, we know and are assured by God's Word that He is a very present help.

Amid your discouragement, tell yourself, "I am going to get through this. This is not going to beat me." That is practicing positive self-talk. Tell yourself you can do this through Christ who gives you strength (Phil. 4:13). The source of our strength is God. David triumphantly wrote, "Some trust in chariots and some in horses, but we will remember the name of the Lord our God" (Ps. 20:7).

Sometimes things come at you that are not right. Sometimes you know you have done the best you can, and the world still does not understand. Sometimes even the church does not understand. In those times, you may feel depression and discouragement coming on. Just encourage yourself in the Lord your God. Remember, it is a spirit of discouragement coming on you, so rebuke it in the name of Jesus Christ. Bring that thought captive to the obedience of Christ.

As born-again believers, we can accomplish great things through Christ, who enables us to do so. There really is nothing in our DNA that tells us we cannot accomplish great things, or that predisposes us to failure. Instead, what we have living on the inside of us is the power of the Almighty God. Discouragement only comes to distract us and to neutralize the real power that we have in us.

Whatever disadvantage we believe we were born with can be gotten rid of when viewed through the prism of God's Word. Discouragement knocks at the doors of all of us from time to time. We must learn how not to open the door to this invading force. When you hear it knocking and see its ugly head through the peephole, do not open the door. Simply apply God's Word to keep it on the other side of the door.

Discouragement happens to most of us. I remember listening to the radio some years ago, in the days when evangelist R. W. Schambach was quite popular. He related a story about a woman from his church who came up to him and complained that she was not happy about something in her life. She told him that she needed help because she was discouraged and depressed.

He told her to lean on his shoulder so they could both cry together. He told her, "I am not happy either." He told her that he was upset, discouraged, and dejected just as she was.

She exclaimed, "What do you mean? You are the preacher."

He told her that indeed he was the preacher, but that day was not going very well for him either. He had just received a one-thousand-dollar oil bill, and he did not have the means to pay it. He told her that she needed to exercise some faith and trust in God.

Brother Schambach always closed his radio broadcast with these words: "You don't have any trouble; all you need is faith in God."[31] That may seem a bit too easy. But is it? Isn't God bigger than all our troubles? Indeed, if we put our faith and confidence in God, we, like David, can encourage ourselves in the face of the most discouraging situations.

There is a chorus to a Southern gospel song that I like to hear. It speaks to the fact that God is bigger than our issues. It does not really matter what those issues are, God is much bigger than they are. The Lord says, "Behold, I am the LORD, the God of all flesh: is there anything too hard for me?" (Jer. 32:27). Clearly, the answer is a resounding no.

We need to come to a place in God where faith and confidence is our default position. Faith is not built on what we see. Indeed, as Scripture tells us, "Now faith is the substance of things hoped for, the evidence of things not seen" (Heb. 11:1). Let us not underestimate the power of God within us.

I like the admonition of Isaiah to God's people regarding the strength that they had: "Awake, awake; put on thy strength, O Zion; put on thy beautiful garments, O Jerusalem, the holy city: for henceforth there shall no more come into thee the uncircumcised and the unclean. Shake thyself from the dust; arise, and sit down, O Jerusalem: loose thyself from the bands of thy neck, O captive daughter of Zion" (Isa. 52:1–2). We have the power in us to break those yokes—those things that bind us to melancholy, those things that bind us to discouragement. What are you doing in the dust? Shake yourself from out of the dust of despair and discouragement, and "look to God who is the author and finisher of our faith" (Heb. 12:2).

One method I have used to help me to break the grip of discouragement is to sing the songs of Zion. When you have read the Word and prayed to God, it is now time to sing for joy. Singing during our most discouraging situations has a way of lifting our spirits. I am always struck by the story in Acts of the Apostles where Paul and Silas were thrown in jail for preaching the Word of God. Although beaten and bruised, the Bible says that at midnight, they began to sing. They did not sing because their troubles were over, for in fact they were still in deep trouble. They did not sing because they knew that in the morning, some rich benefactor would come and bail them out of jail. They sang without knowing how, if, or when they would be released.

What caused them to sing? I believe they sang because their faith rested not in the resources of human beings, but in the faithfulness of an all-resourceful God.

I love the old hymn that reads:

> Why should I feel discouraged,
> Why should the shadows come,
> Why should my heart be lonely,
> And long for heaven, heaven and home,
> When Jesus is my portion,
> My constant Friend is He;
> Oh, oh-oh, his eye is on the sparrow,
> And I know He watched, watched it over me
> (Civilla D. Martin).

In our daily walk with Christ, let us be cognizant that many things will come to discourage us. Even the most faithful person from time to time is beset by discouraging thoughts. Let us remember, however, that discouragement is par for the course. It is said that Thomas Edison failed ten thousand times before he finally succeeded in inventing the light bulb. I suspect that most of us would have given up after the fourth or faith failure. But for Edison, each failure buoyed him. In his mind, those previous failures would never be repeated.

It takes faith to look in the face of defeat and see victory. I wish, as Christian believers, that we could possess such a mind-set. When discouraging thoughts come to your minds, bring those thoughts captive to the obedience of Christ. God is bigger, much bigger than our circumstances.

A Prayer

Heavenly Father, sometimes when we try and fail, we become discouraged. We lose the impetus to go on. At other times, we are discouraged by criticisms of us and of our work, and as a result, we lose our spiritual energy. Help us, dear Father, to bring every discouraging thought captive to the obedience of Christ, understanding that You will never leave us or forsake us (Heb. 13:5). In Jesus's name. Amen.

CHAPTER 10

Bring Every Fearful Thought Captive to the Obedience of Christ

The only thing we have to fear is fear itself.
—Franklin D. Roosevelt

In this section we will wrestle with another issue with which so many of us are plagued on a regular basis—that is, the issue of fear. I wish I could declare here and now that when a person accepts Jesus Christ as Lord and Savior and receives the infilling of the Holy Ghost, all that person's fears are gone. Unfortunately, this is not the case. Even people who are committed Christians face the phenomenon of fear.

It is unfortunate because fear is not of God. The Bible clearly states, "There is no fear in love; but perfect love casteth out fear: because fear hath torment. He that feareth is not made perfect in love" (1 John 4:18). So, according to Scripture, the remedy for fear is the love of God.

In this text, John provides a very interesting and profound analysis of the root cause of fear. It says that if we experience fear, we truly have not experienced God's love, for fear has to do with punishment. We fear because we believe that something bad will happen to us. But God tells us that if we truly experience and embrace His love, it will expel fear. When we truly experience God's love and understand such love in all its implications, we are assured that God protects us from all threatening elements in our lives, even from eternal punishment.

If it were possible for me to conduct a poll of those reading this book and ask whether you have ever experienced fear, I think the answer would be overwhelmingly yes. Many of us fear many things. I suppose sometimes our fears are justified and grounded in reality. But at other times our fears are ungrounded and without any basis in fact. Stated differently, many times our fears are a product of faulty thinking.

Let us begin by defining fear. What is it? According to Merriam-Webster, *fear* is a verb that means to be afraid of or apprehensive of something. The adjective, *fearful*, describes something or someone who experiences fear. For example, if we describe a fearful storm, we are describing a natural phenomenon that causes or is likely to cause dread or fear. Fear is fright of something, especially because of that thing's dangerous potential. If you have ever been through a hurricane, you do not want to go through another one. The experience of having gone through a hurricane results in fear of hurricanes.

Now, that fear could be excessive, such that in a rainstorm with a little bit of wind, the fearful person could panic and make inappropriate decisions. A healthy fear of hurricanes, however, would cause someone to make reasonable preparations. Such a person could ensure that there are batteries, water, an adequate supply of food, a radio, and other necessities to ride out the storm. Also, a healthy fear of hurricane dictates that if you live in low-lying areas or by the ocean, you will move inland to avoid the wrath of the storm.

Some fears are without merit and are irrational. My grandmother was afraid of bodies of water at night. She could not pass over a body of water at night if you paid her, because in her mind, that body of water was as deep as a bottomless pit. It did not matter that during the day, she could cross over it without undue fear. That describes an irrational fear.

What are some of the things that we fear? Well, some folks are fearful of a coming storm, fearful of their boss, fearful of their spouse, fearful of public speaking, fearful of death, or fearful of life itself. A young man in high school with me approached me a month or so prior to our graduation and confessed that he was deeply afraid of leaving high school and having to face life. He was amazed that I did not share the same fear. Perhaps being concerned about the future is reasonable, but being crippled by fear of it to the point of inaction is irrational.

Why do we fear? There are many reasons people fear things. Let us take the fear of death for example. Why do we fear death? People fear death because they are afraid of heavenly punishment. People who hear the gospel of Jesus Christ, and refuse to accept it fear the prospect of dying, because they are afraid of just retribution. Although they are not willing to change, they do not savor the prospect of going to hell. Not only does the unregenerate sinner fear death, but sadly, also even some who have put their faith in Christ still fear death.

It amuses me sometimes to hear the bold, wonderful testimonies of believers. They sing and testify that they want to go to heaven and rest, that this world is not their home, that they are tired of living this life, and other such wonderful hymns. They read with such fervor and enthusiasm the passage from John 14 that speaks of the many mansions in heaven awaiting them. They affirm their belief in this text and testify how they long for this reality. Then, when they fall sick and get bad news from the doctors, they cry, moan, and live in fear of dying. That response to the doctor's negative report about their health is so contradictory to their testimony of faith.

I do not mean to disparage anyone who has received negative reports about their health and are fearful. I simply point this out to show that the presence of unreasonable fear makes a mockery of our testimony of faith.

Some parents fear dying because they worry about their children and other relatives. One of the fears my mother had of dying was the fear of leaving us young children behind. That is not an unreasonable fear. I shared her sentiments when my children were young. I felt that my wife and I were best suited to raise them, and the prospect of dying prematurely was a deep concern of ours. In response to that fear, we made appropriate provisions with some close relatives to raise the children in case we parents died early. We also purchased an adequate amount of life insurance to ensure the children would be supported financially. This was a reasonable response to a reasonable fear.

Some people fear dying because they feel that they have too many sins. They are afraid that maybe God will not or cannot forgive them. You would think that such a fear would drive them to seek God, but that is not always the case. Others fear dying because they do not want to leave behind secular pleasures. Others fear death because they have failed to perform their pious duties and obligations. Some fear death because it entails so many aches, pains, and unknown issues. They are afraid of the torture of the grave. When I was a child, my fear of dying was that if I went to the grave, I might suffocate. Obviously, that was an unreasonable fear. If I am already dead, I need not worry about being unable to breathe.

Some fear death because of what they will leave behind: their wealth, their friends, and their valuables. If you are a billionaire and you are going to die at age forty-five, you may fear that eventuality terribly because you are leaving so much behind.

There is the fear of loss of self and identity in death. Death puts an end to our plans, objectives, and that which makes us uniquely who we are.

Some people fear dying because of the legacy they will leave behind. The playwright William Shakespeare once observed, "The evil that men do lives after them, the good is often interred with their bones."[32] If that is true, it stands to reason that some fear their bad deeds will be made manifest, and that people will remember them in a negative light forever. It is conceivable that the infamous Judas had done some good in his life prior to betraying Jesus, but no one remembers any of that. That singular evil deed has sealed his character and reputation for almost two thousand years and counting.

Physical death is inevitable. It is not reasonable to be afraid of death, because we cannot change death by being afraid. I think some people hurry on toward their deaths by fearing death so much. All the stress that is associated with fear can hasten the death event. Fear of death, far from extending life, tends to cut life short.

I remember visiting the sickroom of a person I knew some years ago. She had been admitted to the hospital and hoped to be released in a few days. But things turned for the worse when she overheard the doctors talking about her case. Their prognosis was not good. Whether they did not care or were not aware that she was listening, they made it clear to her that they expected she would not survive long.

Upon hearing that, she went into a panic and died within hours, perhaps a day. She died from cardiac arrest and not from the disease that had occasioned her hospitalization. How much longer she might have lived had she not overheard the doctors talking is conjectural, but we know this much: her cause of death was not her disease.

Fearing death cannot stop the inevitable. Shakespeare, writing in the voice of Julius Caesar, made what I think is a cogent observation about death: "Cowards die many times before their deaths; the valiant never taste of death but once. Of all the wonders that I yet have heard, It seems to me most strange that men should fear; seeing that death, a necessary end, will come when it will come."[33]

Let us be honest here. Death is associated with many unknowns, which leads to fear. But if we think clearly about death, why should we fear it? There is not much we can do about it anyway. Some people fear death so much that they virtually stop living. I do not mean to argue that there is no dread in death, but to be obsessed with it to the point of making yourself sick is unhealthy.

When the grim reaper comes, no matter how much we scream or try to avoid him, he will take us out. You may be ninety years old or nine, but when death comes, no amount of fear or unreasonable trauma will change anything.

Some time ago, a young man I knew was dying. Even in the last week of his life, he absolutely refused to accept the inevitable. He kept saying that he was going to live. What may have seemed like an expression of faith was in fact fear. Fearing death, he refused to accept the inevitable.

Loud words and boisterous behaviors can mask deep-seated fear. When you know it is time to die, surrender to God boldly. If you do not know it is time to die, and you believe that God is really going to heal you, I beg you to hold on to that faith. There comes a time, however, when a person knows it is time. Fearing it does not help.

What are some of the effects of fear? Fear immobilizes a person. If you are fearful enough, this can remove your will to act in your own self-interest.

Years ago, I was home alone, and I thought I heard a troublesome noise downstairs at two o'clock in the morning. The noise really shocked me, but instead of going downstairs to investigate what the problem was, I stayed in the bed and could not move. Everything in me instinctively told me that I needed to go investigate, but I could not because fear crippled me.

Finally, I decided that whatever it was down there, I needed to find out. I had to be the man of the house and do the only thing that was right.

So I reached under the bed, picked up my machete, and gingerly walked downstairs, all the while hoping that there was nothing there. I found that there was nothing wrong, so I was able to relax. I felt better then, but truly, I had been immobilized for a moment by fear of the unknown. It took every ounce of courage in me, as well as all the willpower I could muster, to get me to go and investigate.

Fear causes physical problems: your heart pounds faster and your blood pressure goes up. Fear cripples a person and opens the door for the Devil to do his work.

Where did fear come from? The Bible tells us that "God has not given us the spirit of fear, but of power and of love and of a sound mind" (2 Tim. 1:7). If we have the spirit of fear in us, it did not come from God. If fear did not come from God, it must come from the Devil. We need to rebuke that spirit of fear that comes in to terrify us.

Fear brings confusion. It causes us to hide, and it causes us to abandon our love for others. I have seen people who really love others, but because of fear, they cannot allow themselves to express love. They fear that if they express their love, it may not be reciprocated. Because of that fear, many relationships that could have been absolutely rewarding and fulfilling never materialize. A person such as this is fearful of the implications of loving. Some people also fear loving others because they perceive that there is vulnerability in loving.

I knew a pastor some years ago who, having loved his congregants as we are commanded to, was hurt in some relationships. He became gripped by fear of being hurt again. Because of this, he hardly ever expressed love. He was a lovely man who loved God and truly served Him well, but he was terrified.

As I observed him in ministry, I saw the devastating effect that fear had on him. I requested a meeting with him because I thought it imperative that I at least attempt to help him with this problem. As I was sitting with him, something dropped in my spirit. I said, "He who dares to love possesses a window of vulnerability. When a person loves and embraces another, one of two things may happen. First, he may be loved and embraced in return. Second, he may be embraced and stabbed in his back." I told him that as a leader, he did not have the luxury of not loving or of not expressing his love to others.

The presence of fear in the life of the believer has some serious spiritual implications. Fear keeps us from serving God fully and to the best of our abilities. I have heard people say that they do not wish to get too close to the center of leadership or even too deep in their relationship with God, for fear of what will be required of them to sustain such closeness. Some people in our churches are gifted and could do wonderful work in ministry, but they do everything to sabotage that ministry for fear of its responsibilities. Some folks fear that if they are actively engaged in ministry, people may think that they are pushing for status, and so they draw back.

Fear causes us to flee when we should stand and fight. This is known as the flight or fight dilemma. In solving the fight or flight dilemma, one must assess the risks and opportunities in the environment. Sometimes, prudence will dictate that one must flee the scene. That is not necessarily due to fear. If the odds against one are overwhelming, and if standing to fight would mean destruction, then it is important to remove oneself from the scene.

But if one refuses to fight because one is crippled by fear, and not because one has real ground to believe that one may not win, that is a dysfunctional and undue fear that must be addressed in the context of Scripture. Believers must know when to stand up and fight. In this fight against sin and the Devil, we cannot afford to turn tail and run. Fear cripples us. We must face our enemies and challenges with boldness and resolution.

Back in the old days, we sang the hymn by Bessie F. Hatcher titled, "Keep on the Firing Line," The first stanza and chorus read as follows:

> If you're in the battle for the Lord and right,
> Keep on the firing line;
> If you win, my brother, surely you must fight,
> Keep on the firing line;
> There are many dangers that we all must face,
> If we die still fighting it is no disgrace;
> Cowards in the service will not find a place,
> So keep on the firing line.

Refrain:
Oh, you must fight, be brave against all evil,
Never run, nor even lag behind;
If you would win for God and the right,
Just keep on the firing line.[34]

That should be the attitude of those of us who are God's children. We do not have the luxury of retreating or running away and hiding. God is calling upon us to put aside our fears and do His work. So when the thoughts of fear come into our minds, we must be careful to bring them captive to the obedience of Christ. Fear is a weapon of Satan designed to cripple us. We must recognize it for what it is, and when necessary, take prudent precautions. But we must never let fear cripple us to the point of inertia.

One of the most dysfunctional fears that people possess is fear of another human being. This becomes such a negative force that even when a person's whole experience tells them otherwise, they surrender to the one they fear. It's necessary to stand up for what you believe in, or you will fall for anything. If you surrender to another person whom you perceive as superior, you will become eclipsed. You will no longer be recognizable.

Many years ago, I worked for a tyrant of a boss. I do not know if she thought she had something to prove, but every opportunity she got, she simply terrorized the managers who reported to her. I was one of those managers, and it appeared to me, as well as to others in the office, that she was particularly hard on me. I had a young family, and this was a well-paid job. I thought I needed to keep this job so I could provide for my family. Also, my upbringing dictated that I ought to be respectful of those over me. These factors caused me to fear and dread her. I was terrified of going to work. I knew I feared her, for when she was not at work, I functioned better and was much more productive and relaxed.

One day she yelled at me, not in the privacy of her office, but in the open, where the representatives who reported to me were able to observe it. At lunchtime, I went to the conference room alone, hurt, embarrassed, and dejected. I felt like a failure. I also felt trapped. My desire to care for my family and avoid unemployment had caused me to take this emotional abuse.

But as I sat in that conference room brooding, something triggered my fighting spirit. I knew that I had to put a stop to this. I had to overcome my fear of her and my fear of unemployment, and deal with the matter then and there.

I got up, went to her office, and told her I wanted to speak to her. She made some excuse that she was too busy and could not talk with me, but I would not take no for an answer. I sat down and told her in a respectful but firm tone of my displeasure with the way she was treating me. The more I spoke, the less fear I had. By the time I was done, she had apologized profusely for her behavior.

I thought, "Why did I wait so long? Why did I suffer for so long under her tyrannical rule?" It was my fear. You know, as it turned out, she was not a bad person. She eventually became one of my biggest allies.

What is it about fearing another human being to the point that when they tell us to do any ridiculous thing, we do it? Some of you may remember the tragedy at Jonestown, Guyana, in the late 1970s. A so-called spiritual leader, Jim Jones, convinced over a thousand people to sell their possessions, leave the United States, and move with him to the jungles of Guyana in South America. This man held his followers captive by sheer force of will and their fear of him.

Mr. Jones was brought under investigation by a congressional committee. Some members of that committee went to Guyana to discover the inner working of this sect. Mr. Jones thought the best way out was for all his followers to commit suicide with him. He offered them poison, and they drank the poison and died.

Why did they obey this empty-headed man even to their graves? I believe it was because of a deep-seated fear of him. Of course, there were likely other psychological factors at work. Some of them no doubt had become convinced that drinking cyanide would usher them into a brighter future. Nevertheless, I believe that fear of one person was at the root of their action.

There are some people in positions of leadership who want you to fear them. They seem to believe that when you fear them, you love them. I was teaching in Bible study some years ago, and a gentleman from another country came in as a guest in my class. The topic was the relationship between husbands and wives. We took the biblical view that husbands should love their wives as Christ loves the church, and that wives should submit themselves to their husbands. I was careful to point out that this submission does not mean that the woman is inferior to the man. I made it clear that the wife's submission presupposes that the husband is acting in a godly way, loving his wife as Christ loves the church.

The visiting gentleman interrupted me and told us that American women had too much say in everything. According to him, some thirty years earlier, he had just arrived in the USA with his wife. He and some male friends were having a political discussion at home. His wife, who was busy serving them, dared to presume to interject her opinion, which was contrary to what her husband believed. He immediately boxed her face and told her never again to contradict him. He claimed that from that day forward, she never contradicted him again. He said she loved and feared him. He then asked me, "Pastor, what do you think? Don't you think women should fear and love their husbands?"

You can imagine how the women in our church were looking at me to see what my response was going to be.

We need to make a distinction between respect and fear, particularly when it comes to human relationships. We must control our fear of our fellow humans, or else our fellow humans will control our minds.

Let me be clear. Each of us must learn to respect and honor our leaders. The Bible tells us that we ought to obey those who have the rule over us (Heb. 13:17). But that is not the same as losing yourself and your ability to make decisions to another human being. It is not the same as surrendering your freedom to another person under the guise of obedience. Even Paul told those in Corinth to follow him as he followed Christ (1 Cor. 11:1). We need to respect our leaders, but God comes first. When your leader stops following Christ and makes themselves the center of your church, it is time to leave.

Some people do not like to follow any rules. That is not what I am talking about. There are rules in every organization, and they must be followed. Furthermore, these rules must be enforced by someone. God gives to us leaders to protect us, and this means at times they must enforce godly rules.

But if a leader has clearly assumed a place in your life that is far beyond what is reasonable, it is time to step away. Obey godly rules? Yes. Obey godly leaders? Yes. Honor godly leaders as God's representatives? Yes again. But we must not allow ourselves to be subjugated or brainwashed to the point of not being able to make intelligent choices for ourselves.

Some degree of fear is appropriate. What should we fear? The Bible says, "Let us hear the conclusion of the whole matter: Fear God, and keep his commandments: for this is the whole duty of man" (Eccles.12:13). Jesus Christ says, "And fear not them which kill the body, but are not able to kill the soul: but rather fear him which is able to destroy both soul and body in hell" (Matt. 10:28). We have a duty and an obligation to fear God. In that light, we need to honor and respect God's servants, whom He has placed over us. If the fear of another human being is carefully nuanced in that context, then I suppose it is an appropriate fear. But we must cast aside the fear that robs us of our true selves.

As children of the living God, we ought to live without crippling fear. Our thought lives ought to be informed by what God's Word says to us. If our lives are hiding with Christ in God (Col. 3:1), then we should be able to say, like David, "Yea, though I walk through the valley of the shadow of death, I will fear no evil: for thou art with me; thy rod and thy staff they comfort me" (Ps. 23:4). Instead of fearing evil or our bosses, we should fear God.

What does the Bible say about fear? Throughout, we are instructed to fear the Lord. For example, we find in Psalm 5, "But as for me, I will come into thy house in the multitude of thy mercy: and in thy fear will I worship toward thy holy temple" (Ps. 5:7).

When thoughts of fear come into our minds, we should rethink the basis of our fears. We must regulate our thinking. In the final analysis, we must ask ourselves, what can other human beings really do to us, from an eternal perspective?

In Psalm 118, we read, "The LORD is on my side; I will not fear: what can man do unto me?" (Ps. 118:6). What, indeed can man do unto me? Can people hurt us in this life? Yes, they can. Can they make our lives difficult in the here and now? Yes, they can. But consider that you serve the living God. God will not allow anyone to inflict pain or suffering on you beyond that which you are able to bear.

When we are tempted to fear human beings, let us remember the promises of God. I am often encouraged by this very popular passage of Scripture found in Isaiah: "No weapon that is formed against thee shall prosper; and every tongue that shall rise against thee in judgment thou shalt condemn. This is the heritage of the servants of the LORD, and their righteousness is of me, saith the LORD" (Isa. 54:17). We repeat this Scripture passage with expressiveness, but when we are faced with difficult problems, we seem to forget its promises. "No weapons" means no weapons. Nothing the Devil throws at us can prosper if we trust in our mighty God. So why fear?

Sometimes, unfortunately, we fear people on the job so much that they make us do things we would not otherwise think about doing. Let me give you an example. You are a Christian and would not think about going to the corner store to buy a pack of cigarettes. No one in your immediate social circle could get you to buy a pack of cigarettes for them. Yet your boss at work asks you to buy cigarettes, and guess what? You do it for fear of losing favor with the boss. All the while as you walk to the store, you pray that nobody from your church sees you.

In this example, fear causes you to compromise your principles. If your thought life was properly centered on Christ, when your boss asked you to go buy this item, you would have respectfully said, "Sorry, I cannot do that." And if they asked why not, you would have been bold enough to tell them that this is a religious matter for you. But I suppose some of us, notwithstanding our testimonies, are in fact closet Christians.

I have said before that there is appropriate fear. We need to fear God and keep His commandments. The Bible tells us that we are wise to fear God: "The fear of the Lord is the beginning of wisdom: and the knowledge of the holy is understanding" (Prov. 9:10). This fear of God motivates us to learn more about God and His ways, and in learning His ways, we become wise.

The presence of unfounded and unreasonable fear demonstrates a lack of trust in God's Word. The Bible tells us, "Be not afraid of sudden fear, neither of the desolation of the wicked, when it cometh. For the

Lord shall be thy confidence and shall keep thy foot from being taken" (Prov. 3:25–26). I guess the question is, why do we fear an impending disaster that is designed for the wicked and not for the righteous? The Word says, "Have no fear of sudden disaster or of the ruin that overtakes the wicked" (Prov. 3:25, NIV). Since you and I are not the wicked then we should not fear these things for we belong to God.

The Bible tells us in Psalm 91 that if we dwell in the secret place of the Most High, we shall abide under the shadow of the Almighty. That passage goes on to say, "Thou shalt not be afraid for the terror by night; nor for the arrow that flieth by day; Nor for the pestilence that walketh in darkness; nor for the destruction that wasteth at noonday. A thousand shall fall at thy side, and ten thousand at thy right hand; but it shall not come nigh thee. Only with thine eyes shalt thou behold and see the reward of the wicked" (Ps. 91:5–8).

The punishment of the wicked will not be visited upon us. The terror that is designed to discomfit the people of the world should not make us be afraid, because we know that we belong to God. The NIV renders verse 8 as follows: "You will only observe with your eyes and see the punishment of the wicked." In other words, you will live to see the wicked punished, but you will not be subjected to such punishment because you belong to God.

Listen, there are dreadful and fearful events in the world in which we live. Mass murders take place in schools, shopping malls, subways, and so on. These are dreadful things. The world has a right to fear them. But as children of God, we must prepare ourselves to face fearful things with the full understanding that throughout all of this, our great God stands by our side. He shields us in these dreadful circumstances. The Bible tells us in Psalm 20 that the Lord hears us in the day of trouble, and the name of the God of Jacob will defends us.

God is our defense and our strong tower. When sudden fear comes, we can stand firm and trust God, for He is our defense. He is our confidence, He is our rock, and in Him will we trust. David prayed that when his soul was overwhelmed within him, God would lead him to the rock that was higher (see Ps. 61:2). There is a Rock that is higher than we are, and we can run to Him and be safe (Prov. 18:10). In that strong tower which is our God, we can afford to demonstrate our strength and to discard our fears.

When I was a little boy back in Jamaica, people had dogs that were rather loud and boisterous when they were safely behind the fence of their masters' properties. But if you met those same dogs on the outside and made threatening gestures at them, they would scamper away screaming, because they were outside their tower of strength. To overcome our fears, we need to get behind our Tower of Strength.

Although some of God's people are plagued by fear and dread, there is hope that in time we can overcome such fears. The Lord promised that He would rid us of our fears at a future time: "And it shall come to pass in the day that the Lord shall give thee rest from thy sorrow, and from thy fear, and from the hard bondage wherein thou wast made to serve" (Isa. 14:3). Isn't that a wonderful promise? God is going to deliver us from our sorrows and from our fears.

Listen also to Isaiah: "Say to them that are of a fearful heart, be strong, fear not: behold your God will come with vengeance, even God with a recompense; he will come and save you" (Isa. 35:4). This is a rather reassuring thought. When the Enemy comes against us, the Bible says, fear not. Your God will come with vengeance. This vengeance is not aimed toward His children. Rather, the vengeance is against the forces of darkness that would trouble God's people. It seems to me, then, that we should take hope and become confident in the promises of God, even in the face of our fears.

It really does not matter what is going on in your life. The things that make you upset and disturb your peace are inconsequential. According to the Bible, God is coming to deliver you, and He comes with vengeance. The person who stands in the way of God's people is in need of pity, because God is coming to deliver you and me.

Jesus told His disciples, "But whoso shall offend one of these little ones which believe in me, it were better for him that a millstone were hanged about his neck, and that he were drowned in the depth of the sea" (Matt. 18:6). With this assurance, why should we fear? What can human beings do unto us when God is on our side?

I acknowledge that there are fearful situations that, as Christians, we must confront almost daily. I am not asking that we suspend our instincts or be unconcerned about our safety. I am not asking that we delude ourselves into thinking that there are no fearful situations in our environment. That would be unrealistic. What I do ask is that we acknowledge those fears and then face them boldly, armed with God's Word.

Some years ago, we had a preacher from Malawi, Africa, visiting our church. He preached a message that uplifted the entire congregation. I was blessed by it too. But to tell you the truth, the only thing I remember about it now is his admonition that we should face our problems and speak to them. In other words, acknowledge a problem, call it by name, and then speak to it. In the case of fear, you acknowledge it by saying, "Fearful situation, I know you are there, but now I speak to you in the name of Jesus Christ. By God's Word, take flight and go." We do not deny the problem; instead, we face it with courage.

I wish to make another point about fear. Fear feeds on the fearful at heart. Fear is like a big schoolyard bully who preys on weaklings. When you run from a bully, he chases you down and beats you up. But I know this for sure: most schoolyard bullies are cowards themselves. The moment you stand up to a bully, he is no longer a bully. Even when a bully is stronger than you, if you put up a strong enough fight, he will generally leave you alone.

There was a fellow at my school of whom I was rather afraid. I thought he could whip me at any time. I stayed far away from him and hoped that he would not pick on me. I made sure I did not get into a fight with him.

One day at lunchtime, I was sitting in my class after eating. A friend of mine, who was on all accounts a weakling, was being beaten up by this bully. Another classmate of mine, recognizing what was going on, reported the situation to me. But he did not tell me who it was that was beating up my friend. Perhaps if I had known, I would not have gone out there. Not knowing who it was, I ran out in the schoolyard in great fury, expecting someone I could easily handle. Guess who I found beating up my friend?

By the time I realized who it was, I was already committed to the fight. I was running and yelling so loudly that I could not stop. So I continued and faced the bully head-on, fully expecting to be engaged in the fight of my life.

To my surprise, when this boy saw me coming, he backed away, stopped hitting my friend, and apologized. You do not know how powerful I felt at that moment. From that day until I left that school, I had no more fear of that bully. My friends thought I was bold. Truth be told, I really was not that bold. I simply put on a bold face, and it worked.

I was prepared to defend my weak friend because I knew that I had some friends who would probably help me if I got into trouble. I had, as we in Jamaica would say, "backative" (meaning "we've got help"). But can you imagine living our lives with the realization that God is our backative? It really does not matter what we are going through; God will help us. Isaiah 43:1–3 tells us not to fear, for when we pass though the waters, God is with us, so that the waters will not overwhelm us. Even though we are going through the fire, we shall not be burned. How is that possible? Because we serve a miracle-working God who is impervious to flood and fire. Far from being afraid of them, He controls them, for He is God.

I have consistently argued that these issues we face germinate in our minds or thought lives. We therefore need to recondition our minds so that we can better deal with these things. Applying God's Word to our situation is the best way to overcome. When fear comes, we must ask ourselves, what does the Bible say about fear? "For ye have not received the spirit of bondage again to fear; but ye have received the spirit of adoption, whereby we cry, Abba, Father" (Rom. 8:15). When you feel afraid, go to Abba. When the Devil sends out his hosts against you, and the fearful pestilence comes upon you, cry out, "Abba!"

Abba is an Aramaic word meaning "father." According to the *HarperCollins Bible Dictionary*, the word is properly translated as "my father" or "our father." *Abba* suggests familial intimacy. When we cry out, "Abba, Father," it is more than simply praying to an impartial deity. Rather, when we pray to Abba, we are talking to our loving Father. This is the reason that when Jesus taught His disciples to pray, He told then to start, "Our Father which art in heaven."

I started this chapter with a very famous quotation from President Franklin Delano Roosevelt, who said, "You have nothing to fear but fear itself." That statement on some level is true. Sometimes our fear of a person or thing makes that person or thing more prodigious than they really are.

God does not want His children to live in fear all their lives. The greatest fear that humanity faces is the fear of death. But even death has lost its ability to terrorize God's people, because of the resurrection of Jesus Christ from the dead.

The author of the book of Hebrews tells us that Jesus partook of flesh and blood so that He could die for us. In dying and being raised from the dead, Jesus destroyed the Devil, who had the power of death. By His death, Jesus delivers us who, through fear of death, were subject to bondage our entire lives (Heb. 2:14–15).

So if the final enemy—that fearful, terrorizing phenomenon of death—has lost its power over us, does it not stand to reason that as God's people, we should not really fear anything? If the one thing that could rob us of our personhood and consciousness has been defeated, what else could there be in our lives that we cannot overcome? When thoughts of fear come into our minds, we must bring such thoughts captive to the obedience of Christ, knowing that not even death itself spells our doom.

A Prayer

Dear Lord, sometimes we forget that You have "not given us the spirit of fear; but of power, and of love, and of a sound mind" (2 Tim. 1:7). As a result, we are crippled by fear. Please help us, dear Father, when next the thought of fearfulness creeps into our minds, to bring that thought captive to obey Your Word. In Jesus's name. Amen.

CHAPTER 11

Bring Every Doubtful Thought Captive to the Obedience of Christ

Doubt is a pain too lonely to know that faith is his twin brother.

—Kahlil Gibran

Would it not be nice if, when an evil thought comes to us, we could immediately take that thought and bring it to the feet of Jesus? Sometimes we entertain thoughts that inflame us and make us upset, fearful, or doubtful. If we could just stop those thoughts at the door, they would not have that impact upon us. The key is to stop those thoughts from entering our cognitive processes in the first place. From a human perspective, however, that is easier said than done.

Doubtful thoughts plague our minds and render us ineffective. Like the other issues we have talked about, we must bring doubtful thoughts captive to the obedience of Christ.

I must qualify my warning against doubt by saying that some forms of doubt are healthy. For example, it is perfectly legitimate to have a healthy skepticism of what some politicians tell us. Politicians like to win, so they make lots of promises that only a naive person would embrace without skepticism. When a president does not fulfill, in four years or even eight years, the promises made during the campaign, we will not be surprised if we have held skepticism about those promises all along.

Another area of doubt that is appropriate is applied when we hear stories about believers in the church. We need to be skeptical when brethren tell us about somebody else. In fact, I argue that we should dispose of the stories altogether. The Bible tells us that we ought to prove all things and hold to that which is good (1 Thess. 5:21). So doubt is appropriate in this situation. A good principle by which to live is to examine the motive of the person spreading the rumor.

When it comes to God's Word, however, we must cast aside all doubts and embrace the Word with all enthusiasm. When my sons were children, if I told them that I was going to do something for them, they believed it. As their dad, I would not want them to doubt me, so I was careful to deliver that which I promised. God likewise honors His Word to His children. If we doubt Him when He gives us His Word, we are saying we do not trust Him. That is an affront to God. So we need to bring doubtful thoughts captive to the obedience of Christ.

Doubt is the great neutralizer of progress. When we doubt God's Word, we forego the blessings that God has in store for us. By contrast, when we stand upon faith, we will reap the benefits of what is contained in His Word. There is so much in God's Word that addresses our various situations and challenges. If we, for example, can embrace what God says about our health, we will live healthful lives. If we can embrace what God says about our finances, we will not be so broke, because we will be trusting God's Word completely.

Let us examine what God says about giving tithes. The Bible tells us that in giving tithes, we prove God, and He will open the windows of heaven and pour out such blessings upon us that we will not have room enough to receive them. He will rebuke the devourer for our sake and bless the fruits of our ground, and all nations will call us blessed (Mal. 3:8–12). Yet so many believers do not give their tithes. Why is that? I believe there is an element of doubt involved. Such believers doubt that God really will give back if they give 10 percent of their salary.

Recently in our afternoon service, a young man testified about the blessings of giving. He had had only ten dollars left in his wallet, and it was time for the offering. He asked someone to exchange his ten-dollar bill for ten singles, so he could put a couple in the offering plate. The person told him to trust God and give the whole thing. He gave it, not knowing where his next dollar would come from. By Monday or Tuesday of that very week, he had received one hundred dollars in tips from his job.

Someone reading this may say that this was unrealistic or even foolish for him to have given up all the money he had to his name. But he gave it believing that God would take care of him. Hearing that testimony, why would I doubt what Jesus said: "Give, and it shall be given unto you; good measure, pressed down, and shaken together, and running over, shall men give into your bosom. For with the same measure that ye mete withal it shall be measured to you again" (Luke 6:38). And yet, many times we doubt. What is the result of doubt when it comes to giving? We stay broke and do not realize the tremendous blessing contained in being obedient to God's Word.

What would happen, I wonder, if we cast aside our doubt and truly embraced God's Word? We are seeking for the Holy Ghost to infill us and to direct our lives. I wonder what we would be able to accomplish if we simply stopped doubting and believed that the Holy Ghost was given two thousand years ago at Pentecost, and He is around us, beside us, and in us, energizing us and giving us the ability to accomplish great things. What if we simply embraced what God says without doubting? The Bible says, "But as it is written, Eye hath not seen, nor ear heard, neither have entered into the heart of man, the things which God hath prepared for them that love him" (1 Cor. 2:9).

Sometimes we have great mountains in our lives that seem impossible to climb. What has our doubt done to those mountains? The mountains stand like colossi before us. They are huge because we measure them based upon our own capabilities. When we harbor doubt, we see them as evil giants, large and threatening. But when we look at the giants in the way God sees them, they are nothing but little things before us, to be overcome not by might nor by power but by the Spirit of God (Zech. 4:6). Jesus told His disciples that if they had faith like the grain of mustard seed, they would be able to speak to the mountain and command it to be removed, and the mountain would obey them (Matt. 17:20; Luke 17:6).

What is doubt? According to Merriam-Webster's online dictionary, *doubt* is a lack of confidence. It is to be distrustful or to consider something unlikely. Doubt is to waver. To *waver* is to vacillate irresolutely between choices, or to fluctuate in opinions, allegiances, or directions. It is to sway unsteadily. As believers, we do not want to be doubters. James said that a double-minded person is unstable in all their ways (James 1:8).

You cannot go to God with your plan and say, "I want this thing this way." God wants us to depend on Him constantly and exclusively, day by day. When we come to God with our plans and pray about our plans, and things do not work out the way we wanted, then we doubt. To eliminate doubt, we must learn to be obedient to God's Word and seek His will for our lives.

Where did doubt come from? As discussed in chapter 8, I believe that doubt started with the Devil in the garden of Eden. The weapon the Devil used upon Eve was to plant a seed of doubt in her mind. Satan planted the seed of doubt by raising a question: "Did God really say you must not eat the fruit?" Why was that important? Because doubt comes in when we begin to question the veracity of God's Word.

Our spiritual parents were ultimately more successful than many of us are today because they accepted and embraced God's Word unequivocally and without reservation. Many of these men and women were not nearly as educated as contemporary Christians are, but they learned to trust God. Our parents sent us to school to improve us, but instead of using our education to the glory of God, we use our research skills to disprove what our parents taught us about God. Instead of using our education to firm up our faith in God, we use it to find inconsistencies in Scripture—or at least, what seems to us to be inconsistencies in Scripture.

It is never a bad thing to examine Scripture for ourselves, because in some cases our parents did not get it right. But we should not start from a point of doubt and skepticism, with a view toward proving the Bible wrong. If there are passages in Scripture that we do not quite understand, we should approach them from the perspective of faith, trust, obedience, and submission to the Holy Spirit of God. We should ask Him for divine insight into His Word. To start from the perspective of doubt is a prescription for failure.

Doubt comes by questioning the objective Word of God. What does the Bible teach about doubt? It teaches, among other things, that we should ask in faith without doubting or wavering (James 1:5–6). I am guilty of harboring doubt from time to time. This is a painful admission to make, for I truly believe God. That seems like a contradiction. If I truly believe God, I should never doubt what He has to say to me. Yet sometimes I try to come up with solutions to my own problems. Late at night, I am up trying to figure out how I am going to accomplish this or that. I think, "I can do this," but after many hours of twisting and turning, I find that the problem really is bigger than me.

Suddenly, when I am exhausted, the Holy Spirit taps me on the shoulder and says, "Why don't you just give this one to me now and let me solve it. Stop doubting my words and go to sleep. I will take care of this." Even then at times I find it very difficult to let go.

Sometimes we try to handle what belongs to God. We must realize that this is not our business, and we should allow God to deal with it. It belongs to Him, and all we are doing is running interference. There are some things that God will do for Himself without our help. We do not need to try and help God.

I remember some years ago, a delegation from our church in the USA visited our churches in Nigeria. The compound where we stayed had a diesel generator that produced electricity. Our host turned on the generator around two o'clock each afternoon and ran it for a few hours to cool the things in the refrigerator. Then he would shut it down. When the ice that had formed in the freezer ran out, we had to wait until the next afternoon to get more. We were never able to get a really cold drink before certain time in the late afternoon.

We thought that we could solve this problem. We went to him and asked if he would allow us to buy a drum of diesel fuel, so the electricity could stay on all day. His response was very gracious, but firm and unmistakable. He said, "My lords, this is not your business. This is my business."

We had observed what to us was a need, and we thought we could help him solve it. Our gesture suggested to him that we thought he did not have the resources to buy fuel. We assumed that he would not mind us making such an offer. We also assumed that by making such an offer, we would please him rather than offend him. We were all wrong on all counts.

It had never dawned on us that perhaps the reason the electricity was turned off at night was to ensure that the students got to bed at a reasonable time. There might have been a host of other reasons that our host chose to turn off the electricity. We didn't think about any of them.

Regrettably, that is how we operate with God at times. We are trying to put fuel in God's tank, in a manner of speaking, but this is not our business. We need to leave it to God! We are trying to help God, as though God needs our help.

God asked Job some profound questions to show His divine sovereignty over all things. Job pursued God for justice, seeking to understand God's ways. God said, "Where were you when I laid the earth's foundation? Tell me, if you understand. Who marked off its dimensions? Surely you know! Who stretched a measuring line across it? On what were its footings set, or who laid its cornerstone—while the morning stars sang together and all the angels shouted for joy?" (Job 38:3–7 NIV).

Where indeed were you and I when God created the universe? Did God consult with us? When He said, "Let there be light," and light came into being, did God ask our opinion? Did He ask us to go light candles? He said, "Let there be light," and light came. That was obviously easy for Him because He is the light. He spoke light into being because light came from within Himself (John 1:7, 8:12, 9:5, 12:46). When God speaks into our lives, therefore, let us not doubt Him.

Let us not doubt that God is our Shepherd. People will try to hurt you, and the Devil is trying to kill you, but remember to trust our God, who is our El Roi. David declared, "The Lord is my shepherd, I shall not want" (Ps. 23:1). When doubt comes, tell doubt, "No, no, no, I believe God."

Paul was in the ship, on his way to Rome, and the ship was falling apart because of a severe storm, and the people on board would not eat for fourteen days. Paul got up and said (I am paraphrasing here), "Sirs, do not let your hearts be troubled. I believe God. He whom I serve stood by me tonight. He told me that if you abide in the ship, not one soul will be lost" (Acts 27).

When we have a petition to ask of God, we need to come to Him with boldness and confidence that He will give us what we need. To harbor doubt in our minds is a precursor of failure. James tells us that we must ask God, who gives to all men liberally (James 1:5–8). James also states that a doubting person should not think they will receive anything of God (James 1:7). When we come to God, we must do so with the confidence that He is a "rewarder of them that diligently seek him" (Heb. 11:6).

You will notice Scripture does not say that those who come to God must first receive blessings from God, and then they can trust Him. The Word says if you come, you must first believe that *God is.* Those who come to God must first believe that God exists. Once we settle the question about God's existence, with all its implications for us, then we believe that He "rewards those who earnestly seek him" (NIV).

Furthermore, we must trust what God did in Jesus Christ for us, and say to Him, "Lord, I surrender all to you." We give Him everything and trust Him implicitly with everything. We must give Him our lives and say, "Your Word says this or that, and I will not waver, I will not doubt." We should resolve that whatever it costs us to trust God, we should be willing to do it, for in the end, we are confident that He will do for us more than we can even imagine.

I can think of no better promise to form the basis of our trust than Christ's Word to us in Luke 12:27–31. There the Lord compares us to the lilies that are better dressed than King Solomon with all his riches. He instructs us not to worry about material things, but rather to "seek ye the kingdom of God; and all these things shall be added unto you" (v. 31).

What an assurance! We need to begin to believe God more than we believe in or fear our circumstances. If we believe God and do not become flustered by what we do not have in the storehouse, God will supply all our needs.

A person who has faith and who trusts in God's faithfulness is one who rejoices even when they have nothing to rejoice about from the human perspective. Frankly, anybody can rejoice when they have great jobs, kids, and health. Such a person can come to church and testify that God is a provider, a healer, and so on. It is easy then to say, like David, "I will bless the Lord at all times: his praise shall continually be in my mouth" (Ps. 34:1).

But what do you do when the doctor confirms that you have brain cancer? Do you now turn from God and say, "Why did God do this to me?" Do you now lose your faith and trust in Him? Do you complain, "I've served Him since I was so-many years old, and now look what He has allowed to happen to me?"

Or do you stand up and say, like Job, "Though he slay me yet will I trust him" (Job 13:15)? Can you say, even in face of such a devastating diagnosis, "I believe His Word, 'I am the Lord that healeth thee'" (Exod. 15:26)?

I was blessed to have met a young man some years ago who was in total renal failure. When we first met, he testified that six months earlier, his doctors had given him six months to live. But he said triumphantly, "Here I am, six months later!"

Five years later, I saw him again. He said that five years earlier, his doctor had given him six months to live, and "Here I am." He was still in renal failure, but he was still trusting God.

Twenty years later, he was still in renal failure, but he was still trusting God and he still maintained his joy.

To make a long story short, the brother died after twenty-one years of being told he had six months to live. One can only wonder how long this man would have lived if, when he heard of his devastating prognosis, he had given up and stopped trusting God. I am confident that his faith, optimism, and trust in God defied his prognosis and extended his life. As far as I know, his trust in God caused him not just to exist, but rather to live a full life, rich with thanksgiving.

Learning to trust God does not mean that we never face challenges. The fact of the matter is that we will face many challenges. As believers, we will at times face existential questions, such as "Where is God? Why am I here? Why did this happen to me? Did I do something wrong to deserve this illness?" These questions and many others will come. But in spite of that, at the end of the day we must find ourselves not doubting. We must trust the Almighty God.

My late wife Erica got to the point in her illness when she learned to trust God in everything. When she was first diagnosed with multiple myeloma, we fought with all we had. We fought with conventional medicine as well as alternative medicine, all the while trusting that God would heal her body.

Then Erica began to say, "Lord, whatever you want for my life, I'm going to trust you." She prayed and we all prayed until it became clear to her that God was calling her home. When the doctor told us the bad news that there was no hope, my wife trusted God. She embraced Him and His will for her life.

Her trust in God did not fade away. From my observation, she held on to Him until the eve of her passing, when she slipped away into unconsciousness. I think in Erica's illness, not one day did the Devil get any glory out of it. When you asked her how she was doing, her response no matter what was "I'm okay." Was she being unrealistic? Was she in denial? She was not. I believe she trusted God and never doubted His faithfulness to her, despite her pains.

Like many of the other emotions that I have written about, the seeds of doubt are planted in the rich soil of our thinking. Once planted, they germinate, spring up, and grow into plants producing fruits of doubt. Doubt feeds on and perpetuates itself. Therefore we must bring every doubtful thought captive to the obedience of Christ. We must look doubt in the face and say, "Doubt, I reject you and rebuke you. I take authority over you. I am going to walk in faith, I am going to walk in trust, and I am going to walk in confidence."

The Hebrews author encouraged his readers not to throw away their confidence, because such confidence would be rewarded richly. He urged patience because Christ will come and will not delay (see Heb. 10:35–37).

If we say we believe God for something, we cannot at the same time harbor any doubt and yet expect to receive it. Doubt is the killer of faith. That is what James calls being double-minded: "A double minded man is unstable in all his ways" (James 1:8).

I wish to reiterate that there are some things we should doubt. For example, we should doubt the bad-news stories that are spread about a brother or sister. When faced with those negative bits of information, we should discard them and instead hold to that which is good.

On the other hand, it is never okay to doubt God's Word. His words are eternally sealed in heaven. There is no wavering on God's part. He will do what He has promised. The Bible teaches, "For all the promises of God in him *are* yea, and in him Amen, unto the glory of God by us" (2 Cor. 1:20). Therefore, if God says it, He means it and will bring it to pass. We should therefore bring doubtful thoughts captive to the obedience of Christ.

A Prayer

Lord, we are many times plagued with doubtful thoughts, not recognizing that when we doubt, we make a clear statement about the state of our faith. By doubting rather that trusting You, we become ineffective. Dear Lord, please help us to bring every doubting thought captive to the obedience of Christ. In Jesus's name. Amen.

CHAPTER 12

Bring Every Disobedient Thought Captive to the Obedience of Christ

One act of obedience is better than one hundred sermons.
—Dietrich Bonhoeffer

We have come a long way in dealing with many of the dysfunctional thoughts that render us a lot less effective than we could otherwise be. If we learn to control these thoughts, we will find ourselves much more powerful Christians.

In this chapter, I wish to deal with the matter of disobedience. I believe it is accurate to assert that disobedience was the first sin. God gave Adam a specific command and prohibition. Instead of doing what God told him to do, Adam disobeyed. That single act of disobedience set in motion a world of pain. It introduced sin into the world, and as a result humanity is still suffering. One act of disobedience on the part of one man caused all humanity to sin, but the obedience of one man, Jesus Christ, brought righteousness to all those who believe in Him, according to the apostle Paul (Rom. 5:18–19).

As believers, if we could be totally obedient to God and to those set over us, most of our problems in terms of our walk with God would be solved. More often than not, the act of sin is volitional and germinates in our thought lives. James tells us that a person is tempted when he is drawn away by his lust, and when lust has run its full course, it ends in death (James 1:13–15). For lust to run its full course, it must germinate and grow in the mind.

If one examines the struggles that we as Christians face, one discovers right away that the heart of our problem lies in the fact that we are disobedient and self-willed. Some acts of sin and disobedience are spontaneous. Some acts of disobedience happen because people get caught unawares; they were not thinking, and so they are overtaken. These are not deliberate acts of sin. Sometimes a person was just at the wrong place at the wrong time. Such people, when they realize that they have sinned, immediately take responsibility and run to God for forgiveness. They are not prone to blaming others. They recognize that the fault was their own, and they alone bear the responsibility.

But I argue that most sins we commit are not because we are taken unaware. Instead, such acts were first conjured up in our thought lives and then manifested in the conscious decisions that we make. Let us take the act of adultery as an example. If two people decide that they are going to violate their marriage vows, they must first convince themselves and each other that this is something they want to do. They must consider how they are going to hide their act from their spouses, children, church, and neighbors. They must arrange a convenient time and place, and then they must make excuses as to why they were not where they would ordinarily be. These are only a few of the forethoughts that must be put into one act of adultery.

According to James, a person cannot blame God when he yields to temptation. "Let no man say when he is tempted, I am tempted of God: for God cannot be tempted with evil, neither tempteth he any man: but every man is tempted, when he is drawn away of his own lust, and enticed. Then when lust hath conceived, it bringeth forth sin: and sin, when it is finished, bringeth forth death" (James 1:13-15). That is, we are tempted when we are governed by our own desires. Where do we get our desires from? Our desires come from our thinking process. We see someone with a beautiful car, and we think we would look good in that car. The next step is to think how we can get that car. We work ourselves up to a place where, although we know we cannot afford that automobile, we will find a way to get it.

Of course, the problem comes when we cannot afford to make the monthly payments. But that downward spiral into more debt started in our minds. It was our lust for a thing that set in motion our relentless efforts to acquire it, even though we knew that we really could not afford it.

It is no different with willful acts of disobedience. We think that we know what is right for us. We are drawn away by the lust for personal freedom. We justify getting into certain acts which are clearly violations of God's holy standards. We know what the Word of God says, but we decide that we want to go in another direction.

Some of us are convinced about the theology or instruction from the Bible, but because someone else tells us that we ought to go down that path, we rebel. We simply defy them in the name of freedom and do our own thing. I believe that at times, if someone had not told us not to do such and such a thing, we might not have done it. But because somebody dared to presume to instruct us, we decided that we would not listen. We might lose face. We reason that if we do what they suggest, they may take credit for it.

What is disobedience? According to *Merriam-Webster's Dictionary*, disobedience is refusal or neglect to obey. Webster's provides some related words: contrariness, defiance, forwardness, insubordination, intractability, rebellion, rebelliousness, recalcitrance, unruliness, waywardness, and willfulness, among others.

Disobedience is a willful act of insubordination designed to communicate one's assertion of one's right to govern oneself, notwithstanding the consequences. In the context of the Christian's ethical responsibilities, disobedience to God's Word is a tacit declaration that we will not be governed by anyone—not even God. We become self-centered rather than God-centered, self-pleasing as opposed to God-pleasing.

When people argue that they cannot submit to church rules or to a pastor, they are treading on dangerous ground. Sometimes we disobey our leaders because we figure that we are older, more educated, or more experienced than they are, and therefore they cannot presume to tell us what to do. This is particularly true of young people who go off to colleges and universities and learn some philosophy. Often they return home with the attitude that their parents and church leaders are living in the Dark Ages. Pastors and the older adults in their lives are, they say, totally out of touch.

A little humility goes a long way. From my own perspective, I have learned much more from the older people in my life than from any textbook. My grandmother was my first teacher, although she did not go beyond the third grade. She continues to have a profound impact upon my life long after her death. Notwithstanding the degrees that I hold, my grandmother Susan Mitchell has framed my worldview and the way I conduct my life more than any professor. Those of us who rebel against our leaders because we feel that we know more than they do are missing the point altogether.

Many of us cannot be charged with adultery, fornication, stealing, or lying—any of the so-called big sins. But most of us can be charged with disobedience, self-will, and stiff-neckedness. God promises blessings for obedience. We therefore need to examine ourselves and be careful not to miss out on those blessings because of our disobedience. The Bible tells us, "If ye be willing and obedient, ye shall eat the good of the land: But if ye refuse and rebel, ye shall be devoured with the sword: for the mouth of the LORD hath spoken it" (Isa. 1:19–20). When thoughts of disobedience come, we would do well to recall this passage of Scripture.

The *Harper Collins Bible Dictionary* defines *obedience* as "submitting to the will and authority of another." That could be parents, pastor, youth director, Sunday school teacher, or ultimately, of course, God. To be obedient, we must bring our will under subjection. We must recognize that someone else has the upper hand—that we take the lower seat, so to speak.

I can think of no better example of humility and obedience than that of Jesus Christ. He was God, but when He became a man, for the purpose of bringing redemption to disobedient humanity, He subjected Himself to the heavenly Father and was obedient unto death. On the eve of His crucifixion, when He knew that His hour was coming, as a man He felt the anguish and pain of carrying our sins upon Himself and of facing that cruel cross. Crucifixion was one of the most excruciating ways of dying known to humanity. Let us face it: Jesus was not looking forward to the pain. We observe in Scripture His expression of agony. Jesus said, "My soul is exceeding sorrowful, even unto death" (Matt. 26:38; Mark 14:34). Notwithstanding His agony, sorrow, and anxiety, Jesus prayed that His Father's will be done (Matt. 26:39). That is obedience, and we would do well to follow Jesus's example.

The apostle Paul encouraged the Philippian brethren to have the attitude of Jesus Christ. He instructed them that in their relationships with one another, they should have the same mind-set as Christ Jesus. That mind-set took Him to the cross, but in the end God exalted Him (Phil. 2:5–11). As imitators of Christ, we must have that same attitude of obedience. As we seek to answer the question, "What does it mean to be a Christian?" we must be willing to look to Christ's example of obedience and do as He did.

The apostle Paul encouraged Titus to "put them in mind to be subject to principalities and powers, to obey magistrates, to be ready to every good work" (Titus 3:1). To children, Paul wrote, "Obey your parents in all things: for this is well pleasing unto the Lord" (Col. 3:20; see also Eph. 6:1). To servants, he wrote, "Obey in all things your masters according to the flesh; not with eye service, as men pleasers; but in singleness of heart, fearing God" (Col. 3:22). Paul instructed the believers at Rome to subject themselves to the higher powers, for God ordained the authorities that existed. Paul made it clear that those who resisted the authorities resisted God (Rom. 13:1–4).

There are consequences for disobedience. No matter who we are, whether bishop or newly baptized, we need to obey. Here is the attitude of some church folks: "I am smart enough, I will read Scripture myself. I am not going to listen to what a human being says, for that person is only human, just like me. I will make my own determination as to what I will do."

If that is our attitude, we are wrong! It does not matter the age of the person who is assigned to lead us. He or she may be younger than our youngest child, but we still have a responsibility to obey as unto the Lord.

Samuel was only eight years of age when he began to hear from God. It is safe to say that when Eli was no longer hearing from God, the eight-year old boy heard the divine voice, although he was not able to distinguish it. When Eli heard what the Lord had told Samuel, Eli submitted to it. We need to understand that obedience means to submit, even to those whom we may regard as less capable than ourselves.

That is hard for some people to do. I was doing premarital counseling with a couple some years ago, and I told the woman that as a wife, she was to submit to and obey her husband. She was floored! She exclaimed, "What, Pastor, submit? What does that even mean? And obey?"

I said, "It means you submit to and obey your husband. It means the man is the head of the house, and you submit to and obey him, even as there is mutual submission between the both of you."

She said she had been on her own for many years, calling the shots without having to consult with anyone. Submitting to and obeying anyone would prove to be a very difficult thing to do.

I told her that now that she had decided to change her status from single to married, she would need to submit to her husband's authority. She was awfully upset by that, but I would not let her off the hook. I told her that obedience and submission are God's requirements for marriage. Then I told the husband that according to the Bible, he must love his wife as Christ loves the church. Christ gave Himself for the church. I further instructed him that when he had given her everything he had—attention, love, compassion, financial resources—then he would have earned her submission and obedience.

Let us look again at what the Bible teaches about obedience and disobedience. "And Samuel replied, does the Lord delight in burnt offerings and sacrifices, as much as in obeying the voice of the Lord? To obey is better than sacrifice, and to heed is better than the fat of rams" (1 Sam. 5:22 NIV). Saul was told to go to the Amalekites. The Amalekites were the enemies of Israel. God's instruction was to smite and utterly destroy the Amalekites (1 Sam. 15:3).

This command seems quite clear to me. There is no room for misunderstanding. This command may be draconian, and it may insult our twenty-first-century sensibilities, but let us not question God's decisions. This is what God told Saul to do. The command was to destroy everything.

What was Saul's response to God's unequivocal order? He spared Agag, an Amalekite leader, and the best things the Amalekites had. Saul destroyed only the not-so-nice things (1 Sam. 15:9). Saul made his own decision about who should live and who should die. That was not his job. God's command was to destroy everything. We cannot presume to countermand God's commands, for in doing so, we are placing ourselves above God's wisdom and sovereignty. We are in effect saying that we know better than God what is best for us.

Disobedience to God is an opening for the Devil to possess us, because constant disobedience to God is the product of a hardened heart. In Exodus we read, "And he hardened Pharaoh's heart, that he hearkened not unto them; as the Lord had said" (Exod. 7:13). Why did Pharaoh not obey God's commands? He did not obey because his heart was hardened. One may argue that in Pharaoh's case, God hardened him so that he would not obey, but as a general principle, this is not the case. God does not capriciously decide to harden a person's heart, although He certainly could. Generally, people become hardened when they persist in their disobedience.

Let us think on that again for a moment. God does leave disobedient people to their own vices. This is another way of saying that they were hardened and callous. Paul tells us that when people fail to retain God in their knowledge, God gives them over to depraved minds (Rom. 1:28).

I stated earlier that disobedience to God is an opening for the Devil to possess us. The apostle Paul wrote to Timothy, "Now the Spirit speaketh expressly, that in the latter times some shall depart from the faith, giving heed to seducing spirits, and doctrines of devils; Speaking lies in hypocrisy; having their conscience seared with a hot iron" (1 Tim. 4:1–2). Did you notice that those who departed from the faith gave heed to seducing spirits? Those who have a habit of obeying God do not give heed to seducing spirits.

Please notice the last clause of this verse. It reads, "having their conscience seared with a hot iron." That means their consciences are dead. I believe it is safe to say that if one's conscience is dead, one has been hardened. There are consequences for disobedience, and Scripture makes that abundantly clear. "He, that being often reproved hardeneth his neck, shall suddenly be destroyed, and that without remedy" (Prov. 29:1).

Most acts of disobedience come out of our hearts. So if you find yourself not able to comply with the God's Word, examine the state of your heart. You will most likely find that there is something wrong with it. Some of us pride ourselves on being stubborn. But stubbornness in the face of truth betrays a bad heart toward God. Such a heart needs to be circumcised. The Lord told Israel, "Circumcise therefore the foreskin of your heart, and be no more stiffnecked" (Deut. 10:16). A heart that is circumcised is one that has had the metaphorical foreskin removed. Such a heart is sensitive to the things of God.

God's people should not follow every wind of doctrine. Different people may have various interpretations for a particular passage of Scripture. It would be inappropriate to embrace these various interpretations. Rather, we must search Scripture for ourselves. With the help of the Holy Spirit and the guidance of a godly spiritual leader, we will arrive at truth. When we are faced with the truth but reject the truth because it departs from our presuppositions, that amounts to stubbornness and disobedience.

I see this in marriages quite often. People stake out their positions. The husband takes a position that is opposite to his wife's, and will stick to that position even when faced with overwhelming information that disproves it. His attitude is "I cannot look bad before my wife." So, out of pride, he feels obliged to stick to his position no matter the cost to the marriage.

In other cases, the wife knows that her husband is right, but her attitude is "I will not give him the satisfaction of knowing that he is right." And she continues to hold her position at the expense of their relationship.

When Christians do such things, we are being disobedient to God's Word, which instructs us to be submissive to each other in the fear of God (Eph. 5:21).

When presented with new information, there are times a person honestly does not see it. If you do not see what the other person is saying, you need to examine the facts for yourself. The ability to make decision is a God-given attribute of humanity, in consequence of humans having been made in God's image. As good stewards of this image-bearing status, we are required to think critically and arrive at intelligent decisions. We must be willing to admit when we are wrong.

But what if you cannot readily see what the other person is telling you—what should you do? What if it is your pastor who is urgently telling you to do or not do something? What should you do? As followers of God, there are times when a thing is so critical that even though we do not see it, we need to follow the direction of our trusted spiritual leaders. Of course, this presupposes that you have godly pastors.

Unfortunately, some Christians are stubborn and disobedient, and will do what they want to do no matter what the consequences may be. Nehemiah lamented the disobedience of the people of Israel. God had given them bread from heaven, provided water out of the rock, and promised their fathers a land. Sadly, however, instead of listening to God, they dealt proudly and hardened their necks, and did not follow God's commandment (Neh. 9:15–17).

Thank God, He has given us His lovingkindness and His tender mercy. Even in our rebellion, there is still hope that we can be saved. Even in our disobedience, there is still time for us to repent. However, we must remember that we do not have unlimited time. God's children need to come to the place where we do not get settled in our old, sinful ways, where we become callous and unresponsive to God's Word. When we are disobedient, we open ourselves to another spirit to work in us. The apostle Paul refers to this as "the spirit that now worketh in the children of disobedience" (Eph. 2:2).

When we find ourselves obdurate and implacable, we are not operating in the Spirit of Christ, for disobedience is from Satan. It is interesting that, among the many sins for which the apostle Paul says people are worthy of death, disobedience is named. God sees disobedience as a grave sin. Adam and Eve were thrown out of the garden of Eden for it, and Israel's first king, Saul, lost his throne and any possibility of dynastic rule because of it. At the root of all types of sin, therefore, is the spirit of disobedience.

Some believers are so stubborn and so set in their ways that not even God's Word itself can bend them. They refuse to allow the Word to have its effect on their lives. When the Bible says that some people are left over to the reprobate minds, we think first or almost exclusively of homosexuality. But the context of Romans 1 makes it clear that it is not just homosexuality or other sexual deviance for which people are worthy of death. It is rather about disobedience on all levels.

According to Paul, those who know that God's justice demands that disobedient people who commit such acts are worthy of death, not only do those acts themselves, but also have pleasure in people who do those things (Rom. 1:32). In other words, they keep company with other disobedient people, and cheer them on when they do disobedient acts. A disobedient Christian is no safer than the sexually deviant person. So if we are judging a gay person, but we are ourselves disobedient, then both we and the gay person are worthy of God's judgment, because we are both disobedient to God.

In a section of the second warning passage in Hebrews, chapters 3:7–4:13, we are warned to take heed lest we miss the promise of entering into God's rest. The author points out that the Old Testament believers did not enter into rest because of unbelief (Heb. 4:1–2). The Old Testament believers heard God's Word, but they did not abide by it. They heard it with their ears but not with their hearts. They did not process it and did not obey it. Perhaps the messenger may not be to our liking, yet we must look beyond the one delivering the message and take heed of the message. We must bring every disobedient thought captive to the obedience of Christ.

A true prescription for spiritual disaster is disobedience. At the root of every failing saint or Christian organization is disobedience. Nothing the pastor says will ever move some people until or unless they are prepared to be obedient to God's Word. Marriages break up because couples are not prepared to follow God's prescription for their lives. Family relationships break down because children would rather listen to the sentiments of the latest hip-hop artist than follow their parents. Disobedience betrays a prideful heart that says, "I know what's best for me."

There resides in people who are disobedient the "prince of the power of the air, the spirit that now worketh in the children of disobedience" (Eph. 2:2). This is a very difficult truth to admit, but we must be honest with ourselves. Disobedience does not come from Christ. He was obedient to His Father even to death on the cross (Phil. 2:8). When we find ourselves having a difficult time obeying God's Word, we need to start rebuking that spirit.

As children, when we were obedient to our parents, they were more generous to us because we pleased them. The most obedient and truth-telling child in the home was the one who got the most favors. Some of us who were not very compliant got punished more severely. Jesus says that the servant who knows his lord's will but does not do it will be "beaten with many stripes" (Luke 12:47). Our parents operated on this principle.

My grandmother never spanked us without first warning us. She would first declare unto us her will. We knew what she wanted from us, but somehow, we were either unwilling or unable to be obedient, and so we suffered the consequences.

Disobedience has dire consequences. We read in Jeremiah that the Lord sent His servants to warn His people to depart from their wickedness, but they were disobedient and failed to listen. The result was that God's fury was poured out upon them, and they were left waste and desolate (Jer. 44: 4–6).

In his Romans epistle, the apostle Paul wrote, "By one man's disobedience many were made sinners" (Rom. 5:19). Do you not see the dire consequence of the evil of disobedience? This one man, Adam, sinned by disobeying God, and everyone else since that day has suffered as a result. If any of us, particularly those of us in leadership positions, are living in disobedience and deluding ourselves that it does not have consequences, we need only to look at Adam's example.

Let us examine Romans 5:19 in its entirety. It reads, "For as by one man's disobedience many were made sinners, so by the obedience of one shall many be made righteous." There are corporate, lasting, and far-reaching implications for both obedience and disobedience. Obedience is a learned behavior; it is something we need to learn. Most of us were not born to be obedient. We were born with Adam's nature, a nature characterized by disobedience and rebellion. That is where our problem started. The first couple had everything they needed for sustenance and comfort. The known world was their domain, except for one single tree. Yet they could not obey God and keep their hands off that forbidden fruit.

Because obedience is a learned behavior, when Jesus Christ took on human nature, He learned to obey. In speaking about Jesus, the Hebrews writer observes, "Though he were a Son, yet learned he obedience by the things which he suffered" (Heb. 5:8). This verse demonstrates the true humanity of Jesus Christ. It tells us that through His suffering, He learned to obey. It gives us hope that we, like Him, can learn to be obedient.

If Jesus had to learn how to obey, so must we. Some may comment that since He was also God, why did He not simply evoked His divinity and say, "I am God; I don't have to obey anything." Some may ask,

"How do we know that Jesus's total obedience was not simply a result of His divinity"? In other words, did He not simply switch to His divinity when faced with difficulty choices, so that He could obey?

Such questions betray an ignorance of Jesus's true humanity. He could no more cast off His humanity than you or I can. Although He was truly divine, Jesus did the work of redemption in the flesh. Jesus "condemned sin in the flesh" (Rom. 8:3). One commentator writes, "In the human nature of his own Son, God broke the power of sin."[35]

Charles Hodge, the famous nineteenth-century Princeton theologian, states that Paul's argument in Romans 8:1–3 is that "there is no condemnation to us, because God condemned sin in Christ."[36]

Craig Keener writes, "For God to 'condemn sin in the flesh' was for him to execute judgment on it in Jesus's person."[37]

In other words, by His obedience, Jesus became a sin offering for us (2 Cor. 5:21). In the eternal council of the Godhead, the divine decision was made that Jesus would take on the sin of the world to redeem God's elect. The fulfilment of God's redemptive plan rested on the obedience of Jesus Christ.

Because of indwelling sin in humanity, the law condemned us, but because of the obedience of Christ, sin itself is condemned. It is not as though sin no longer exists, or that it no longer has any effect on God's people. We all wish that were the case. What it does mean is that, although sin is still rampant in the world and still affects God's people, it no longer has dominion over those of us who are under grace (Rom. 6:14). All this is made possible because of the obedience of Jesus Christ.

Contrary to what we often believe, it is a lot less painful to be obedient to God than to be disobedient. When God wants something out of our lives, He will not let us off the hook by compromising His righteous standards. God will not bend or break. He will bend and break us until we conform to His plan for our lives.

For example, if God has gifted you with evangelism, He is going to bring that to reality despite how much you try to be disobedient to that call. You have the choice of doing it the easy way or the hard way, but in the end, God will get His way. You might as well just obey Him now and avoid the unnecessary pain.

I was once watching a religious program on television, and there was a gentleman speaking. He was hard to look upon because of the severe disfigurement of his face. Whatever had happened to him, it had caused his face to be twisted to one side. He told the audience that he thanked God for his disfigurement, because without it, he would never have submitted to God's will. He confessed that it was this awful disfigurement that had helped him surrender to God, and from it God got the glory. It need not be that way with us if we are obedient from the beginning.

It is never advisable to resist God, for He never loses. He gets the last word. God gets to write the last chapter and the epilogue to your life's story. The Lord invites His children into a relationship of obedience. In the Old Testament, God called Israel to obedience, and by extension He is calling us to that same life.

The Bible tells us that although our sin stain may be great, we can be made clean if we are willing and obedient, and shall eat the good off the land. If, however, we are disobedient, we shall be devoured with the sword (Isa. 1:18–20). God will perfect us, but we must participate in the perfecting process by being obedient to Christ.

My late pastor told us a story about a young lady in Jamaica who came to his tent meeting to hear him preach the gospel. The people with whom she lived were strictly against her being part of a Pentecostal church, because in those days, Pentecostalism was not accepted in Jamaica. But when she heard the Word of God that night, she felt that she could not resist God's call. God touched her heart and called her to himself. As the Holy Spirit ignited a flame in her heart, she cried out, "Yes, Lord, I will obey thee." And with the tears rolling down her face, she knelt at the altar and surrendered her life to Christ.

After almost sixty years, and having lost her husband at an early age, she is still obeying the Lord. Her son happens to be a member of the church where I currently pastor. He, like his mother so many years earlier, had his own transforming encounter with the risen Lord, and has surrendered his life to Christ. There is a blessing and a reward in obeying God.

Let us come to that place where we say, like Jesus, "Father, if thou be willing, remove this cup from me: nevertheless not my will, but thine, be done" (Luke 22:42). There is an old hymn that we do not hear much anymore, but it speaks well about this idea of being obedient. Two of the verses read as follows:

> Have thine own way, Lord! Have thine own way!
> Thou art the potter, I am the clay.
> Mold me and make me after thy will,
> while I am waiting, yielded and still.
>
> Have thine own way, Lord! Have thine own way!
> Hold o'er my being absolute sway.
> Fill with thy Spirit till all shall see
> Christ only, always, living in me![38]

God's will must hold absolute sway over our own. When we are tempted to disobey, we must remember that disobedience comes from the thought life. We should bring that disobedient thought captive to the obedience of Christ. It is worth repeating over and over again: "For though we walk in the flesh, we do not war after the flesh: For the weapon of our warfare are not carnal, but mighty through God to the pulling down of strong holds; Casting down imaginations, and every high thing that exalteth itself against the knowledge of God, and bringing into captivity every thought to the obedience of Christ" (2 Cor. 10:3–5).

A Prayer

Heavenly Father, like Adam, we are disobedient many times. Lord, we understand that "by one man's disobedience many were made sinners," but we rejoice in the fact that Christ, the second Adam, has changed our nature so that we can become obedient children (Rom. 5:19). So, Lord, when the disobedient thoughts come, help us to bring such thoughts captive to the obedience of Christ. In Jesus's name. Amen.

CHAPTER 13

Bring Every Defeatist Thought Captive to the Obedience of Christ

The mind is an intricate mechanism that can be run on the fuels of both victory and defeatism.

—Pat Conroy

We now turn our attention to another debilitating thought that prevents God's people from realizing their full potential—that is, defeatist thoughts. Many times, the greatest of potentials are snuffed out because of our defeatist thinking.

What is defeatist thinking, or defeatism? Defeatist thinking is evident when a person gives up before they even get started. If, for example, a boxer thinks that his opponent is better than himself, and that he does not stand a chance against this opponent, he will most likely lose the fight. He was already defeated before he stepped into ring. The boxer's most formidable opponent is not the opposing boxer, but his defeatist thinking.

As a mental health counselor, I encounter many people who are plagued with defeatist thinking that prevents them from enjoying life. Often it is clear that these are otherwise bright people who could do almost anything that they put their minds to, but somehow they tell themselves that they cannot do such and such a thing.

I recall vividly one smart client who was in the health-care field. She had become involved in a marketing business in addition, and had done very well. By the time she came to see me, she had been promoted and had several people reporting to her. She panicked and could no longer produce. Not only her marketing business but also her position in health care was in jeopardy, because she was no longer productive in either place.

After about three sessions, I asked her what was responsible for the precipitous slide in her performance. She admitted that she was afraid of success. Her experience up to that point had been that her performance was average at best. When she began to experience above-average performance, she became afraid that she could not sustain that success over time.

This dear lady talked herself out of her success. Her defeatist attitude eventually cost her the job in the health-care industry, and her marketing business suffered as well. She even contemplated moving back home with her mother.

Like the other negative thoughts about which we have been talking, we must bring every defeatist thought captive to the obedience of Christ. The Bible says that for as a man thinks in his heart, so is he (Prov. 23:7). Jesus Christ had a lot to say about the heart. He taught that our behaviors are a result of the thoughts that we possess in the heart. He told His audience on one occasion that what comes out of one's mouth actually comes from the heart, and that these things defile the person (Matt. 15:18–20).

To be successful, we must reframe and reform our thinking. We begin this process by replacing negative self-talk with positive self-talk. I am not advocating pop psychology or engagement in self-help programs, in which we are supposed to find the answers to all our problems. Rather, the positive self-talk that I advocate is one based on God's Word. The question is: what does God's Word have to say about your situation?

We are always talking to ourselves anyway. We might as well do so based on God's Word. So if you are facing really bad news from your doctor, there is nothing wrong with affirming to yourself that by His stripes, you are healed (Isa. 53:5). If your spouse has just left you and you feel lonely, why not tell yourself that God said: "I will never leave thee, nor forsake thee" (Heb. 13:5). If you are thinking of starting a business or embarking on a career, why not tell yourself that "all these blessings shall come on thee, and overtake thee, if thou shalt hearken unto the voice of the Lord thy God" (Deut. 28:2). If you know that you are being obedient to God's Word, why not have great expectations from Him? God cannot lie. What He has promised, He will do.

I am told that I am a good preacher. Although I am sure that I am not as good as some people make me out to be, I believe in my heart that there is a measure of effectiveness present in my preaching. Long before I was given the opportunity to preach, I believed in my heart that I was called to preach. I had seen good preachers and had always wanted to emulate them, so I told myself that I could preach. Before I started preaching in church, I preached to myself in the shower, as I walked the streets, and later in my car. In my judgment, I preached some of my best sermons in these venues. Unfortunately, no one heard them.

I told myself that I could preach and then I did what it took to become a preacher. I did not simply talk. I enrolled in seminary and earned a master's degree in divinity and a PhD in theology. As I believed in my heart that I would one day become a good preacher, I did the hard work of studying to make sure that I was prepared to fulfill my dreams.

In the early years of my ministry, some of my sermons were not very good. Sometimes after I was done, I felt embarrassed. I had to battle the negative self-talk that I would never be any good at this preaching thing. I had to keep telling myself that my best sermons were yet to be preached. No matter where you are in life, you need to affirm continually that you can do even better. I still believe that my best days are ahead of me. My best sermons are still to be preached.

Throughout this book, I have attempted to admonish the reader to bring several dysfunctional thoughts captive to the obedience of Christ. We do this by bringing the whole weight of Scripture to bear.

Let us look a bit closer at defeatism. According to the *Webster's Dictionary*, *defeatism* is "an attitude accepting, expecting or being resigned to defeat." Dictionary.com says that defeatism is the "attitude, policy or conduct of a person who admits, expects or no longer resists defeat because of a conviction that further struggle or effort is futile."

It is a pessimistic person who accepts defeat as the only option. Pessimists accept defeat as something that is a foregone conclusion. It is an attitude of accepting, expecting, or being resigned to the inevitable. Defeatism is a very impoverished way to live. There may be mounting evidence that things may turn out wrong, but we need not accept that conclusion. The facts may be daunting, but the truth of God's Word says that we are more than conquerors (Rom. 8:37).

Sometimes our defeatist attitude has an external source, and at other times it comes from within us. Some folks, out of good intentions, will tell us that we cannot do such and such a thing. "It is too risky," they say. Sometimes we tell ourselves that we do not have the capabilities, resources, or support that we need, so we simply quit and bury our dreams. We need an attitude adjustment. Many people with great natural abilities die without realizing their full potential, because of a defeatist attitude.

In contrast, there are many people with average abilities and insufficient resources who have soared to great heights because of the right attitude. Jesse Jackson Sr., the civil rights leader, once observed in his poetic style that one's aptitude plus one's attitude equals one's altitude. Aptitude is your natural ability to learn. It is your intelligence quotient (IQ). Your aptitude is extremely important to your success, but aptitude alone will not get you anywhere unless you have a good attitude to match. Attitude is defined by Merriam-Webster as "the way you think and feel about someone or something, a feeling or way of thinking that affects a person's behavior." In other words, no matter the aptitude that you possess, if your attitude is that you are a failure, you will become a failure.

I suspect that there are many doctors, scientists, bankers, and other people from all walks of life who have lower IQs than some homeless people on the streets who have superior IQs. The difference between these two groups is attitude. The successful person has a can-do attitude. A person who fails despite their aptitude possesses a defeatist attitude that says, "I can't do this." There are many books that could have be written—but were not. There are many businesses that could have been started—but were not. There are many brilliant careers that were never realized because of people's defeatist attitude. Defeatism has the uncanny ability to snatch defeat out of the mouth of victory.

What is the cause of defeatism? And how do we overcome a defeatist attitude? Defeatism occurs when a person has doubts about their abilities or is uncertain about their state of mind. Defeatism starts in the mind.

Sometimes the thoughts are subconscious. We may not even be aware of why we feel the way we do. It is important, therefore, to examine our thinking. We must think about our thoughts.

You may not be able to control all the many thoughts that are constantly running through your mind, but you can choose which thought or thoughts will control your behaviors. If you invest most of your time thinking self-defeating thoughts, you should not be surprised if you develop a defeatist attitude.

It is easy, when things seem very difficult, to just go with the flow and say, "This is how it is going to be, so I might as well accept my fate." But I like the Old Testament story of two former slaves from Egypt who were part of the great Exodus. Their names were Caleb and Joshua. When the multitude of freed slaves had reached the desert of Paran, their leader, Moses, wanted to assess their challenges and opportunities in the Promised Land, so he sent twelve spies to scout. Among these were Joshua and Caleb. Despite the bounty the scouts observed, ten of them discouraged the Israelites by telling them that there were giants in the land, and that Israel was not capable of defeating them.

But Caleb took the optimistic view. His advice to Moses was "Let us go up at once and possess it; for we are well able to overcome it" (Num. 13:30). The reports of the other ten spies had made the people doubt and had caused a rebellion in the camp, Joshua and Caleb stood up and put the appropriate perspective on the matter. They properly assessed that the land was an exceedingly good land. They made it clear that if the Lord delighted in them, He would bring them into the land (Num. 14:6–9). Their perspective was an optimistic one, an optimism based on God's faithfulness.

Defeatism is a state of mind that must be attended to in order to break the cycle of fear of failure and resignation to one's fate. Let me be clear: there are times when the tasks that face us and the threats that hang over us are daunting. But no power that threatens us is greater than the power of the Holy Spirit within us. The apostle Paul wrote, "Now unto him that is able to do exceeding abundantly above all that we ask or think, according to the power that worketh in us" (Eph. 3:20). The power is not of us. It is of God and works within us.

The power of God within us helps us to overcome defeatist thoughts.

The Bible tells us that if we observed the wind or regarded the clouds, we would neither sow nor reap (Eccles. 11:4). Sometimes in the season of our sowing, the winds are boisterous, and many times when we should be harvesting, the threatening clouds hang low. But we must know when to disregard those threats and proceed to do what God has commanded us to do.

Perhaps there is something that you have always wanted to accomplish in your life, but you have not done so because someone—maybe even yourself—told you that you could not accomplish it. Please do yourself the favor of rethinking that. In the process, commit Ephesians 3:20 to memory and let it guide your thought life. It is worth reading again. It affirms that God is able to do much more than we are able to ask for or even conceive. The power of God works in us to accomplish great things. The apostle Paul tells us, "It is God who works in you to will and to act in order to fulfill his good purpose" (Phil. 2:13 NIV).

There is nothing that you cannot accomplish if you set your mind to it. Many of you have accepted mediocrity and defeat long enough. It is time to walk in dominion. We must learn how to defeat defeatism. The things that lock you up in the prison of your defeatism must be defeated.

A defeatist attitude contradicts the plan of God for our lives. We should not accept what seems to be inevitable from the human perspective. God may have another way out for us. Do not compromise your dreams or accept something less because you think what you have is the best you can do under the circumstances. Seek, by God's empowerment, to control those circumstances.

If you are a young lady who wants to get married, do not compromise your standards because you think you are getting old and cannot do better. If you believe and wait on God, He has something better for you. Do not overlook prodigious flaws in a man because you think you cannot do better. If he looks like a frog, sounds like a frog, jumps like a frog, and croaks like a frog, do not try to convince yourself that he is a prince. He is a frog, however loudly you may have told yourself to settle.

Do not settle for something that is not yours. God has a better and bigger plan for your life. God declares, "For I know the plans I have for you," declares the Lord, "plans to prosper you and not to harm you, plans to give you hope and a future" (Jer. 29:11 NIV). I like the prayer of Jabez. He asked God to enlarge his coasts and to make him greater than he was, and that his increase would not grieve him (1 Chron. 4:10).

There is a story in 2 Kings about four lepers who faced a critical decision. A severe famine gripped the land, and they felt stuck between a rock and a hard place. They reasoned, "If we go into the city of Samaria, we are going to die because there is no food there. If we stay here, we will die because there is no food here. The Syrians may not be having the same kind of drought we are having, so if we get to their camp, they may give us some food. If they give us food, we will live. If they do not give us food, will die. But we are going to die in the other scenarios anyway. Let's take a chance and do something." (See 2 Kings 7:3–8.)

These men did not assume a defeatist attitude. They grasped at any glimmer of hope. The defeatists resign themselves to their fates, often determined by what they see with the natural eyes or by what they feel. Let us remember, "We walk by faith, not by sight" (2 Cor. 5:7). Faith in God's Word is one way of overcoming defeatism.

These lepers could have accepted their fate and stayed where they were, or they could have gone into the city they knew and faced sure death along with many others. Their story is inspiring because they decided to face the unknown with hopefulness. In the meantime, while they were contemplating this, God confused the Syrians. He let them hear what they thought were the chariots of a mighty army. In their horror and dread of being overwhelmed by Israel, the Syrians ran away and left all their stuff: their horses, their silver, their gold, and the food in the camp.

The four lepers went into the camp and discovered all they needed to sustain life. The only way this could have happened was because those lepers refused to accept defeat. No matter how desperate the situation may be, we must continue to cling to hope. My grandmother repeated this saying: "While there is life, there is hope." She would say this in the most hopeless of situations. This still hold true today. Hope is another key to overcoming defeatist thoughts.

I recall a specific situation that seemed hopeless, one in which my grandmother's refusal to accept defeat, I think, made a difference. My aunt and uncle had migrated to England for economic reasons, and had left their four children in Jamaica, with Grandma. Meanwhile, my mother was living in Kingston with my stepfather, and because they were so poor, they had no place for me to live with them. So Grandma had custody of me also.

One rainy season, one of my cousins became gravely ill and got rapidly worse with the passing hours. The closest doctor to us was some eight miles away. Our only mode of transportation, apart from walking, was one donkey.

My cousin became unresponsive. Her breathing was labored for a while, and then she seemed to stop breathing altogether. Her eyes rolled back in her head. Things looked hopeless. This was about ten o'clock at night, and it was pouring rain. The look on my grandmother's face revealed that she was deeply concerned.

But she did not give up. After doing what she could for the child, she dropped to her knees and began to pray. Her words were something to this effect: "Lord, I believe that you can do all things. Please heal this child. Lord, I will not write my daughter and tell her that her child is dead, so please perform a miracle."

Grandma covered up the child and kept vigil over her all night, praying and believing that God would keep the child alive. By six o'clock in the morning, it was still raining, and the child was still alive.

Grandma then asked the Lord to hold up the rain long enough for us to get the doctor. In about a half an hour, the rain stopped falling. She saddled the donkey with two hamper-like wicker baskets, one on each side, in which she placed the two youngest children. A third child rode in the saddle. My older cousin, Grandma, and I walked alongside. It was eight miles to the doctor. After being attended to by the doctor, we headed back home. As soon as we arrived and unsaddled the donkey, the skies reopened and the rain resumed.

The happy ending is that in a few days, my cousin began to recover. Years later, that same cousin and I were baptized on the same day. Now she is living in England, quite healthy.

This event, I believe, was an example of someone who absolutely refused to accept defeat. When faced with disaster, my grandmother prayed. Prayer is another tool available to us to defeat the defeatist thoughts.

It does not really matter where you are today. You may be facing your own crisis. Indeed, you may be spiritually a leper, feeling as though you are an outcast. But there is food in the camp for you. Your relief is only a matter of time. There is victory ahead. Do not give up and walk away. Do not leave until God blesses you. And when He tells you to move on into a new dimension of grace, just follow where He leads.

The apostle Paul, writing to the Corinthians, commented, "And God is able to bless you abundantly, so that in all things at all times, having all that you need, you will abound in every good work" (2 Cor. 9:8 NIV). It may not feel that way at times, but as believers, we must go with the truth of God's Word and not be guided by our feelings.

I will go further to say that in rejecting defeatism, we should not settle for the leftovers. Do not settle for crumbs. Seek for the "exceeding," "abundant," and "above" blessings (Eph. 3:20). If it is all the same to the naysayers, they can keep their crumbs. I want something better! I want something richer! I want something of a more lasting value than they are offering!

Sometimes, to move away from a defeatist disposition into one of action and faith, we must be pushed. I think of Esther, a Jewish girl in Persia, who rose to the lofty position of being queen to Xerxes (Ahasuerus, KJV). Her predecessor, Vashti, refused to display her beauty before the drunken king and his nobles, as a result of which she was banished (see Esther 1). Esther then became queen. Meantime, her cousin Mordecai, who had raised her, uncovered a diabolic plot to assassinate King Xerxes, and the king bestowed upon Mordecai great honor. These two circumstances engendered much hatred, not just for Mordecai and Esther, but also for the entire Jewish population throughout the 127 provinces that constituted the Persian Empire.

When Mordecai alerted Esther to the plot that arose against the Jews, her response was defeatist in nature. Some may say that she was bound by protocol, or that she was insensitive to the plight of her people, since she was safe as queen. Whatever may have been her motivation, she was resigned to the Jews' fate. That was defeatist. She focused on the fact that to approach the king when she was not called could jeopardize her own life.

Mordecai's sobering response to her was just what she needed to snap her out of her complacent and defeatist attitude. He said she should not feel safe in the palace compared to the Jews in the provinces. He prophesied that if she did not act, God would still deliver His people, but she and her father's house would be destroyed (Esther 4:13–14). Mordecai refused to accept Esther's first response, because to accept it would be to accept defeat and dire consequences.

Meanwhile, Haman was constructing the gallows on which to hang Mordecai, certain of the destruction of the Jews. Unfortunately for Haman, the gallows he had built served as the instrument of his own execution.

Perhaps even now the Enemy is fashioning the instrument of your demise, but do not accept defeat. The Enemy does not get the last word. An attitude of defeatism cripples us and robs us of the blessings available to us. There is a plan for every one of you. You may not be a preacher, and you may not be able to sing, but God has a plan for you.

It is critical that we be aware of our self-talk—that is, what we tell ourselves. Is your self-talk self-sabotaging? Self-talk such as "I'm good for nothing. I'm so weak. I'm not going to amount to anything" are self-fulfilling prophecies. You become what you think and confess. Other people will also put you down and have low expectations of you. Do not accept their opinion. They do not get to define you. That is God's job, not theirs.

As a child, I was disparaged by several people for a variety of reasons. When I was about age five, my grandmother and I entered a small grocery store. One of the patrons inquired, "A who fa pickney dis?" (Translation: whose child is this?) Another responded that I was Susan's grandson.

Yet another shopper had the unmitigated gall to offer, "After Sue (my grandmother) and Robert (my grandfather) could not have anything better looking than this." These people were not satisfied with insulting only me, but they meant to inflict the highest disrespect on my entire family, including my grandparents. As would be expected, my grandmother was most offended by this dismissive remark. She left the store and headed home, praying in her heart for me. She reached home, sat me on the edge of the bed, knelt before me, and began to bombard the throne of grace. She prayed against every negative thought and speech directed against me.

Many years later, I went back to Jamaica to attend the funeral of a family member. Many folks from my childhood were in attendance. I spoke at the funeral to a crowd of about seventeen hundred people, and they heard me speak but did not recognize who I was.

I went to the house afterward for the repast. During our socializing, someone called me by my name. One fellow who had known me in those early days and was perhaps one of those who had not expected me to amount to much could not believe the transformation in me. He kept asking, "A Barry dis? No, a Barry dis?" (Translation: Is this Barry? No, is this Barry?)

What was it that baffled them? My grandmother believed I was smart and handsome and could make it, in spite of my many disadvantages. She refused to let the local people define her boy. Instead of adopting a defeatist attitude toward me, Grandma held firmly to her belief that I could do anything to which I put my mind.

When you are tempted to engage in negative self-talk, just remember what God thinks of you and your prospects. "For I know the thoughts that I think toward you, saith the Lord, thoughts of peace, and not of evil, to give you an expected end" (Jer. 29:11). I also like the NIV's rendition, which says, "I know the plans I have for you." Not only is God thinking of you, but He has a plan for you to do you good.

All the fears that you have in life, God has a plan to disperse. All the weaknesses you feel in your spirit today, God has a plan to make strong. God has a plan to make the darkness light before you and to make the crooked path straight before you. With the knowledge that God has a plan for you, you can move away from the plains of defeatism unto the mountaintop of victory. You can escape the littleness of your fears and rejoice in the bigness of who God is. You can get away from the shallowness of your idiosyncrasies and insecurities and launch out into the depths of God's bountiful blessings. When Jesus says, "Lo, I am with you always, even unto the end of the world," this is grounds enough to move you away from defeatism to the lofty heights of victorious living (Matt. 28:20).

Once again, we go back to our theme text: "For though we walk in the flesh, we do not war after the flesh: For the weapons of our warfare are not carnal, but mighty through God to the pulling down of strong holds: Casting down imaginations, and every high thing that exalteth itself against the knowledge of God, and bringing into captivity every thought to the obedience of Christ" (2 Cor. 10: 3–5). With that text in mind, please tell every defeatist thought goodbye. And with that, sing this old hymn:

> I'm pressing on the upward way,
> New heights I'm gaining every day;
> Still praying as I onward bound,
> "Lord, plant my feet on higher ground."
>
> *Chorus*
> Lord, lift me up, and let me stand
> By faith on Canaan's tableland;
> A higher plane than I have found,
> Lord, plant my feet on higher ground.
>
> My heart has no desire to stay
> Where doubts arise and fears dismay;
> Though some may dwell where these abound,
> My prayer, my aim, is higher ground.[39]

A Prayer

Dear Lord, sometimes we see the glass as being half-empty as opposed to half-full. We often see the negative rather than the positive in life. As a result, we develop defeatist thoughts. Please help us to see things from Your point of view. In Jesus's name. Amen.

CHAPTER 14

Bring Every Proud Thought Captive to the Obedience of Christ

Pride goeth before destruction, and an haughty spirit before a fall.

—Proverbs 16:18

We now examine the thinking behind pride, with a view toward bringing prideful thoughts captive to the obedience of Christ. It is safe to say that in all of us, there is some measure of pride. Pride may not have originated in humanity, but we inherited it from Satan, and we seem to have no shortage of it. Pride boils down to an overappraisal of one's self. It is a belief that we are greater, prettier, more likable, and more worthwhile than we really are. This thinking has its origin in Satan. It was he who, in his prideful thinking, declared that he would exalt his throne above the stars of God and be like the Most High (Isa. 14:12–15).

As with the other dysfunctional thoughts and behaviors, prideful thought must be brought captive to the obedience of Christ. I argue that few things are more destructive and devastating to our Christian walk than an attitude of pride. To the extent that pride comes from within us, we must bring those thoughts captive to the obedience of Christ. Prideful thinking is the precursor for destruction. Solomon tells us, "Pride goeth before destruction, and an haughty spirit before a fall" (Prov. 16:18).

One way to minimize pride is to remind ourselves that our accomplishments are of God and not of us. Every gift and every talent that we have are gracious gifts from God, and must be used for His glory, not ours.

The Bible points out six things that God hates. When a seventh is added to that list, the whole thing becomes abominable to God. In other words, these seven things together are perfectly abhorrent to the nature of God.

Among these seven things is pride. Here's what the Word of God says: "These six things doth the Lord hate: yea, seven are an abomination unto him: *A proud look*, a lying tongue, and hands that shed innocent blood, An heart that deviseth wicked imaginations, feet that be swift in running to mischief, A false witness that speaketh lies, and he that soweth discord among brethren" (Prov. 6:16–19, emphasis added).

Imagine that, of all the things God hates, pride is first on the list. Notice that the list includes a proud look right alongside murder ("hands that shed innocent blood"). You will note also that some of the things we now consider big sins—adultery, witchcraft, theft, and so on—did not make this list. To be sure, the perfect, holy nature of God hates those sins too, but it is as though God is saying, "Of all the things that offend me, these seven are really the worst."

Some of us have a look that may be regarded as proud. I am often critiqued for the way I walk and the way I talk. To some, these come over as proud.

I learned to walk uprightly. It was something that my grandmother taught me a long time ago. Likewise, she insisted that I speak clearly. I try to enunciate as clearly as I can. In some circles, that comes off as prideful, although I do not mean it to be. My inclination is to speak rapidly, and so, to be understood, I slow down and speak distinctly. Because I read a lot, I have developed a vocabulary that is perhaps above average. To some, that seems over the top, so I try to write and speak as simply as I can. The degree to which I have succeeded or failed is for others to judge.

Even though my reasons for speaking the way I do are legitimate and have no prideful intent, I must be aware of my audience and adjust accordingly. If, for example, I am ministering to a group of people who are generally not educated, it would be prideful of me to throw out highfalutin theological words and concepts, knowing full well that I would lose my audience. I might sound smart to them, but my message will have been lost in the maze of prideful speech.

What is pride? Merriam-Webster dictionary renders the word *pride* as "an inordinate self-esteem, a bigger self-esteem than is required; conceit, proud or disdainful behavior or treatment, or ostentatious displays." When some folks walk in a room, you know that they want you to know that they are there. They are flamboyant and ostentatious in their presentation. Their attitude announces, "Look at me! I'm here!" It is like they are saying, "The rest of you little people are not worthy to share the same space with me, so take note."

The Hebrew word for pride is *ga'own* (pronounced gaw-ohn'), which in a negative sense means arrogance. There are at least two Greek words found in the King James Version that are translated as "pride." The first word is *huperephania* (pronounced hoop-er-ay-fan-ee'-ah), found in Mark 7:22. This word has a range of meanings according to NetBible.org: "haughtiness, arrogance, the character of one who, with a swollen estimate of his own powers or merits, looks down on others and even treats them with insolence and contempt."

The other Greek word for "pride" is *typhoo* (pronounced took-o'-o), found in 1 Timothy 3:6. It also has a range of meanings according to NetBible.org. Among them are "to raise a smoke, to make proud, puff up with pride, render insolent, to be puffed up with haughtiness or pride, to blind with pride or conceit, and to render foolish or stupid."

This latter word gives the idea that pride is something superficial. We cover ourselves in a cloud of meaningless smoke when we act a certain way. You may have heard the phrase "smoke and mirrors." It's a metaphor for a deceptive explanation or description. The source of this phrase is based on magicians' tricks, where they make objects seem to appear and disappear by extending or retracting mirrors amid a confusing burst of smoke. These magicians want their audience to believe something that is not true. That is what pride is. It shows off and projects something that is not really the truth. It causes others to believe that we are something that we are not.

Pride emerges from a false sense of self-worth. Let me be clear: having an appropriate level of self-esteem, grounded in the knowledge that all we are and all we have acquired is from God, is important for effective functioning. One of the things that counselors deal with is trying to instill in our clients an appropriate self-esteem. Some clients have been so beaten down for so long by others, and told that they are no good or that they will not amount to anything, that we do need to help them to build up their self-confidence.

Therefore, some appropriate level of pride is important. The right level of pride is essential as people interact with others in a variety of circumstances: to pursue a career, to start and maintain a meaningful romantic relationship, to function in social groups, and to generally feel good about oneself.

But having false pride is quite destructive. I believe an overly proud person is masking some shortcomings in their life. There are some husbands who need to compensate for some inadequacy or another, and therefore they bully their wives and children and blame everyone else. They do not recognize that the problem is not from without, but from within themselves. They feel a need to project themselves in a manner that onlookers may be deceived into believing demonstrates control. This sometimes takes the form of putting others down to build themselves up.

People behave in this manner because their pride will not allow them to admit their shortcomings. Such people compare themselves with others, minimizing their problems and exaggerating those of their opponents. Such comparisons are dysfunctional and betray an insecure person. The apostle Paul's assessment of such people gets to the core of the problem. He writes, "We do not dare to classify or compare ourselves with some who commend themselves. When they measure themselves by themselves and compare themselves with themselves, they are not wise" (2 Cor. 10:12). Such prideful comparisons demonstrate a gross lack of wisdom.

Hubristic pride—that is, overbearing pride—is rooted in narcissism (extreme selfishness, unreasonable self-love, a grandiose view of one's own talents, and an unreasonable craving for admiration). The Bible speaks extensively against pride, because God wants us to have a true sense of who we are, as juxtaposed with who He is.

In the rest of this chapter, I wish to speak about three things: a proud person does not live in the will of God, a proud heart is a precursor to destruction, and the path to exaltation is through humility.

A Proud Person Does Not Live in the Will of God

Despite our profession to the contrary, when we think of ourselves more highly than we should—that is, when we harbor prideful thoughts about ourselves and our accomplishments—we are outside God's will. In such a case, we are truly not seeking God, and we are not seeing ourselves the way God sees us. We may attempt to play the part of a true believer, but those proud thoughts and actions tell a different story altogether.

Here is what the Word of God says about pride: "The wicked, through the pride of his countenance, will not seek after God: God is not in all his thoughts" (Ps. 10:4). Pride is a product of wickedness, and in such a state, the prideful, wicked person does not think of seeking God. There is no room in their heart for God.

A proud Christian is one who does not know the holiness of God, for in the presence of God's refulgent holiness and majesty, we see ourselves for who we really are. When Isaiah encountered the holiness and majesty of God, he cried out, "Woe to me! … I am ruined! For I am a man of unclean lips, and I live among a people of unclean lips, and my eyes have seen the King, the LORD Almighty" (Isa. 6:5 NIV). No matter how great we thought our accomplishments were, no matter how righteous we were led to believe ourselves to be prior to seeing God's holiness, once we recognize it, it makes our holiness look like filthy rags by comparison (Isa. 64:6).

The proud person does not really fear the Lord. If the proud person knew God and His awesome power, which always engenders fear in those closest to Him, how could they walk away feeling or thinking that there is anything about them that is worthwhile? As compared to the Almighty God, what about us could be worthy of pride? When the believer truly fears God, pride is as far from them as the east is from the west. In the book of Proverbs, we read, "The fear of the Lord is to hate evil: pride, and arrogancy, and the evil way, and the froward mouth, do I hate" (Prov. 8:13).

Pride is not a product of God's kingdom. In God's kingdom, which is in the hearts of His children, where He rules and reigns, there is no room for pride. The Bible declares that the pride of life is not of the Father but of the world (1 John 2:16). Where, then, does pride come from? It came from a fallen world in which the Devil now holds sway over unregenerate people. The Bible calls the Devil "the god of this world" (2 Cor. 4:4). As I noted earlier, it was the Devil in his prideful heart in heaven who decided to challenge God. Having been expelled from heaven, he comes to earth and infuses in people's hearts that spirit of pride.

Those possessing a spirit of pride demonstrate the evil spirit of the last days. The apostle Paul forewarned Timothy that this would be the case (2 Tim. 3:1–5). He wrote that in the last days, people will be lovers of their own selves—covetous, boasting, and proud. As believers, we need to avoid these: "from those, turn away" (2 Tim. 3:5).

In case you do not know, each of us has the propensity to be proud. It is in our nature. A person with a prideful heart does not seek after God. If one is not seeking after God, one will never know God's will. Not only is the proud person not in God's will, but pride leads to destruction (Prov. 16:18).

A Proud Heart Is a Precursor to Destruction

All too often we observe men and women at the zenith of their power, popularity, and notoriety. No sooner do they begin to think of themselves as being above the rest and invincible, than they head for a tragic fall from grace. One must wonder to what extent these prideful people hurt others on the way up. Whom did they deprive of their rights? How did they get there? Did God put them there? When they attained their positions of power, did they give glory to God for it? Did they use their power to benefit others or only for self-aggrandizement?

There is nothing wrong with God's people being in positions of power. I immediately think of Daniel, Shadrach, Meshach, and Abednego, who in the land of their captivity rose to positions of prominence. From the biblical evidence, these servants of God remained humble despite their prominence. No doubt these men understood that they were placed in these positions of power because of God's grace, and not because of any inherent goodness. If they had used their power for any other purpose than to glorify God, they would not have had the positive outcomes that they experienced.

When we find ourselves in high positions, there is no place for pride. We should realize that we did not get there because we earned it. When we recognize that it was God who promoted us, we must seek to promote His glory. If we instead turn around and begin to be lifted up in pride, we stand in jeopardy of being disoriented by God. In other words, God may cause confusion in our affairs so that we become a shocking spectacle before the world.

I make the case that a proud heart is a precursor to destruction. Think of Nebuchadnezzar, king of Babylon. He was driven away from people and lived with wild animals for seven years (see Daniel 4). At the root of his troubles was a proud heart. In driving him from his throne and into the fields, the Lord told him, "And seven times shall pass over thee, till thou know that the most High ruleth in the kingdom of men, and giveth it to whomsoever he will" (Dan. 4:25). Evidently Nebuchadnezzar did not understand this, and so the Lord had to show him that the Lord is sovereign, and that Nebuchadnezzar reigned at God's pleasure.

Another sign of a prideful heart is the tendency to forget the people who are in part responsible for the success we have achieved. The concept of a self-made man is a misnomer, if self-made is to be understood to mean that no one else contributed to that success. That is a false notion, rooted in pride. The truth of the matter is, no matter how smart we are, we did not make it all alone. Somebody along the way contributed to our success, be it our parents, siblings, friends, and even strangers.

If you are a great preacher, and you can deliver a sermon better than your pastor, you should realize that first, you owe your abilities to God. He could easily have caused you to have a speech impediment, so that you could not preach. So the first person to be thankful to is God. Then you must be thankful to your pastor, who gave you the opportunity to grow. The same is true for a great singer and for all who possess great gifts.

It is a sign of arrogance for one to assume that one has achieved all one's accomplishments because of one's raw talent alone. This is simply not the case. Many people along the way contributed, one way or another, to your success. My late pastor used to tell me that we, his sons whom he had nurtured, had become better preachers than he ever was. Whatever element of truth there may have been to his observation, it would have been sinful for us to show up our pastor. To us he was still our pastor, and we spoke to him with "yes, sir" and "no, sir," because if he had not given us numerous opportunities to grow, we would not have realized our potentials.

We acknowledge that pride is part of the human nature. But as Christians, we must fight against its manifestation at every turn. Shakespeare observed, through the character of Brutus, "But 'tis a common proof that lowliness is young ambition's ladder, whereto the climber upward turns his face, but when he once attains the upmost round, he then unto the ladder turns his back, looks in the clouds, scorning the base degrees by which he did ascend."[40] What did Shakespeare mean? Simply put, he was saying that it is common knowledge that ambitious young people use humility to go where they want to get in life. Yet when they have arrived at their goals, they turn their backs on those who have helped them along the way. As they reach for the skies they scorn those who helped them get where they are. That is one of the ways pride manifests itself. It causes one to forget the contributions of others to one's success.

At times, our best strategy is to keep a low profile. Sometimes we should stay behind the scenes and wait until God exalts us in due season. Striving to be always on the highest rung may not be the best approach to living. Reaching to that height may lead us to pride, which is a precursor to destruction. Jamaicans have a saying, "The higher the monkey climbs, the more he is exposed." This exposure may not be the best thing. The monkey so exposed presents an excellent target for those who hunt monkeys.

Some people are so hungry for power that they do not wait to be appointed to higher offices. Instead, they are self-appointed. Some years ago, I was invited to preach a revival out of state. On the night of our arrival, I was invited, as the guest preacher, to sit in a reserved chair on the platform.

A few moments later, a young man came into the sanctuary. Having observed me seated in that chair, he came to me and told me in no uncertain terms that I was sitting in his seat, but that he would "allow" me to continue sitting there. I told him that I was so sorry, but I had been escorted to that seat by an usher. He then introduced himself to me as apostle so and so, and then told me that it would be fine if I continued sitting there.

After the revival was over, the pastor solicited my opinion on this fellow. I told the pastor that I thought that he was interesting. The pastor admitted that she was having a difficult time knowing how to handle him. She indicated that she had called his former pastor for a recommendation, and was told that the young man had never been appointed as apostle in that congregation. That church did not even recognize the office of apostle for the contemporary church. As it turned out, this fellow was a novice. He was a self-appointed apostle who thought that, by virtue of this title, he should always have a reserved seat on the platform.

I am confident that most people who clamor after power and recognition are not as blatant as this fellow was. Yet in subtler ways, this type of attitude is displayed more frequently in the body of Christ than should ever be the case. Many are blinded by titles and recognition. They must be addressed by their title or they are offended. The best title that a Christian should crave is to be called "child of God" or "servant of God."

Sometimes the way we preachers are treated leads us to believe that we are more important and greater than we really are. Often when I am invited to preach outside of our church organization, those who extend the invitation ask me for my biography to print in their program. They may read it aloud prior to my preaching. Sometimes when they ask me what I would like to have said about me, I tell them, "I am Brother Barrington Hibbert, I am a child of God, and I love God. Please dispense with the long biography."

My biography may be impressive on paper. Yes, it contains six degrees and some accomplishments, but it does not talk about my flaws and failures. Therefore, it is not a true reflection of who I am. If people knew me as God knows me, perhaps they would not want me in their pulpits, for like all Christians, I am an imperfect man.

Many times when I arrive at these meetings, I am amused by the special treatment that I receive. Sometimes my host assigns me a person as my armor bearer, a sort of an adjutant to walk before me, carrying my Bible. It is as though they are declaring, "Behold, he cometh; be attentive." I have seen this done for others, and then the sermon did not live up to the hype. I suppose some who have heard me preach have come to that same conclusion about me. I would rather carry my own Bible to the pulpit. I would rather dispense with the biography, so long as I am able to have a word from the throne of God to deliver to His people. Just let me have an anointing from God, so when I get done saying, "thus saith the Lord," somebody's heart is touched, some soul is convicted of their sins and turns to Christ, and above all, God always gets the glory.

I earlier quoted Proverbs 16:18, which reads, "Pride goeth before destruction, and an haughty spirit before a fall." If I heard my grandmother repeat this verse once, I heard it from her a thousand times. Every time we children began to act a bit too high-minded, we would hear, "Pride goeth before destruction, and an haughty spirit before a fall."

Grandma never seemed to forget where she came from. Therefore, in her mind, there was no room for foolish pride. We went from living in a two-room house in a rural part of Jamaica, with a detached kitchen, detached toilet, no running water, no electricity, and no shower, to what seemed then to be a big house in the capital city of Kingston. We hired a full-time helper to wash, clean, and cook, and we thought we had arrived. We had a maid now! As children, we had an attitude.

One of these helpers was a relative of ours. My grandmother insisted on treating her as a family member and not as a maid. We thought that was simply ridiculous. In our minds, she was a maid, being paid by us. Therefore, she should be given a lower status than the rest of us.

One Christmas season, this relative wanted to accompany us on an evening walk. We were not having it. She ran in and complained to Grandma of this slight. I was sure that Grandma would tell her to sit herself down. No. Grandma did no such thing. She told us that if that child could not go along with us, none of us would go.

Since we all wanted to go, we begrudgingly told our relative to come along. We straitly commanded her to shut her mouth and not say anything to us. Of course, we did this outside of Grandma's hearing.

As the days progressed, Grandma realized that we needed an

attitude adjustment. She called us together and made it abundantly clear that if we insisted on treating this young lady as a maid, she would send her back to her parents. Should that happen, we would go back to doing that work again. That helped to reshape our thinking about how to treat her.

My grandmother was trying to teach us that we should never forget from whence we came. I personally did not like the young lady because I thought she got too much attention from Grandma. Grandma was not concerned about our feelings. She was trying to teach us something about how we should behave toward each other. In her mind, humility was the way to go.

I needed to remember that I was just a lowly, fatherless boy myself. Just a few years before, I had spent time out of school at ages ten, eleven, and twelve, for six to eight weeks at a time, walking behind a donkey, transporting sugar cane from the field to the main road during the harvest. I made these trips in the heat of the sun, barefooted, from eight in the morning to six at night until the harvest was over. How could I now put anyone down? I really had no basis for doing so, and yet even such a poor boy as me could find room in his heart for pride. Thanks to my godly grandmother, she drove that away from me. But even with her training, if the truth be known, sometimes I still struggle with such feelings.

How destructive is pride? "A man's pride shall bring him low: but honour shall uphold the humble in spirit" (Prov. 29:23). Do you want to succeed in life? Become humble before God and man. The Word tells us that pride will bring a person low. Proud people who abuse other people are not liked very much. People cannot wait to chop them down.

In New York a few years ago, there was a governor who won by a large majority of the votes. He went to Albany saying that he was going to steamroll over anyone who stood in his way. It did not take too long before he was brought low and had to resign. In his pride and arrogance, he had made many enemies along the way. When their opportunity came to get revenge, they showed no mercy.

In the 1980s, there was a very popular television preacher whose talent and zeal were remarkable. He was a singer and preacher of the highest caliber. When he learned that another televangelist's ministry was compromised by some financial irregularities, this preacher went after his rival with a vengeance. As it turned out, this preacher himself had some skeletons in his closet, which came out not long after. He also headed for a fall. While his ministry survived, it was only a fraction of what it had been. The only good thing that came out of this is that from all accounts, this preacher seemed more humble and compassionate afterward than he had been previously. Thank God for His mercies and grace. As pride is a precursor to destruction, let us drop our pride and turn to God in earnest.

The Path to Exaltation Starts with Humility

Since pride is the precursor to destruction, what is the antidote? The antidote, or cure, is humility. The path to exaltation is through humility. At first that may seem counterintuitive. One may ask, "If I wish to advance myself, why should I be humble? Shouldn't I seek to be seen and heard if I want to advance in this world?" Yes, to be sure, that is the way to do it in this world.

I was once told, when I worked at a large telecommunications firm, to "publish or perish." They were telling us that unless we are willing to talk and write about what we were doing, we would experience a *careerous interruptus* (my made-up Latin for "interrupted career").

So keeping a low profile and taking a low seat is not a recommended strategy for people who desire to climb the corporate ladder. And yet that is precisely the path we are asked to take as members of the body of Christ. Jesus once told His audience, "Beware of the scribes, which desire to walk in long robes, and love greetings in the markets, and the highest seats in the synagogues, and the chief rooms at feasts" (Luke 20:46).

Contrary to what the scribes did, Jesus admonished them that when they were invited to a function, they should take a lower seat, so that the only place they could go from there was to a higher seat, at the request of the host. If, on the other hand, they assumed a seat of honor that was not reserved for them, the host would be obliged to relegate them to a lower seat if another person of a higher status was in attendance (Luke 14:8–9). Jesus was not teaching something that He was unwilling to do. This was the way He lived His life.

Paul tells us that Jesus Christ's exaltation came after His humiliating death. He emptied himself of all the trappings of Godness and assumed the office of a servant, made in the form of a man. He became obedient unto death, the most ignominious death of all—death on a cross (Phil. 2:5–11). This emptying of Himself is what theologians call the *kenosis*. Kenosis means that although Jesus was God, He dispensed with the outward manifestations of His majesty, not regarding them a thing to be grasped and exploited for personal gain. Instead, He let them go so that He could identify with humanity, and die to save us.

There is nothing fundamentally sinful about someone wanting to achieve significance or even greatness, if this status can be used for the greater good. If I wish to be a great neurosurgeon to help people and bring glory to God, then that is not in itself a bad thing. If my desire to be an excellent preacher and teacher of God's Word is intended to win souls for Christ, to disciple believers to imitate Christ, and to perfect the saints for the kingdom of Christ, so that God is glorified, then those are noble goals and should be encouraged. If, however, my primary purpose is to gain fame, fortune, and notoriety, then my motives are wrong, and are based on pride and arrogance.

You wish to be great? I think everybody should strive for greatness if greatness is used to God's glory. No matter how talented we are, however, we must recognize that the ultimate source of our greatness is God. All our gifts and talents find their source in God, who graciously bestowed these on us although we are underserving.

People with great intellects have not cultivated intelligence on their own account. They had to start with the basic raw material, and that is a gift of God. It is not hard to see that intellect is not altogether genetic. There are parents with very low IQs who produce brilliant children. The reverse is also true. It is equally easy to find siblings with vastly disparate intelligence. If intelligence were inherited, it would follow that if my father was a genius, then so would I be, but that is not exactly the case. Even if one could make a case that intelligence is passed down in the genes, the baby has nothing to do with the choice in the first place. One has to conclude that God placed the baby there. Therefore, the glory belongs to Him.

The path to exaltation is through humility. This is how things are done in the kingdom of God. In the secular world, there are limited resources. It is like a favorite pie at Thanksgiving. The size of the slice you get will determine what is left over for me; therefore, we fight to get as much we can.

In God's economy, however, there are unlimited resources, so what is mine will be mine, and what is yours is yours. When I receive all that God has designed for me, it will in no way take away from what God has reserved for you. To get what God has for you, all you have to do is "humble yourselves in the sight of the Lord, and he shall lift you up" (James 4:10).

We may be politically astute enough to convince our leaders to lift us up, but if God does not lift us up too, we are going to fall. I am convinced also that if God has determined to bless you, it really does not matter what others have to say about it. They cannot stop the hand of God. The Lord assured His people, "'For I know the plans I have for you,' declares the LORD, 'plans to prosper you and not to harm you, plans to give you hope and a future'" (Jer. 29:11 NIV).

You will recognize this is God's promise to Judah to bring them back from the land of their captivity. Their restoration to the land of their birth was not dependent on the generosity of anyone. Indeed, God would use a future Persian king to facilitate their release, but it was God who initiated and conducted their release, not the Persian king. The king was an instrument in God's hands. God simply drafted him in His orchestrated plan for Judah's release. He had to release Judah, and that on God's timeline, because God made him do it.

That Persian king could have no more objections to God's mandate for Judah's release than the light had in the beginning of the creation when God said, "Let there be light" (Gen. 1:3). When God said, "Let there be light," there was light. There was no debating of the issue. There was no negotiating of terms. By divine imperative, God said it, and it was done. Understanding that no forces in heaven or on earth can resist God's sovereign will should cause His people to humbly rest in Him and allow Him to work on their behalf.

People do not gain grace and favor with God by being proud. On the contrary, as I have been hammering home, humility is the path to exaltation. It has been said that "the way up is the way down." Let me put this another way. If God's people want to stand tall before God and humanity, they must first bow low at God's feet. Peter wrote, "Likewise, ye younger, submit yourselves unto the elder, yea, all of you be subject one to another, and be clothed with humility: for God resisteth the proud, and giveth grace to the humble" (1 Pet. 5:5).

"God resisteth the proud." That is not a hopeful endeavor for the proud. It is interesting that Peter did not say that God ignores the proud, or that God reasons with the proud. God resists the proud. God is not passive toward an attitude of pride. The word *resist* here means that God rages in battle against the proud. In other words, to assume the attitude of pride is to summon God to battle against oneself. That is an awfully silly move. If God is resisting me, He will win every time. And where does that leave me? A loser every time!

As I write this, I am convicted by the Holy Ghost that I still struggle with pride, despite my efforts to rid myself of it. I recognize that I cannot, of myself, entirely eradicate this spiritual cancer. I have not arrived completely at perfection. God is still working on me, and I hope that you allow Him to work on you too.

Yes. I must admit, I do have a little proudish thing going on in me sometimes. It is something I continue to pray about. How does this manifest itself in my life? Well, sometimes when I preach a message, and people seem genuinely blessed by it, the thought enters my mind that this result evidences my good exegetical preparation, focused prayer life, and decent oratory skills. When people make kind compliments to me in these instances, I have to say to them "Thank you, but to God be the glory," and keep saying it to avoid taking the credit for myself.

I pray for humility, for I recognize that God could have confounded me just as easily before the congregation, notwithstanding my preparation. To be sure, this is not an excuse for not being diligent in preparing to speak for God. Study and prayer are indispensable tools in preparing to minister the Word. But the preacher must recognize that the results are all up to God.

God resists the proud. This is an active resistance. He fights against the proud, but He gives grace to the humble. I am reminded of a Broadway musical of the 1970s titled *Your Arms Too Short to Box with God*. Not having seen the play, I can only imagine what the author's intent was. My take on it is simple: if you presume to get into the cosmic ring with the all-eternity Champion of the universe, you will suffer the most crushing defeat of all the ages.

If we hope to succeed as Christians, we must have a change of mind as to who we really are, as juxtaposed to God. We need to bring all proud thoughts captive to the obedience of Christ. I have argued throughout that we fight the battles for our souls in the sphere of our minds. That is where the Devil attacks us first and foremost.

When was the last time you were physically attacked and beaten up in church? Fortunately, very few of us have ever been beaten up anywhere. If we had a church where people came to physically fight each other, that would be dangerous. We would have to have the police at our churches each Sunday to keep the peace. But as bad as that would be, worse than physical fighting is going on in our churches, and sometimes we do not even know where it is coming from. We need to guard our minds and assume a humble mind-set before God.

I wish to say once more that the path to exaltation is through humility. Our primary example is Jesus Christ. His exaltation followed His humiliation (Phil. 2:5–11). The Bible says that because of this humiliation, God has also highly exalted Jesus and given Him a name which is above every name. That at the name of Jesus, every knee should bow. The thief on the cross who was reviling Him must bow. The angels in heaven must bow. The Devil in hell must bow to Him. But before He received that position of exaltation, He humbled Himself and became obedient to death, even death on the cross.

We must bring every proud thought captive to the obedience of Christ. An appropriate Christ-centered appraisal of ourselves will bring us to our knees. Let us remember that our greatness does not come from self-promotion or from putting others down. Far from it! Instead, it comes for humility. Jesus declared, "Whosoever therefore shall humble himself as this little child, the same is greatest in the kingdom of heaven" (Matt. 18:4). Let us bring every proud thought captive to the obedience of Christ.

A Prayer

Heavenly Father, please keep us from embracing thoughts of pride, for Your Word tells us, "Pride goeth before destruction, and an haughty spirit before a fall" (Prov. 16:18). Help us, dear Lord, to stand in humility. In Jesus's name. Amen.

CHAPTER 15

Bring Every Murmuring Thought Captive to the Obedience of Christ

> *A basic cause of murmuring is that too many of us seem to expect that life will flow ever smoothly, featuring an unbroken chain of green lights with empty parking places just in front of our destinations.*
>
> —Neal A. Maxwell

As I earlier disclosed, some years ago, the Lord laid it on my heart to preach about the impact of the thought life upon believers' functioning. What I had planned as a two-part sermon turned out to be something far more comprehensive. For as I exegeted the text 2 Corinthians 10:3–5, it became clear to me that I needed to lay out many of the areas of our lives that we must bring captive to the obedience of Christ. Each week the Lord gave me something additional that we must bring captive to Christ's authority.

Along the way, I talked about the mind, and about the battles that go on there for the control of our souls. I have argued that I believe that these battles are fought and either won or lost in the mind. These battles did not start with us, and they will not end with us. The initial battle started in heaven, where the Devil issued a challenge to the Most High God. Having been summarily dispatched from heaven and destined for hell, the Devil roams about the world, doing his diabolical business. We observe the first glimpse of his handiwork when he deceived Adam and Eve in the garden of Eden. From that time, a cosmic battle has been pitched, and it continues to the present moment.

The biblical evidence for the commencement of the battle is this: "And the LORD God said unto the serpent, Because thou hast done this, thou art cursed above all cattle, and above every beast of the field; upon thy belly shalt thou go, and dust shalt thou eat all the days of thy life: And I will put enmity between thee and the woman, and between thy seed and her seed; it shall bruise thy head, and thou shalt bruise his heel" (Gen. 3:14–15). It is quite clear that this enmity between the seed of the woman and that of the serpent will take its toll. While in the end the seed of the serpent (Satan and his minions) will lose, he will leave his mark in terms of his bruising of the heel of the seed of the woman (Christ, and those that are in Christ). It should be clear that the implements of this warfare are not swords or guns, but ideas. In other words, the battle rages in people's minds.

In this book, I have identified several thoughts that must be brought under Christ's control if we are to live victorious lives. I now examine the tendency of people to murmur and complain when things are not going well. As in previous chapters, my objective is to examine the thinking behind murmuring with a view toward bringing every murmuring thought captive to the obedience of Christ.

These subjects with which we have dealt are not meant to be an exhaustive, all-inclusive list of thoughts about which we need to be concerned. I think that by addressing the ones we have, the Holy Spirit is telling us that we need to shore up our thought lives in these critical areas, so that we can develop transformed kingdom-mentality thinking.

When believers murmur, this is displeasing to God. We see evidence of this in the Old Testament as the children of Israel were passing through the desert (Exod. 15:24, 16:2, 17:3; Num. 14:2, 29, 16:41; Deut. 1:27; Josh. 19:18). There were grave consequences to Israel for murmuring against God. Those who did so were not permitted to enter the Promised Land. The Bible tells us that their carcasses fell in the wilderness (Num. 14:29).

The apostle Paul warned the Corinthians not to murmur, and used the Old Testament as the basis for this warning. Paul pointed out that because of their murmuring, the people were destroyed by serpents (1 Cor. 10:9–11). Paul makes it clear that these things happened for our admonition. In other words, God allowed them to happen, and recorded them in Scripture that we might take heed.

I believe that if we are listening to God's Word, the transformation process of the inner person will have begun. The Holy Spirit's aim, I believe, is to get us to become transformed by renewing of our minds daily. If we can fill our thoughts with positive thinking, positive things will begin to happen to us. We will begin to experience an inner change.

I am not so concerned about outward conformity, which is contrived to satisfy a particular cultural emphasis. I am more concerned about a transformation that takes place in the innermost being. When this transformation takes place, we will find ourselves compliant with the rules of the church. Leaders could be successful in forcing people to conform to outward rules and requirements before the inward person is changed. But as soon as they are no longer being observed by these leaders, the people will revert to what comes naturally to them. When the Holy Spirit has caused a transformation from the inside, believers are much easier to direct.

In this chapter, we will deal with our tendency to murmur, and discuss how to bring those murmuring thoughts captive to the obedience of Christ. What is a murmur? Webster's says that the word *murmur* refers to a half-suppressed or muttered complaint. The Hebrew word that the King's James Version translates as "murmur" is *luwn*, which means to grumble, to complain, or to murmur. There is a Greek word as well, *gongosu*, which simply means to grumble.

Murmuring is not a good trait and does not reflect a good Christian character. Some years ago, my Sunday school teacher told us a story of a lady who married a gentleman and made his life miserable by her constant murmuring. She murmured, complained, and nagged him day after day. No matter how hard he tried, he could never do anything right in her estimation. He could complete a project 98 percent correctly and be proud of his work, but she could not see the 98 percent completion. She focused on the 2 percent left incomplete and was relentless in her complaints.

World War II broke out, and while he did not look forward to the prospect of fighting overseas and possibly dying, the gentleman thought that nothing was as bad as living with his murmuring wife. So he volunteered for military service. He was soon sent to the European theatre, and immediately was engaged in active combat. While there, he looked forward to receiving his mail packet from home. His mother was encouraging and prayerful, but each letter he received from his wife had some complaint. At first, he tried to write her some encouragement, but nothing he said to her through letters made any positive impact. She continued murmuring. Soon, he dreaded opening her letters, because he knew they would make him really depressed.

When he could abide her letters no more, he wrote to her, saying, "Betsy, stop writing me so I could fight this war in peace." To him fighting the war was less dangerous, more peaceful, and less taxing on his psychology and emotions than her relentless murmuring letters.

I read a funny story on the internet about a murmuring, hard-to-please husband. His wife could never satisfy him in anything; he always found something about which to complain. If she fried his egg for breakfast, he complained that she should have boiled it. If she scrambled it, he complained that it was too dry or too moist.

One day, they had only two eggs remaining. The eggs were the same color and same size. He indicated that he wanted a boiled egg and described just the way he wanted it. The poor wife went to the kitchen and made the perfect boiled egg, just the way he wanted it. This man sat down to breakfast. He examined the egg and could find nothing wrong with it, Instead of saying thank you, his response was "Why did you boil the wrong egg?"

These two anecdotes may have been contrived, but they make the point; some people are habitual complainers who cannot be pleased.

I think Moses must have felt something similar when he was trying to lead God's people through the wilderness to the Promised Land. Nothing he did or that God did through him could please those set-apart people of God. One would expect that a people who had witnessed God's mighty hand and strong arms as He manhandled Pharaoh (or rather, "Godhandled" him) would have learned to trust Him and not murmur. Alas, that was not the case. The more God did on their behalf, the more they demanded. The more they got what they wanted, the more they grumbled and complained.

Murmuring demonstrates an unthankful and discontented heart. To murmur is to say we are not happy with what God has done on our behalf. We need to find a way to see the hand of God even in our direst situations.

It is not easy, but we need to say to God, "My life is in your hands. The things that happen to me could never have happened unless you ordained them. And Lord, if you ordain them, they must be for a good purpose."

Not everything that happens to us is good. Frankly, some things are just bad. But the Bible assures us, "And we know that all things work together for good to them that love God, to them who are the called according to *his* purpose" (Rom. 8:28).

The reader will permit me to do some more self-disclosure at this juncture. I am not known to be a murmurer or complainer—at least, not in public. I tend to have a stoic affect in public, but my heart and thought processes are not seen. Some things have happened in my family over the last fifteen years that have shaken me to the very core of my being. And sometimes in my quiet moments, I complain to God. I ask often, "Why me?" I even question God as to whether He has called me to ministry, particularly when things are not going as I think they should.

If there is anything positive about me in these times, it is that I thank God for who He is at the beginning and end of my complaints. But, sadly, I do complain, and I recognize that I must bring that complaining tendency captive to the obedience of Christ.

We should assume the attitude of King David, who, having been chastened and hounded by his enemies, and faced with what seemed to him as certain death, had the presence of mind to write, "Yea, though I walk through the valley of the shadow of death, I will fear no evil: for thou art with me; thy rod and thy staff they comfort me" (Ps. 23:4).

David's perspective was the polar opposite of a murmuring disposition. He recognized the dangers that he was facing, but he knew that if God was with him, he would be fine. Despite his difficulties, David did not become cynical or pessimistic. Rather, he was able to see God's hand in his most desperate situations. Therefore, David decided not to murmur. Even in the psalms of lament, where David poured out his complaints to God, he always bracketed them with acknowledgment of God's sovereignty and his trust in God.

As I observed earlier, the attitude of the Israelites coming through the wilderness was the exact opposite of David's attitude. It did not matter what God had done for them; they just looked for the next opportunity to murmur.

If you have a child you are raising, and that child is always complaining, it is a very heartrending and discouraging thing. People say that the squeaky wheel gets the grease, meaning that if you talk and complain a lot, you will get your way. But sometimes when it comes to parenting, that tactic does not work. A murmuring child annoys his parents and leaves everyone frustrated. A better approach is simply to be grateful for what you have.

I have observed many times in my work as a mental health counselor that children associate gifts with their parents' love. They believe that the more gifts they receive from their parents, the more their parents love them. When parents cannot afford gifts, or when they have decided that gifts are not appropriate, that child becomes extremely upset and concludes that their parents do not love them. They put so much pressure on their parents that sometimes, even though the parents really cannot afford it, the parents relent and put themselves in debt to stop the murmuring child. Some children feel that they must have the latest sneakers that cost hundreds of dollars, or the latest electronic game and all the accessories. If the parents refuse to give those things to them, they murmur and ask, "Why not? Everyone has it." They feel that their lives are ruined because they do not have the latest trendy thing.

The murmuring attitude comes about when people feel that they must have instant gratification. The attitude of "I want what I want when I want it" or "I want it because I deserve it" is not godly. There are times when God simply tells us to wait. David wrote, "Wait on the LORD: be of good courage, and he shall strengthen thine heart: wait, I say, on the LORD" (Ps. 27:14). Sometimes the answer is "Wait." At other times it is simply "no." Sometimes the answer is neither yes nor no, but silence. Even then, believers are called upon to trust God and not to murmur.

When Israel was going through the wilderness for forty years, they constantly murmured against God and against Moses. One would think that, given these biblical examples, Christians today would know better than to murmur. Alas, we are no different from those who preceded us in many particulars. Sometimes we look at our leaders and think they must cross all their *T*s and dot all their *I*s. When those leaders make one mistake, we cut them down to nothing. We murmur and are ready to assemble a search committee for a new pastor. We seem often to fail to realize that leaders are human beings who need our support.

The question is, why are we complaining to the leaders of our churches and not to God? Rather than murmuring and complaining to the leaders and about the leaders, we should be talking to God. When we complain, grumble, and murmur to people, we make ourselves and them miserable, because people cannot help us in the way we need to be helped. The Psalms provide us ample examples of people pouring out their complaints to God, and that should be our model. Please read Psalm 142, which serves as a good example of pouring out to God.

David's complaint during his troubles was directed to God and not unto man. Further, his complaint shows a reliance on God for his deliverance. "I cried unto thee, O LORD: I said, Thou art my refuge and my portion in the land of the living" (Ps. 142:5). The argument against murmuring is not to suggest that a person has no outlet to express their pain. Rather, it is to suggest that the tendency to murmur over things, rather than bringing our troubles to God, must be brought under Christ's control.

In high school, I would murmur and complain every day to my Spanish teacher because of what I perceived to be her inability to control her class. I would say, "Miss ______, why can't you get this class in order? Why can't you get these children to keep the class clean?"

I believe that my murmuring, well-intentioned as it was, was as much a source of annoyance to this teacher as was the rowdiness of these students. She would say to me in her deep accent, and with such frustration, "Barrington, every day you come to class, I am telling you go directly to your seat. Don't complain to me; complain to the principal. Barrington, you talk, talk, talk too much. You talk like an old lady." She would sometimes throw her hands in the air, look up to the ceiling, and exclaim, "O God, give me strength." She would go on to threaten me: "Sweetie, you give me trouble in the class, I'll give you trouble in your grades. Okay, sweetie—laugh now, cry later."

My murmuring and complaining got us nowhere. All I accomplished was frustrating her and jeopardizing my grades. As a matter of fact, one marking period she lowered my grade from my usual *A* to a *B*. When I went to her to complain, she laughed at me and reminded me that she had warned me. She said, "Barrington, now I am laughing and you are crying. Go take your seat."

Later, when I got home, I complained to my mother about the grade. I also told her why the teacher had graded me that way. Far from being sympathetic to me, the looks my mother gave me left me with the distinct impression that she was going to seriously hurt me. So my protestation was brief, and I slid out of her presence lest evil should befall me there and then. As a Christian boy, instead of murmuring to this teacher, I should have been praying that God would give her strength.

When we face difficult circumstances in our lives, instead of complaining to the wrong person, we need to bring the thought of murmuring to Christ. We need to look to God and say, "God, I want to give you my life and its affairs. Please help me to fully put my trust in you and to not become anxious, murmur, or complain over things I cannot change."

I am convinced that as Christians, we talk entirely too much. Particularly those of us who live in the West struggle with silence and quiet contemplation and meditation. Our days are filled with activities—work, social media, family, friends—and little or no time to be with God and self in quiet musings. When things are not going our way, we become agitated, and we find an outlet to complain and murmur.

But simply by being still and quiet in God's presence, we may find the meaning and solutions to our struggles. Listen to the psalmist's observation and admonition: "He maketh wars to cease unto the end of the earth; he breaketh the bow, and cutteth the spear in sunder; he burneth the chariot in the fire. Be still, and know that I am God: I will be exalted among the heathen, I will be exalted in the earth. The LORD of hosts is with us; the God of Jacob is our refuge. Selah" (Ps. 46:9–11).

Allow me to presume to enter the inner sanctum of the Godhead and capture an imaginary dialogue when God sees His redeemed children murmuring and complaining. "I created them in love. When they rejected me, in love I sent my Son to die for them. I have given the Holy Ghost to protect them. I have given them my Word to preserve them. I have given them my promises to assure them. But every time something seems to be going wrong, they murmur and complain. What else must I do with these murmuring people?" A murmuring disposition does not endear us to God. It displeases Him much.

The attitude of murmuring shows a forgetful and ungrateful heart that evokes the wrath of God. In the book of Numbers, we see this at work. The people murmured against Moses and against God not long after they had been miraculously released from centuries of slavery by God's mighty hand. One would think that these people, having seen the awesome power of God break the will of the king of Egypt and destroy his army in the Red Sea, would trust God implicitly. Their murmuring was so great that God proposed to kill them all in the wilderness. It took the intercessory prayers of Moses to stay God's wrath.

Even though God relented from executing His purpose of killing them in short order, He implemented a different punishment. Of all those who left Egypt and were over twenty years old, He only permitted Joshua and Caleb to enter the Promised Land. So when God threatened to kill them, He did not really change His mind. He simply delayed the execution of His plan to save His name, lest the nations around should have said, that whereas He had the power to take them out of Egypt, He was not capable of taking them into the promised place of rest.

Even God's chosen vessel, Moses, did not make it to the Promised Land. It was not by reason of his murmurings, but because the murmuring and complaining people caused him to sin. Moses's failure to enter the Promised Land is very much to be lamented. If the people had simply been contented with God's provision and willing to trust Him, Moses would not have gotten so angry as to strike the rock twice.

The rock that Moses struck represented Christ. When the people lacked water, God instructed Moses to strike the rock, which he did, and fresh, clean water came. The striking of the rock and the refreshing, life-giving water that gushed from it signify the shedding of the blood of Jesus Christ, by which blood His chosen people would receive eternal life. Moses, therefore, had the authority to strike the rock once, for Jesus Christ would be struck (crucified) just once.

When Israel moved on to another place in their journey, where once again there was no water for drinking, they murmured against Moses. God told Moses to speak to the rock. Moses became so agitated with his murmuring people that, instead of speaking to the rock as he was instructed to do, he struck it. In His gracious kindness to His people,

God again allowed water to come from that rock, although Moses had violated His instruction. Striking the rock a second time violated the plan of salvation, according to which Jesus Christ would make a once and for all sacrifice for sin. The dire consequence was that Moses, this wonderful and meek man of God, did not get to inherit the Promised Land of which he had so long dreamed.

When I urge believers not to murmur or complain, this is not to say there should never be any expression of grief. As human beings, when we suffer loss, we need an avenue of outlet, without which we could implode psychologically and emotionally. At times the pain that is visited upon me leads me to wonder exactly where God is leading me, or what lessons He wishes to teach me. Sometimes the will of God is opaque—that is, not very clear to us—and we are confused and hurt. Lamenting before the Lord, in full assurance of His ability to act on our behalf in our very painful situations, is perfectly appropriate for the Christian. However, even in our lament, we must be willing, like Jesus, to say, "Thy will be done" (Matt. 26:42; Luke 22:42).

As a keen observer of people, and given my age and experience as a mental health therapist, I hold some suspicions of those people who seem to have everything lined up just right. They seem to always have a smooth explanation for everything that happens in their lives. They seem to know exactly where God is leading. They can interpret everything in a hyperspiritual context. They seem to have a simple and easy answer for everything in your life and theirs.

Often, however, life is not that tidy. Sometimes life is messy and confusing, and there are not always nice answers. Christians must at times learn to live with ambiguities and uncertainties, and simply trust that God knows best.

Something tragic, like a healthy seventeen-year-old child dying suddenly, is a messy business and defies frivolous explanations. When people tell the grieving parent not to cry, but to give God the glory, one can be forgiven for ignoring them. At such times, I have heard statements to the effect that this death should cause the bereaved to rejoice, because God was creating His bouquet in heaven and wanted the prettiest flower He could find. The implication is that this child was that flower. When I hear that, I want to say to them, "So what's wrong with *your* child? If this death is such a glorious thing for that other person's child, why did God not take your child to adorn His bouquet?"

I have often wondered, had God chosen to take their "flower," if they would have been equally prepared to spew out such philosophical and theological platitudes. I suspect that if God came to take their child, they would not be so quick to admonish themselves not to cry.

I will never forget when my dear cousin lost her seventeen-year-old daughter. On the day of the funeral, a well-meaning lady accosted her, who was so numb with pain, and began to tell her not to grieve. I was so annoyed that I simply took my cousin away to another room and embraced her.

Or how could I forget going to the home of a dear, saintly couple who was about to bury the third of their five children? In the space of thirty years, they had lost three—one just about every ten years.

The mother assumed the role of an instrumental griever—that is, she grieved by doing things. She planned the funeral and entertained her many guests. The father was the opposite. He was inconsolable. He had stopped eating or taking his medication and seemed hopeless.

On the morning of the funeral, when all the preparations were done for the repast and the mother was getting dressed for church, she finally broke down and let out a bitter wail. Someone standing by cried out, "No man, she can't go on like that," and was moving toward her room with the intent of telling her so.

I immediately intercepted him and said, "Yes, man, she can and must go on like that." I was very relieved to see her give vent to the pain, because that was natural.

The injunction against murmuring is not to pretend that we have an answer for every situation that we face. There are some things we do not know, and we must simply leave it at that. We are not required to know everything about everything, but we are required to trust God in everything, for He is our strength and deliverer. We trust Him even in our uncertainties, with all the ambiguities and pain, though we do not fully understand Him.

I have been saved and serving God for over forty years. I have studied theology and read the Bible. But the more I know about God, the more I realize that I do not know much at all, because His knowledge is unfathomable. In contemplating the wisdom of God, the apostle Paul could do no less than break out in doxology: "Oh, the depth of the riches of the wisdom and knowledge of God! How unsearchable his judgments, and his paths beyond tracing out! Who has known the mind of the Lord? Or who has been his counselor?" (Rom. 11:33–34 NIV). I say, "Amen! Amen! Amen!"

In our grief, we do not offer up meaningless platitudes, pretending to understand everything. We grieve the loss as appropriate. In our grieving, we must be careful to consider God's will. The beloved hymn "It Is Well with My Soul" was written by Horatio Spafford in the aftermath of having lost his children at sea. His response, while singular in its absolute expression of trust in God, nevertheless should serve as a model of what a non-murmurer looks like.

It is said that after the news of the deaths of his children, Spafford took ship to go to Europe and had to pass the same place in the Atlantic Ocean where they drowned. The captain of the ship took him on deck and showed him approximately where his children perished. Spafford went back to his cabin and wrote the hymn that is known the world over. It reads:

When peace like a river, attendeth my way,
When sorrows like sea billows roll
Whatever my lot, thou hast taught me to say
It is well, it is well, with my soul

Though Satan should buffet, though trials should come,
Let this blest assurance control,
That Christ has regarded my helpless estate,
And hath shed His own blood for my soul

My sin, oh, the bliss of this glorious thought
My sin, not in part but the whole,
Is nailed to the cross, and I bear it no more,
Praise the Lord, praise the Lord, o my soul

It is well (it is well)
With my soul (with my soul)
It is well, it is well with my soul.

If anybody had anything to complain about, Horatio Spafford did. But instead of murmuring or complaining, the Holy Spirit gave him a hymn that has been a blessing for the body of Christ for years. Out of his deep sorrow and pain emerged a blessed hymn that has comforted the hearts of millions.

An attitude of gratitude is the remedy for murmuring. I loved buying gifts for my late wife Erica and her mother. No matter what I purchased for them, they made me feel as though I had given them the most expensive gift ever seen, because they embraced those gifts with such appreciation. When my late mother-in-law received any gift from us, no matter how inexpensive, (and in the early days of our marriage, we were so poor that all our gifts were inexpensive, but rich in love), she would smile and say, "Come here, Papa, and give Mummy a kiss." She would thank us so many times that it was embarrassing. You would have thought we had given her twenty thousand dollars and a trip to Jamaica in the middle of a northeastern winter.

Some of us are waiting to get the million dollars before we start worshipping God. We are waiting to get the big job, the big home, the wonderful car, or the right spouse before we start glorifying God. But in bringing every murmuring thought captive to the obedience of Christ, we must be thankful for even the little that we have, knowing that "little is much when God is in it," as someone once observed.

Circumstances may work in such a way as to cause us to be in career situations that are well below our abilities. You may know very well that you have the ability to be a nurse, a doctor, or an engineer, but because of lack of opportunity or weight of family obligations, you find yourself a housekeeper or a janitor. You may feel justified in murmuring and complaining about your unfortunate situation, and from a human perspective, who could blame you?

But in our fight with the world and the circumstances it throws at us, we are not to use carnal weapons. If you find yourself a housekeeper, and you know that you have the potential for bigger and better things, instead of murmuring, give God thanks and, if possible, pursue your dream. When you get in the house and your employers are away and you are alone, begin to glorify God.

The apostle Paul writes, "Be careful [or *anxious,* NIV] for nothing; but in every thing by prayer and supplication with thanksgiving let your requests be made known unto God" (Phil. 4:6). Give Him the glory in your circumstances, trusting all the while that God can pick you up when He sees fit. When God sees that we are grateful and thankful in the little things, He will trust us with bigger things. When He sees that you are thankful for the housecleaning job, God may reward you with a contract to clean office buildings, making hundreds of thousands of dollars rather than minimum wage. You could then become an employer rather than an employee.

You may want to be a doctor, and you know you can grasp the material, but at this time you are a nurse's aide. Just thank God that you can provide a vital service to the sick in your present capacity. As you work in your current situation, pray, give thanks, and find opportunities to advance your education. When your heart is in the right place and your ways are pleasing with God, He will put people in your path who will grant you favors even when they do not know why they are doing so.

Some years ago, we were building our home in West Milford, New Jersey. We did the right thing by first praying about the move, then putting our current home up for sale. We ensured that we had a signed contract from a qualified buyer before we entered into contract to build the new home.

Everything was moving smoothly until one evening, some two or three days before the closing on the house we were selling and five days before the closing on the house we were building, I got a call from the realtor. He told us that our buyer had canceled. To make matters worse, my selling agent had not collected the requisite deposit from this buyer, so all they had from him was a thousand dollars.

I needed forty thousand dollars to close the deal on the new house, and we had no more than ten thousand dollars in the bank. What were we supposed to do? We had been counting on the proceeds from the sale of our house to satisfy the down payment on the new house.

We had no alternatives. Forty thousand dollars in 1989 was a lot of money for everyone we knew. Even if we had known anyone who had that kind of money, we were too ashamed to ask for a temporary loan.

We did the only thing we knew how to do. Erica and I knelt at our bedside and told God our dilemma. We reminded Him that before we embarked on this project, we had consulted Him. We told Him that we did not know what to do, so we were simply going to leave it in His capable hands. For me, this was very hard to do, but I really had no other alternatives. So I committed the matter to God.

I went to work the next day, and I was so numb that I could not mention my dilemma to anyone. At around ten o'clock in the morning, my realtor called to ask if I had been able to raise the money. I told him that we had not even tried, for we had no idea where to turn. He asked me what we planned to do, and again, I told him that we had no idea.

There was a pause, and then he said, "Mr. Hibbert, what I am about to do, I have never done before. I am Jewish, and I do not lend money. But I feel so bad that I will lend you the forty thousand dollars, interest-free, so you can close on your new home."

He continued, "I will sell your existing house within six months. If it is not sold by then, I will buy it from you." It was a two-family dwelling, and we were occupying one of the apartments. So he added, "The apartment you are moving out of, don't rent it. I want it empty so I can show it more easily." He blew my mind even further by concluding, "I will pay you whatever the reasonable rent is for that apartment until the house is sold."

I asked him if he would be willing to put that in writing. He readily consented, and faxed me the loan agreement that very day. We were able to close on time, and he paid us rent for about four months until the house was sold. We repaid his loan interest-free as he had promised.

This was a situation that was murmur-evoking, and I believe normally I would have worried and murmured and complained. But this time the Holy Spirit led us in another direction—a direction of trusting in the almighty God, and He did exceeding, abundantly above what we were able to conceive.

I believe that we are giving up our victory when we murmur and complain. We are letting the Devil into our secret thoughts when we murmur. In place of murmuring, let us praise the Lord and be thankful.

It occurred to me recently that the attitude of ingratitude is a grave sin. The apostle Paul makes his case in the book of Romans against the sinfulness of all humanity. One of the litanies of sins for which people reaped God's wrath was that of unthankfulness. Paul observes, "Because that, when they knew God, they glorified him not as God, neither were *thankful*; but became vain in their imaginations, and their foolish heart was darkened" (Rom. 1:21, emphasis added).

Murmuring signifies that the murmurer is not satisfied with what God is doing in their life. They are not thankful for God's provision. This robs God of His glory, for which we all will be accountable if we persist in murmuring. The three Hebrew boys who were thrown in the fire, Danial in the lion's den, and Paul and Silas, among many other biblical examples, should be our models for trusting God.

Having traveled to several countries, I have come to realize that we who live in the United States and many Western countries are rich by comparison to others. We sometimes complain about the car that we have, while other people have no car and are hopping along on one leg because they have lost the other in an accident or in war.

Some years ago, I was in Jamaica, where I met a family member. This woman had had a broken foot for many years, which was never fixed. For some reason, the leg with the broken foot had, over time, become shorter than the other leg. This dear lady hopped along on one leg, going up and down hills. She was busy working and making a living, never complaining about her condition, and never finding excuse for not working. By not sitting down, and by using the good leg daily, it had become very strong. This allowed her to go about her daily activities.

So if it seems that in our lives, God has removed one of our legs, we need to learn how to build up the strength in the other leg. We must give God the glory on our one leg. When we get tired of hopping around on the one leg, we can sit down if we must, but in that posture, still give God glory.

In place of murmuring, let us develop a childlike trust in God. When my sons were young, they trusted me totally. If I promised them something, they would remember it. They trusted my words and my ability to do wonderful things for them.

I used to play a game with them as I drove them from place to place. I would see a red traffic light ahead, and I would slow down and say, "Let this light be green." The light would change to green—not because it obeyed my voice, but because I had slowed down and timed my approach to catch the green light. I would then roll through the green light. This would fascinate my boys. They thought I had the power to change the light from red to green.

This happened until one day I tried it, and they noticed that I had slowed down. One of them burst out, "Dad, come on, man, why are you slowing down? Just drive as usual." It became clear to them that I really had no power over the lights. Until they recognized my inability to change the lights, they believed. Only after this realization did they complain that I could not do that miraculous thing.

The question to us is, when did God lose His ability to effect change in our lives? When did He lose His power to change red lights to green ones? If we know Him to be the omnipotent God, then let us trust Him and not complain.

My sons rightly became skeptical and untrusting of my ability to change traffic lights from red to green at a word. They learned that I was a fake and joker on that head, and we all had a good laugh. But we must learn to trust God. When there are red lights before us, let us trust Him to change them. When there are closed doors before us and God says walk through them, we simply must obey Him. When there are Red Seas before us and there seems to be no way of escape, we must simply move forward and trust God without murmuring or complaining.

Life is difficult, but we serve an awesome God. Often our minds play tricks on us. If we are not careful, we will be defeated—first in our minds, and then in our decisions and actions. We must therefore take precautions to guard our minds from being invaded by negative thinking. We must control our thought lives.

We end where we began: "For though we walk in the flesh, we do not war after the flesh: for the weapons of our warfare are not carnal, but mighty through God to the pulling down of strong holds; Casting down imaginations, and every high thing that exalteth itself against the knowledge of God, and bringing into captivity every thought to the obedience of Christ" (2 Cor.10:3–5).

A Prayer

Heavenly Father, we murmur when we should praise You. When things are not going our way, we complain instead of trusting You. Please forgive us. Help us to trust You to keep us and provide for us, even as we have trusted You for salvation. In Jesus's name. Amen.

Definition of Terms

Cognitive restructuring: A process of learning to identify and dispute irrational or maladaptive thoughts, and in their place, develop more rational and adaptive patterns of thinking.

Flooding: A form of behavior therapy. It is also referred to as *exposure therapy* or *prolonged exposure therapy*. It is used to treat phobia and anxiety disorders, including post-traumatic stress disorder. It works by exposing the patient to their painful memories, with the goal of reintegrating their repressed emotions with their current awareness, thus minimizing or removing the fear.

Mechanized infantry unit: Infantry equipped with armored personnel carriers (APCs) or infantry fighting vehicles (IFVs) for transport and combat.

Self-actualization: A psychological construct that teaches that what a person can be, they must be. It is based on employing one's abilities to reach one's potential. This potential differs from person to person.

Bibliography

"Controlling Anger Before It Controls You." American Psychological Association. Accessed April 12, 2018. http://www.apa.org/topics/anger/control.aspx.

Anders, Max. *Holman New Testament Commentary: Galatians, Ephesians, Philippians, Colossians.* Nashville, TN: B&H Publishing Group, 1999. Kindle.

Andrews, Bernice, and Chris Brown. "Predicting PTSD Symptoms in Victims of Violent Crime: The Role of Shame, Anger, and Childhood Abuse." *Journal of Abnormal Psychology,* 109, no.1 (2000): 69-73.

Berkhof, Louis. *Systematic Theology.* Grand Rapids, MI: William B. Eerdmans Publishing, 1996.

Calvin, John. *Institutes of the Christian Religion.* Translated by Henry Beveridge. Grand Rapids, MI: Christian Classic Ethereal Library. Accessed April 15, 2018. http://www.ccel.org/c/calvin/institutes/institutes.html.

Erickson, Millard J. *Christian Theology.* Grand Rapids, MI: Baker Academic, 2013.

Gebel, Erika. "The Role of Sleep in Type 2 Diabetes." Diabetesforecast.org. Accessed December 13, 2018. http://www.diabetesforecast.org/2011/may/the-role-of-sleep-in-type-2-diabetes.html.

Harris, Alex H. S. and Carl E. Thoresen. "Forgiveness, Unforgiveness, Health, and Disease." Academia.edu. Accessed December 12, 2018. http://www.academia.edu/1407727/Forgiveness_unforgiveness_health_and_disease.

Hodge, Charles. *Commentary on the Epistle to the Romans.* WORD*search*. Com. Accessed December 12, 2018. *https://www.wordsearchbible.com/customers/1337005/owned_products.*

Hodge, Charles. *A Commentary on Ephesians.* WORD*search*.Com. Accessed December 12, 2018). *https://www.wordsearchbible.com/customers/1337005/owned_products.*

Hunter, Christie. "The Negative Effects of Unforgiveness on Mental Health." Theravive.com. Accessed December 12, 2018. https://www.theravive.com/today/post/the-negative-effects-of-unforgiveness-on-mental-health-0001467.aspx.

Keener, Craig. S. *A New Covenant Commentary, Series 6: Romans.* Eugene, OR: Cascade Books, 2009.

Norman, Kathi, "Forgiveness: How it Manifests in our Health, Well-being, and Longevity." Repository.upenn.edu. Accessed November 2, 2018. http://repository.upenn.edu/mapp_capstone/122.

Reeves, Mark. *300 Ghandi Best Quotes.* Amazon Digital Services LLC, 2012. Kindle Locations 107-108.

Schmidt, William E. "President Praises Carter at Library." *The New York Times.* October 2, 1986. Accessed December 20, 2018. https://www.nytimes.com/1986/10/02/us/president-praises-carter-at-library.html.

Shambash, R. W. "How To Raise The Dead." 1991. Tent Meeting, South Bronx, NYC. Youtube Video. Accessed December 20, 2018. https://www.youtube.com/watch?v=-fgkJTUWvAs.

Snodgrass, Klyne. *The NIV Application Commentary: Ephesians*. Edited by Terry C. Muck. Grand Rapids, MI: Zondervan, 1996. Kindle.

Sutliff, Usha. "Liars' Brains Wired Differently." News.usc. Accessed December 19, 2018 .https://news.usc.edu/22586/Liars-Brains-Wired-Differently/.

Voss, Michael. "Bay of Pigs: The 'Perfect Failure' of Cuba Invasion."BBC.Com, April 14, 2011. Accessed November 25, 2018. http://www.bbc.com/news/world-latin-america-13066561.

Vance, David E., Barbara A. Smith, Judith L. Neidig, and Michael T. Weaver. "The Effects of Anger on Psychomotor Performance in Adults with HIV: A Pilot Study." *Social Work in Mental Health* 6, no. 2 (2008): 83–98.

Wang, Joseph S. "God's Righteousness Provides Salvation (3:21–8:39)." In *Asbury Bible Commentary, Part III:* III. Biblegateway.com. Accessed August 1, 2018. https://www.biblegateway.com/resources/asbury-bible-commentary/Life-Spirit.

Wood, George O. "The High Cost of Unforgiveness: Healing Life's Hurts." Assemblies of God. Accessed July 8, 2018. http://sermons.georgeowood.com/.

Yilmaz, Onurcan, Dilay Z. Karadöller, and Gamze Sofuoglu. "Analytic Thinking, Religion, and Prejudice: An Experimental Test of the Dual-Process Model of Mind." *The International Journal For The Psychology Of Religion* 26, no. 4 (October 2016): 360–369.

Endnotes

Introduction

1 Millard J. Erickson, *Christian Theology* (Grand Rapids, MI: Baker Academic, 2013), 463.
2 Louis Berkhof, *Systematic Theology* (Grand Rapids, MI: William B. Eerdmans Publishing Co., 1996), 203-205.
3 Max Anders, *Holman New Testament Commentary: Galatians, Ephesians, Philippians, Colossians* 8 (B&H Publishing Group, 1999), Kindle Location 5253.
4 Onurcan Yilmaz, Dilay Z. Karadöller, and Gamze Sofuoglu, "Analytic Thinking, Religion, and Prejudice: An Experimental Test of the Dual-Process Model of Mind," *The International Journal for The Psychology of Religion* 26, no. 4 (October 2016): 361.

Chapter 1

5 William Shakespeare, *The Complete Works of William Shakespeare, - Julius Caesar,* Act 2, Scene 3, eds. Irving Ribner and George L. Kitteredge (Lexington, MA: Xerox College Publishing, 1971), 1014.
6 Michael Voss, "Bay of Pigs: The 'Perfect Failure' of Cuba Invasion," BBC. Com, April 14, 2011, accessed November 25, 2018, http://www.bbc.com/news/world-latin-america-13066561.
7 John Calvin, "Institutes of the Christian Religion," translated by Henry Beveridge, Grand Rapids, MI: Christian, Christian Classic Ethereal Library. Org, accessed December 12, 2018, http://www.ccel.org/c/calvin/institutes/institutes.html.

Chapter 2

8 Klyne Snodgrass, *The NIV Application Commentary: Ephesians,* ed. Terry C. Muck (Grand Rapids, MI: Zondervan, 1996), 342.

9 Charles Hodge, *A Commentary on Ephesians*. WORD*search*. Com., accessed December 12, 2018), https://www.wordsearchbible.com/1337005/owned_products.

10 Hodge, *A Commentary on Ephesians,* Database © 2004 WORD*search* Corp.

11 Anders, *Holman New Testament Commentary,* Kindle Location 3858.

12 Snodgrass, *The NIV Application Commentary: Ephesians,* 342–343.

13 Ibid., 343.

14 Ibid., 343.

15 Anders, *Holman New Testament Commentary,* Kindle Locations 3863–3866.

16 Hodge, *A Commentary on Ephesians,* Database © 2004 WORD*search* Corp.

17 Hodge, *A Commentary on Ephesians,* Database © 2004 WORD*search* Corp.

18 Joseph S Wang, God's Righteousness Provides Salvation (3:21–8:39)," in *Asbury Bible Commentary, Part III*: III, Biblegateway.com, access August 1, 2018, https://www.biblegateway.com/resources/asbury-bible-commentary/Life-Spirit.

Chapter 4

19 Harris, Alex H. S. and Carl E. Thoresen, "Forgiveness, Unforgiveness, Health, and Disease," Academia.edu., accessed December 12, 2018, http://www.academia.edu/1407727/Forgiveness_unforgiveness_health_and_disease
Pdf.

20 Erika Gebel, "The Role of Sleep in Type 2 Diabetes," Diabetesforecast.org., accessed December 13, 2018, http://www.diabetesforecast.org/2011/may/the-role-of-sleep-in-type-2-diabetes.html.

21 Kathi Norman, "Forgiveness: How it Manifests in our Health, Well-being, and Longevity," Repository.upenn.edu., accessed November 2, 2018, http://repository.upenn.edu/mapp_capstone/122.

22 Christie Hunter, "The Negative Effects of Unforgiveness on Mental Health," Theravive.com, accessed December 12, 2018, https://www.theravive.com/today/post/the-negative-effects-of-unforgiveness-on-mental-health-0001467.aspx.

23 George O Wood, "The High Cost of Unforgiveness: Healing Life's Hurts," Assemblies of God, accessed July 8, 2018, http://sermons.georgeowood.com/.

24 Mark Reeves, *300 Ghandi Best Quotes* (Amazon Digital Services LLC, 2012), Kindle Locations 107-108.

Chapter 5

25 Law.com, accessed December 15, 2018, https://dictionary.law.com/Default.aspx?selected=1969.

Chapter 6

26 David E. Vance, Barbara A. Smith, Judith L. Neidig, and Michael T. Weaver, "The Effects of Anger on Psychomotor Performance in Adults with HIV: A Pilot Study," *Social Work in Mental Health* 6, no. 2 (2008), 83.

27 Bernice Andrews and Chris Brown, "Predicting PTSD Symptoms in Victims of Violent Crime: The Role of Shame, Anger, and Childhood Abuse," *Journal of Abnormal Psychology,* 109, no.1 (2000): 69.

28 "Controlling Anger Before It Controls You," American Psychological Association, accessed April 12, 2019, http://www.apa.org/topics/anger/control.aspx.

Chapter 8

29 Usha Sutliff, "Liars' Brains Wired Differently," News.usc, accessed December 19, 2018, https://news.usc.edu/22586/Liars-Brains-Wired-Differently/.

Chapter 9

30 William E. Schmidt, "President Praises Carter at Library," *The New York Times.* October 2, 1986, accessed December 20, 2018, https://www.nytimes.com/1986/10/02/us/president-praises-carter-at-library.html.

31 R. W. Shambash, "How To Raise The Dead," 1991, Tent Meeting, South Bronx, NYC, Youtube Video, accessed December 20, 2018, https://www.youtube.com/watch?v=-fgkJTUWvAs.

Chapter 10

32 Shakespeare, *The Complete Works of William Shakespeare, - Julius Caesar,* Act 3, Scene 2.

33 *Julius Caesar,* Act 2 Scene 2.

34 "Keep on the Firing Line" (No. 212) in Banner Hymns (Cleveland, TN: White Wing Publishing House, 1957).

Chapter 12

35 Joseph S Wang, "God's Righteousness Provides Salvation (3:21–8:39)," in *Asbury Bible Commentary, Part III:* III, Biblegateway.com., access August 1, 2018, https://www.biblegateway.com/resources/asbury-bible-commentary/Life-Spirit.

36 Charles Hodge, *Commentary on the Epistle to the Romans,* WORD*search*. Com., accessed December 12, 2018, *https://www.wordsearchbible.com/customers/1337005/owned_products.*

37 Craig S. Keener, *A New Covenant Commentary, Series 6: Romans* (Eugene, OR: Cascade Books, 2009), 99.

38 "Have Thine Own Way" (No. 3) in Banner Hymns (Cleveland, TN: White Wing Publishing House, 1957).

Chapter 13

39 "Higher Ground" (No. 625) in Seventh Day Advent Hymnal, Sdahymnals.com, accessed December 23, 2018, http://sdahymnals.com/Hymnal/625-higher-ground.

Chapter 14

40 William Shakespeare, *The Complete Works of William Shakespeare, Julius Caesar,* Act 2, Scene 2, eds. Irving Ribner and George L. Kitteredge (Lexington, MA: Xerox College Publishing, 1971), 1014.

About the Author

The author recognizes that there are many published works dealing with the mind, and was somewhat reluctant to add another one to the plethora of books in this genre. However, he believes that his training and experience as a board certified, licensed mental health counselor, and a pastor, uniquely qualifies him to comment on how people think and act. He has earned four masters degrees, one of which was in mental health counseling, and one, a masters of divinity in pastoral counseling. He also holds a PhD in theology. In addition to being currently the senior pastor of a growing church, he also provides mental health counseling as an independent contractor.

The author believes that the mind is the center, not only of one's thoughts, but also of the emotions, and is responsible for one's behaviors. Controlling the mind therefore, is key to controlling how one feels and acts. In the context of being a Christian, the author holds that it is all the more important that the believer controls his or her thought life by applying God's Word to every dysfunctional thought that comes to mind. Christ died primarily to save our souls, but in the atonement, He also provides healing for the body and mind. The Bible teaches: "For God hath not given us the spirit of fear; but of power, and of love, and of a sound mind" (2Tim. 1:7). It is therefore, possible and desirable that Christians possess healthy minds. The author has labored under this conviction in his ministry and counseling work, and now offers this book with a conviction that when prayerfully read, it will help the reader to improve his or her functioning on many objective measures.

Printed and bound by PG in the USA

USA2019PGIL